WOMEN AND POWER
in the
NONPROFIT SECTOR

Teresa Odendahl

Michael O'Neill

Editors

WOMEN AND POWER
in the
NONPROFIT SECTOR

Jossey-Bass Publishers • San Francisco

Substantial discounts on bulk quantities of Jossey-Bass books are available to corporations, professional associations, and other organizations. For details and discount information, contact the special sales department at Jossey-Bass Inc., Publishers. (415) 433-1740; Fax (415) 433-0499.

For sales outside the United States, contact Maxwell Macmillan International Publishing Group, 866 Third Avenue, New York, New York 10022.

Manufactured in the United States of America. Nearly all Jossey-Bass books and jackets are printed on recycled paper containing at least 50 percent recycled waste, including 10 percent postconsumer waste. Many of our materials are also printed with vegetable-based ink; during the printing process these inks emit fewer volatile organic compounds (VOCs) than petroleum-based inks. VOCs contribute to the formation of smog.

Library of Congress Cataloging-in-Publication Data

Women and power in the nonprofit sector / Teresa Odendahl, Michael O'Neill, editors.
    p. cm. — (The Jossey-Bass nonprofit sector series)
    Papers from a conference held in Menlo Park, Calif., Nov. 1992.
    Includes bibliographical references and index.
    ISBN 1-55542-650-6
    1. Women in nonprofit organizations—United States—Congresses.
I. Odendahl, Teresa Jean. II. O'Neill, Michael. III. Series.
HD2769.2.U6W66   1994
331.4'81658048—dc20
                                        93–47558
                                          CIP

FIRST EDITION
HB Printing   10 9 8 7 6 5 4 3 2 1   *Code 9444*

The Jossey-Bass Nonprofit Series

CONTENTS

Preface   xi

The Editors   xv

The Contributors   xvii

Introduction: The Paradox of Women and Power
   in the Nonprofit Sector   1
   Michael O'Neill

1. The History of Women in the Nonprofit
   Sector: Changing Interpretations   17
   Kathleen D. McCarthy

2. Women in the Nonprofit Labor Market   39
   Anne E. Preston

ix

3. Pay Equity in Nonprofit Organizations:
    Making Women's Work Visible   79
    Ronnie J. Steinberg and Jerry A. Jacobs

4. The Occupational Structure of Nonprofit
    Industries: Implications for Women   121
    Lynn C. Burbridge

5. Women, Changing Demographics, and the
    Redefinition of Power   155
    Juanita Tamayo Lott

6. Women on Nonprofit Boards   183
    Teresa Odendahl and Sabrina Youmans

7. Women as Professional Fundraisers   223
    Joseph R. Mixer

8. A Latina's Experience of the Nonprofit
    Sector   255
    Antonia Hernández

9. Women and Volunteer Activity: One
    Practitioner's Adventures in Leadership   267
    Barbara C. Roper

10. Women's Power, Nonprofits, and the Future   295
    Teresa Odendahl

    Conference Participants   313

    Index   317

PREFACE

This book explores the roles of women in the nonprofit sector in the United States. The special theme is power. Has the nonprofit sector empowered women, and if so in what ways? Have women working in the nonprofit sector had an effect on power in American society, and if so in what ways? As is bound to happen in such a large and previously unexamined area of study, we have raised more questions than we have been able to answer.

It has long been assumed that the American nonprofit sector was the primary source of empowerment for women, minorities, immigrants, and other groups in societally weak positions. The empowerment theme has become part of the creed of many nonprofit-sector supporters. Yet the empowerment assumption, with regard to women, has not received the critical attention it deserves. The aim of this book is to summarize and analyze the principal data sources on this assumption and to report the personal experiences of some women leaders in the nonprofit sector.

The book grew out of a national invitational conference, Women, Power, and Status in the Nonprofit Sector, held in Menlo Park, California, in November 1992. In attendance were forty scholars, funders, nonprofit executives, volunteers, policy makers, and others with interest and expertise in the subject. The conference was sponsored by the Institute for Nonprofit Organization Management at the University of San Francisco and supported by grants from the AT&T Foundation, the Hunt Alternatives Fund, the James Irvine Foundation, the W.K. Kellogg Foundation, the Sophia Fund, and an anonymous donor.

Audience

Women and Power in the Nonprofit Sector will be of interest to women's organizations, faculty and students in women's studies programs, funders of women's issues, and nonprofit policy-and-research organizations. The board, staff, and volunteer issues raised here affect virtually all nonprofit organizations.

Overview of the Contents

Following an introductory chapter by Michael O'Neill on the principal issue of the book, five scholars analyze the issue from different disciplinary backgrounds. Kathleen McCarthy summarizes the historical literature on women and the voluntary sphere in Chapter One. In Chapter Two, economist Anne Preston traces the changing status of women in the nonprofit and general labor market during the 1970s and 1980s. In Chapter Three, sociologists Ronnie Steinberg and Jerry Jacobs use a case study to illuminate the complexity of the labor market issue for nonprofit women. Lynn Burbridge analyzes the occupational structure and career choices of women in the nonprofit sector in Chapter Four. And in Chapter Five, Juanita Tamayo Lott discusses the implications of demographic shifts for the nonprofit work of women and relates her findings to the question of power.

The next four chapters take up topics of practical importance in the field. Teresa Odendahl and Sabrina Youmans discuss the literature on women on nonprofit boards in Chapter Six. Joseph Mixer presents data on the rapidly changing role of women fundraisers in Chapter Seven. In Chapter Eight, Antonia Hernández, president of and general counsel to the Mexican American Legal Defense and Educational Fund, uses personal anecdotes to illuminate the challenges facing women of color in the nonprofit world. Then in Chapter Nine, Barbara Roper, the first woman president of the national board of the YMCA, uses her experiences to develop several principles for women volunteers in nonprofit agencies.

In the final chapter, Teresa Odendahl reflects on the book's findings and their implications for the future of women, power, and status in the nonprofit sector.

Acknowledgments

The editors express their deep appreciation to the six funders who made the conference and book possible. In addition, we wish to thank the members of the planning committee, who assisted with the development of the conference concept and programmatic details, and staff members of the Institute for Nonprofit Organization Management for their work on the conference. In particular, we wish to thank Susan Richardson, assistant to the director of the institute, for her work in handling conference logistics.

THE EDITORS

Teresa Odendahl is executive director of the National Network of Grantmakers. Prior to this position she served on the faculty of the Women's Studies Program at the University of California at San Diego, and as director of development at a local social service agency. She received her B.A. degree (1974) in anthropology from San Diego State University and her M.A. (1976) and Ph.D. (1982) degrees in anthropology from the University of Colorado at Boulder. Her books include *Charity Begins at Home: Generosity and Self-interest Among the Philanthropic Elite* (1990), *America's Wealthy and the Future of Foundations* (1987, editor and contributor), and *Working in Foundations: Career Patterns of Women and Men* (1985, with E. Boris and A. K. Daniels). She has been a consultant to nonprofit organizations around the country, was the first staff director of the Women's Foundation of Colorado, and worked for several years at the Business and Professional Women's Foundation in Washington, D.C.

Michael O'Neill is professor and director of the Institute for Nonprofit Organization Management in the College of Professional Studies at the University of San Francisco. He earned his B.A. degree (1960) in philosophy at St. Thomas College, his M.A. degree (1964) in education from the Catholic University of America, and his Ed.D. degree (1967) from Harvard University. He is author of *The Third America: The Emergence of the Nonprofit Sector in the United States* (1989) and editor of *Educating Managers of Nonprofit Organizations* (1988, with D. R. Young), *Hispanics and the Nonprofit Sector* (1991, with H. E. Gallegos), and *Ethics in Nonprofit Management* (1990). He is an associate editor of the journal *Nonprofit Management and Leadership*.

THE CONTRIBUTORS

Lynn C. Burbridge is deputy director of the Center for Research on Women at Wellesley College. She received her B.A. degree (1970) in social and political theory from the University of California at Berkeley and her M.A. (1980) and Ph.D. (1984) degrees in economics from Stanford University. Before coming to Wellesley, she spent eight years as a researcher and policy analyst at the Urban Institute and a year at the Joint Center for Political and Economic Studies, both in Washington, D.C. Her research has focused on the effect of public policy on minorities, low-income women, and youth.

Antonia Hernández is president of and general counsel to the Mexican American Legal Defense and Educational Fund (MALDEF). She earned her B.A. degree (1970) in history and her J.D. degree (1974) from the University of California at Los Angeles. Before coming to MALDEF, she was a staff attorney at the Los Angeles Center for Law and Justice, directing attorney for the Lincoln Heights Office of the Legal Aid Foundation of Los Angeles, and staff counsel to the United States Senate Committee on the Judiciary. She serves on the boards of the Federal Reserve Bank of San Francisco, California Leadership, Los Angeles 2000, and the Latino Museum of History, Art, and Culture.

Jerry A. Jacobs is a visiting scholar at the Russell Sage Foundation and associate professor of sociology at the University of Pennsylvania. He received his A.B. (1977) and Ph.D. (1983) degrees in sociology from Harvard University. His publications include *Sex Segregation and Gender Stratification* (1994, editor and contributor), *Revolving Doors: Sex Segregation and Women's Careers* (1989), and several journal articles on gender and occupations.

Juanita Tamayo Lott is president of Tamayo Lott Associates, a public policy firm in Silver Spring, Maryland, and senior research associate at the National Academy of Sciences in Washington, D.C. She earned her B.A. degree (1970) in sociology from San Francisco State University and her A.M. degree (1973) in social sciences from the University of Chicago. Her books include *Knowledge and Access: A Study of Asian and Pacific American Communities in the Washington Metropolitan Area* (1989), and she has written several articles and papers on the Asian-American community. She has worked for the U.S. Department of Health,

Education, and Welfare and for the U.S. Commission on Civil Rights. She chaired the U.S. Census Bureau Advisory Committee on Asian and Pacific Islander Populations for the 1990 census.

Kathleen D. McCarthy is professor of history and director of the Center for the Study of Philanthropy at the Graduate School of the City University of New York. She received her B.A. degree (1972) in history from the University of Illinois and her M.A. (1973) and Ph.D. (1980) degrees in history from the University of Chicago. Her books include *The Nonprofit Sector in the Global Community: Voices from Many Nations* (1992, with V. A. Hodgkinson and R. Sumariwalla), *Women's Culture: American Philanthropy and Art, 1830–1930* (1991), *Lady Bountiful Revisited: Women, Power, and Philanthropy* (1990, editor and contributor), *Philanthropy and Culture: The International Foundation Prespective* (1984, editor and contributor), and *Noblesse Oblige: Charity and Cultural Philanthropy in Chicago, 1849–1929* (1982). She serves on the Research Committee of INDEPENDENT SECTOR, the editorial boards of *Nonprofit and Voluntary Sector Quarterly* and *Voluntas,* and is president-elect of the Association for Research on Nonprofit Organizations and Voluntary Action.

Joseph R. Mixer is a consultant on fundraising, board and staff training, and nonprofit management in Berkeley, California. He received his B.A. degree (1943) in economics from the University of California, Berkeley; his M.B.A. degree (1949) from Ohio State University; and his Ph.D.

degree (1977) in higher education administration from the University of California, Berkeley. He started the development office at the Berkeley campus and was cofounder and associate director of the Fund-Raising School based in San Rafael, California. He is an adjunct faculty member in the Master of Nonprofit Administration program at the University of San Francisco and was a lecturer in the School of Social Welfare at the University of California at Berkeley from 1987 to 1990. He is the author of *Principles of Professional Fundraising: Useful Foundations for Successful Practice* (1993).

Anne E. Preston is associate professor at the W. Averell Harriman School for Management and Policy at the State University of New York at Stony Brook. She received her B.A. degree (1977) from Princeton University and her M.A. (1981) and Ph.D. (1983) degrees from Harvard University, all in economics. Her publications include *The Competitive Edge: Managing Human Resources in Nonunion and Union Firms* (1989, with C. Ichniowski) and several articles and papers on the nonprofit labor market, with special attention to women workers. She received the Peter F. Drucker Prize for the best article in *Nonprofit Management and Leadership* in 1990.

Barbara C. Roper is president of Contour Groves, Inc., and Tops N Travel, Inc., in Winter Garden, Florida, and was the first woman to chair the National Board of YMCA of the USA. Her extensive volunteer work includes board positions with the Public Broadcasting System, the National Safety Council, WMFE-TV public broadcasting in Florida, and the Central Florida Commission on the Status of Women. She received her B.A. degree (1950) in economics from Pennsylvania State University.

Ronnie J. Steinberg is associate professor of sociology and women's studies at Temple University. She received her B.A. degree (1969) in psychology from Bennington College and her M.A. (1973) and Ph.D. (1977) degrees in sociology from New York University. Her books include *The Politics and Practice of Pay Equity* (1994), *Wages and Hours: Labor and Reform in Twentieth-Century America* (1982), *Equal Employment Policy for Women: Strategies for Implementation in Europe, Canada, United States* (1979, editor), and *Job Training for Women: The Promise and Limits of Public Policies* (1989, coeditor with S. Harlan). She is editor of the series *Women in the Political Economy,* for which thirty two books have been published to date.

Sabrina Youmans is research director at the *San Diego Business Journal,* where she headed the paper's report on San Diego's top women-owned businesses and is currently researching the largest nonprofits in San Diego County. After receiving her B.A. degree (1990) in communication from the University of California at San Diego, she worked for several newspapers and publications, including *San Diego Magazine.* Her background in nonprofits includes serving as public relations coordinator for the San Diego Travelers Aid Society. She worked with Teresa Odendahl on the final stages of *Charity Begins at Home* (1990).

WOMEN AND POWER
━━━━━━ in the ━━━━━━
NONPROFIT SECTOR

Introduction

The Paradox of Women and Power in the Nonprofit Sector

Michael O'Neill

The American nonprofit sector, unlike the for-profit and government sectors, has always been based on a primarily female work force, paid and unpaid. Of the 7.8 million employees of the nonprofit sector in 1990, two thirds were women (Hodgkinson and Weitzman, 1993; Hodgkinson, Weitzman, Toppe, and Noga, 1992, p. 129). More than half of the sector's 90 million volunteers were women (Hodgkinson and others, 1992, pp. 71, 73). And, as the chapters of this book make clear, women have had a statistically predominant role in the nonprofit sector throughout American history. Yet there is serious question whether the influence of women in and through the nonprofit sector is as great as their statistical predominance.

The traditional and still widely held view is that women, people of color, immigrants, the poor, and other such

1

groups have found in the nonprofit sector opportunities for leadership, power, and influence not available to them in the business and government sectors. For example, women in nonprofit organizations have played a major role in shaping public policy in the nineteenth and twentieth centuries in such areas as women's political and economic rights and child welfare; on the local level, women have exercised leadership in thousands of arts, social service, religious, and other nonprofit organizations.

A more recent but less widely accepted view is that women's access to power in the nonprofit sector is nearly as limited as it is in business and government. Proponents hold that women may constitute the majority of the nonprofit work force but that they are typically prevented from reaching top executive and policy-making positions in nonprofit agencies, especially the larger, more prestigious, and more influential ones. More generally, the same theorists hold that the centers of real power in America are the economic and political realms, where men dominate. In their view, the nonprofit sector, statistically dominated by women, is removed from real power and confined to service roles, just as women have historically held supporting rather than power roles in families, communities, and societies.

Support for both views can be found throughout the history of what is now called the *nonprofit sector.* Although terminology and statistical usage vary, there is considerable consensus that the nonprofit sector consists of incorporated nongovernment organizations granted tax-exempt status by the Internal Revenue Service and usually state agencies. These include both charitable, or public benefit, organizations such as social service groups, churches, arts organizations, environmental and other advocacy efforts and "mutual benefit" nonprofits such as fraternal organizations, social clubs, political parties, and professional associations. The American nonprofit sector thus defined includes about 1.4 million organizations.

The definition does not include—but one should not forget—the many unincorporated associations such as self-help groups, the activities of which parallel those of nonprofit sector organizations.

Most charitable agencies in the seventeenth, eighteenth, nineteenth, and early twentieth centuries were led and controlled by men. But there were significant exceptions, the most visible of whom were upper-class, Anglo-Saxon Protestant women such as Elizabeth Cady Stanton and other leaders of the women's suffrage movement; Jane Addams and other pioneers of social work as a profession; Dorothea Dix, the great mental health reformer; Clara Barton, founder of the American Red Cross; Mary Baker Eddy, Ellen Gould White, and Mother Elizabeth Seton in religion; Emma Willard, Catherine Beecher, and Mary Lyon in private education; philanthropist Margaret Olivia Slocum Sage, founder of the nation's first general purpose foundation; and supporters of the arts such as Isabella Stewart Gardner and Gertrude Vanderbilt Whitney. Far less visible but of incalculable cumulative influence were women leaders of immigrant, minority, ethnic, religious, rural, and other nonmainstream groups. African-American women formed mutual aid and self-improvement associations such as the Colored Female Religious and Moral Society of Salem, Massachusetts (1818), antislavery societies before the Civil War, and many other agencies after the Civil War. Jewish women who had managed families and family businesses in the shtetls of Eastern Europe and Russia transferred their skills to charitable organizations on New York's Lower East Side. Irish-Catholic women, wives and nuns, exercised considerable influence through religious and other organizations, often quietly working around their husbands and priests.

In more recent times, the accomplishments of women in and through the nonprofit sector touch upon vast areas of American life: women's and children's rights, minority rights, environmentalism, the peace movement, the pro-choice movement, and consumer protection efforts, to name only a few. Some have argued that women, the largest of all "minority" groups, have made significant progress toward full freedom and true equality primarily through the nonprofit sector, and thus have made the sector a powerful instrument for enhancing American democracy. Others hold a more skeptical view, questioning the reality of the progress and suggesting that the nonprofit sector may be an unwitting instrument by which the male power structure continues to exclude women from power. This book explores different aspects of that debate.

Major Themes

Some major themes emerge in the discussion of women and power in the nonprofit sector.

The Category "Nonprofit Sector"

Is it useful to consider women's power or lack thereof with reference to different economic sectors? For instance, is the female-male division of labor with regard to childbearing and child rearing so strongly entrenched in social attitudes and practices that sectoral differences with regard to the issue are relatively trivial? Generally, it may be that opportunities and barriers for women are so deeply embedded in social and economic structures that they remain essentially the same from one sector to another. A different question is whether the nonprofit sector embraces such a diversity of organizations, from hospitals to neighborhood groups, that generalizations about women in the nonprofit sector are relatively useless.

Despite such caveats, several considerations seem to support the usefulness of looking at women's experience through the sectoral lens. The profile of the nonprofit labor force is dramatically different from that of business or government: 65 percent of nonprofit employees are women, as opposed to 44 percent in business and 53 percent in government. Aggregate women's and men's wages are almost at parity in the nonprofit sector, as contrasted with a 20 to 30 percent gap in business and government (see Preston's chapter for a more detailed discussion of this issue). Women are much more likely to be in professional and managerial positions in nonprofit organizations than they are in business or government work. Although all three sectors are far from granting women parity, women are much more likely to head the largest nonprofit organizations than they are to head the largest for-profit or government organizations; for instance, in 1992, sixteen of the nation's one hundred largest nonprofits had chief executive officers who were women (*Nonprofit Times,* 1992), whereas only one Fortune 500 corporation was headed by a woman (Caminiti, 1992). While the data do not settle the question of the usefulness of sectoral analysis, they provide some support for such an approach.

There are many precedents for grouping together what are now called nonprofit organizations, going back at least to Tocqueville's famous discussion of America's "moral and intellectual associations." But there is so much diversity in organizations recognized by the Internal Revenue Service as tax exempt that one might question whether it makes sense to group and discuss the organizations as a sector, with the attendant implication of unique and unifying characteristics. The IRS-recognized nonprofit sector includes such huge financial institutions as Teachers Insurance and Annuity Association/College Retirement Equities Fund (TIAA-CREF) and the Ford Foundation as well as 500,000 groups with annual revenue of less than $25,000 each. It includes major research universities such as the Massachusetts Institute of Technology (MIT) and large research corporations such as Rand and Stanford Research Institute (SRI), as well as tiny associations for the preservation of rare butterflies. And if one defines the nonprofit sector as encompassing all tax-exempt nongovernment organizations and not only the 501(c)(3) "charitables," the sector includes such strange bedfellows as the National

Football League, the New York Stock Exchange, and even the Federal Reserve System, the latter a 501(c)(1).

However, such diversity can also be found in the for-profit sector, which contains not only IBM and General Motors but also the local laundromat and 7-Eleven store and the government sector, which includes the Pentagon and tiny fire and water districts (there are more than eighty thousand local government agencies). On grounds of organizational diversity, it is just as sensible to discuss women in the nonprofit sector as it is to discuss women in the for-profit or government sectors.

Relationship Between the Nonprofit
Sector and the Larger Society

It can hardly be overemphasized that any discussion of women and power in the nonprofit sector is necessarily an artificial abstraction from the complex totality of women's experience in American society. Some of the most powerful factors—changing laws, regulations, and attitudes regarding women; changes in women's educational achievements; increased labor force participation and the opening of professional and managerial occupations formerly closed to women; the decreasing salary gap between men and women; and the increasing political consciousness and power of women—are hardly unique to the nonprofit sector. In her chapter in this book, Lott sketches the importance of recent demographic shifts in any discussions of women in the nonprofit sector. Further, women in the nonprofit sector are greatly affected by what happens to women in business and government. For instance, the increased opportunities for women in the profit world, including some of the more lucrative professions, clearly affect the supply of educated and talented women available to the nonprofit sector. On the other hand, cutbacks in government employment at all levels, the slow rate of increase in government salaries, and the recession of the early 1990s have probably increased the potential female labor supply for the nonprofit sector. More generally, the massive entry of women into all parts of the labor market and the rapidly rising educational levels of women since the late 1960s may have produced a situation in which the supply of educated and skilled women workers met and exceeded the combined demands of all three sectors. Also, there is much evidence of intersector mobility, especially in health, education, and social welfare, the three largest employment groups in the nonprofit sector. Nurses switch from private to public hospitals, faculty members switch from public to private universities, social workers switch from government to nonprofit agencies, and so forth. For these and many related reasons, it is imperative to view the discussion of women and power in the nonprofit sector in a broader economic context.

The social and political context is equally important. Arguably the most significant change since the late 1960s with regard to women in the nonprofit sector is the social position of women as reflected in laws, regulations, court rulings, organizational policies, political party platforms, and the like. Changes in the values and attitudes of individuals are much harder to measure, but it can be argued on the basis of available survey data that change in that area has been considerable as well, with probably the most important change the rising expectations of women themselves. It is highly likely that such broad social changes affect the relative power and status of women in the nonprofit sector, not the least because many changes resulted from the work of women's groups and other nonprofit organizations.

Social Class

Although the gender variable is the principal focus of this book, the various chapters make it clear that the importance of social class is not far behind. Women's philanthropic activity has often been shaped more by social class than by gender. Ostrander (1984), Daniels (1988), Odendahl (1990), and others have argued that upper-class women's philanthropic work is more related to class than to gender, often directly or indirectly supporting the dominance of the upper class in society and of men in the upper class. Further, women's organizations historically were often segregated by social class if not also by race, national origin, religion, and so forth. This is hardly surprising, since class remains a more powerful differentiating factor than any other social variable in American society in virtually all areas of activity; but the issue is important to remember when discussing topics so open to mythologizing as "women in the nonprofit sector" or indeed "women's issues" generally.

Race and Ethnicity

At least one dramatic change was made during the compilation of this book. The participants in the conference on Women, Power, and Status in the Nonprofit Sector

collectively demanded that all presenters give more attention to the issue of race and ethnicity. Both women of color
and white women involved in the conference insisted that
their experiences in the nonprofit sector might be quite
different. They pointed out that the women's movement
is often seen as, in effect, a white women's movement
rather than one that consistently embraces the interests
of all women in American society. As several chapters in
this book make clear, the suspicion that race and ethnicity might differentiate the experience of women in the nonprofit sector finds support in the evidence available. For
instance, Preston found that while women in general made
significant gains in the nonprofit sector during the 1980s,
the same was not true for minority women. Hernández,
although herself the head of an influential national nonprofit agency, strongly questions on the basis of her personal experience the notion that women of color have
fared well in the nonprofit sector. All contributors found
the literature on women of color in nonprofits to be sparse.
But there is certainly enough information to suggest that
the experience of minority women may be different from
that of white women and that the topic is in great need
of further study, policy development, and action. Minority
women on nonprofit boards and in top management positions, especially in large, influential nonprofit organizations, are only two examples of topics that need further
study and action.

Distribution of Power in American Society

McCarthy argues that the issue of women's power in the
nonprofit sector necessarily evokes a much larger ques-

tion about the nature and scope of American democracy. As she says, "If only the political record is examined for the first half of the country's history, the notion of American democracy is little more than a sham. Women, the poor, American Indians, and African Americans were all excluded from direct political action for part or all of the nineteenth century." Women fought for and won enfranchisement and some measure of economic independence by using nonprofit organizations to bring pressure on government and for-profit organizations. In this case as in so many others (minority rights, freedom of speech, environmentalism), the nonprofit sector was a mechanism for dramatic reallocation of power and opportunity in American society. The phenomenon is still visible and strong. As only one example, the striking statistical gains for women candidates in the 1992 elections came in large part from the concerted work of women's groups such as Emily's List. The general issue of women's power in American society must include serious attention to the effect of women's work in nonprofit organizations. There should be nothing surprising in this. In view of the remarkable political and social accomplishments of such people as Dorothea Dix, Margaret Sanger, Clara Barton, and Lucretia Mott more than a century ago, it is ironic that "power" in American society is still conceived in mostly masculine terms and surrounded by male images.

The Meaning and Uses of Power by Women

One question raised at the conference and briefly explored in this book is the question of whether women and men view and use power differently, and if so, what the implications are for the nonprofit sector. There is considerable debate in management and feminist literature as to whether there are gender-based differences in management styles. Some say no; others hold that women managers are more likely than men to practice participative, consensus-oriented decision making, understand and value the personal interests of workers, and eschew hierarchical, authority-based, bureaucratic forms of organization. The jury is still out on this question, because few women have held top executive and policy-making positions in any sector, and because, as some have suggested, even top women executives may have had to suppress their preferred management styles in order to succeed in a male-dominated world. The question of how women view and use power may turn out to be a nonquestion, or it may turn out to be an extraordinarily interesting question.

The issue is particularly relevant for the nonprofit sector, given the large and growing number of women holding managerial positions. According to 1990 census data, 592,000 of the women employed by the nonprofit sector held executive, administrative, and managerial positions, as compared with 431,000 male nonprofit employees who held such positions; that is, women held 58 percent of such positions in the nonprofit sector in 1990. There are no comparable census data for earlier years, because the 1990 census was the first one to differentiate private nonprofit from private for-profit employment. However, by applying Preston's findings (see Table 2.2) on the percentages of women and men holding nonprofit managerial positions in 1969 to Preston's and other estimates of female and male nonprofit sector employment in the late 1960s and early 1970s, we can estimate that women held only about 35 percent of nonprofit managerial positions in 1970, as compared with 58 percent in 1990. While this certainly does not mean that there is parity at all levels of management (or parity of wages at the same level), it does make clear that women in the nonprofit sector now hold a much higher percentage of the positions commonly associated with organizational power than was the case two decades earlier.

Mixer's chapter on women fundraisers provides another interesting study of the changing gender-and-power situation in the nonprofit sector. He points out that women are coming to dominate the critical profession of fundraising, although men still hold many of the top development positions in large nonprofits.

Occupational and Organizational Prestige

Trivialization of the work and roles of women has been a major theme in feminist literature. Any serious discussion of women and the nonprofit sector must ask whether the sector is consciously or unconsciously part of an allocation of status in American society that reserves for men the leadership of the most important organizations and the occupation of the most important careers. Such status allocation would promote the idea that generals are more important than social workers, doctors more important than nurses, lawyers more important than teachers, mechanics more important than day-care workers and therefore would reserve the former roles for men and the latter roles for women. As Burbridge and other contributors point out, the feminization of some occupations has led to their devaluation, and conversely, the increase in prestige of some nonprofit efforts—major social welfare, health, cultural, educational, and funding agencies, for example—has led to their being taken over by men.

A "Gendered" Nonprofit Sector?

Steinberg and Jacobs and Odendahl and Youmans, in their chapters in this book, argue that the nonprofit sector is "gendered female": a large female work force is under the control of an elite male power structure; within the sector, occupations are distributed according to gender (doctors are male, nurses are female; men are financial officers, women are teachers; and so forth); the symbols, images, values, and typical activities of the sector are "female" and "soft"—providing service, being concerned with morality and ethics, producing beauty, and helping people. The gendering of the nonprofit sector, they argue, leads to the devaluation of women's work and subordination of women by men. Relating her experience as a woman volunteer, Roper gives examples that may provide anecdotal support for the gendering theory.

The gendering hypothesis suggests many fruitful lines of inquiry for scholars, policy makers, and practitioners. How or to what extent are nonprofit-sector power and status distributed along gender lines? Is this changing and, if so, in what ways? To what extent do the characteristics of certain tasks (teaching, preaching, counseling, producing art, driving a truck, fighting fires, selling products, heading a government agency) attract and reward people

14

(female or male) with particular interests, values, and occupational orientations? And how are the tasks or jobs distributed within the society and within the nonprofit sector? Finally, if and to the extent that the nonprofit sector is gendered female, what is the full cost-benefit analysis of this situation? Are there positive as well as negative effects for women? And if the effects are totally or mostly negative, why do millions of women continue to choose paid and unpaid roles in the nonprofit sector?

Conclusion

In the simplest terms, this book argues that the experience of 5 million women employees and 50 million women volunteers cannot be ignored. The nonprofit sector plays a major role in the lives of American women, and they play a major role in and through the nonprofit sector. As to the shape, force, and extent of that role, the news is both good and bad, as the book makes clear. But in statistical terms alone, the subject clearly merits much more attention than it has received. We hope this book will be a useful addition to the growing literature on women's issues and nonprofit and voluntary effort. We also hope that the book will provide a stronger basis for policy development and actions directed at making the nonprofit sector fully responsive to its own ideals and best instincts regarding gender equality and empowerment.

References

Caminiti, S., "America's Most Successful Businesswoman." *Fortune,* June 15, 1992, pp. 102–108.
Daniels, A. K. *Invisible Careers: Women Civic Leaders*

15

from the Volunteer World. Chicago: University of Chicago Press, 1988.

Hodgkinson, V. A., and Weitzman, M. S. "A Brief Look at Not-for-Profit Employment from the 1990 Census of Population and Housing." Washington, D.C.: Independent Sector, 1993.

Hodgkinson, V. A., Weitzman, M. S., Toppe, C. M., and Noga, S. M. *Nonprofit Almanac 1992–93: Dimensions of the Independent Sector.* San Francisco: Jossey-Bass, 1992.

Odendahl, T. *Charity Begins at Home: Generosity and Self-interest Among the Philanthropic Elite.* New York: Basic Books, 1990.

Ostrander, S. A. *Women of the Upper Class.* Philadelphia: Temple University Press, 1984.

"The NPT 100: America's Biggest Charities." *Nonprofit Times,* Nov. 1992, pp. 13–21.

1

The History of Women in the Nonprofit Sector: Changing Interpretations

Kathleen D. McCarthy

The historical record of women's philanthropic activities was initially cast in the crucible of sisterhood and the collectivist ethos of the women's movement. From the first contributionist texts that began to identify female movers and shakers to pioneering works by scholars such as Nancy Cott, Anne Firor Scott, Barbara Welter, and Barbara Berg, the emphasis was on collectivism, commonalities, voluntarism, and shared goals. As Nancy Hewitt explains (1985, p. 299), "One of the principal projects of the contemporary feminist movement in the United States has been the development of a sense of community among women, rooted in their common oppression and expressed through a distinctive women's culture . . . [and the conviction] that gender is the primary source of oppression in society and is the model for all other forms of oppression."

Since the beginning of the 1980s, however, the scenario has become more complex, emphasizing fissures within women's organizations and campaigns, as well as common aims. Marxist interpretations have been particularly influential in sharpening scholarly interest in the role of class and race, as well as gender and patriarchy, in shaping women's efforts within nonprofit organizations. Historians have begun to cast their inquiries beyond organizational mandates as well, to explore the hidden political and economic agendas that are concealed by the rhetorical surface of women's giving and voluntarism. The underlying *leitmotif* is power; the result is a fuller vision of the workings of American democracy and the role of women—particularly white, middle- and upper-class women—outside the home.

Ironically, as historical inquiries have become more theoretically challenging, they have also become more insulated from the concerns of women who are working within the nonprofit sector. Practitioners have a wealth of new perspectives and questions to offer feminist historians in their quest to discern the scope, nature, and meaning of women's philanthropy in American life.

Collaboration and Conflict

Although a few scholars raised qualifying voices, the majority of the first histories of women's voluntary associations assumed the tone of Flexner's seminal study *Century of Struggle* (1959), which charts the trials and triumphs of a variety of women's groups, from abolitionist and suffrage organizations to the Women's Christian Temperance Union

(WCTU). While Welter (1966) limns the confining dictates of the pre–Civil War "cult of true womanhood," Cott (1977), Scott (1970), Berg (1978), and others demonstrate the ways in which middle-class white women transcended the confines of their domestic sphere through participation in charities and social reform organizations. Thus, from the outset, feminist scholars have linked women's liberation to participation in nonprofit-sector activities.

Berg was particularly interested in tracing the roots of modern feminism to women's groups in antebellum cities and towns, detailing emerging cross-class alliances that linked middle-class women to the impoverished widows, prostitutes, and battered wives they sought to aid. The more involved they became, Berg (1978, p. 158) argues, the more they sensed the shared disabilities common to all women, whether rich or poor: "Through their work in voluntary societies women became aware of their oppression. . . . In so doing, they slowly came to recognize a unity of all women."

A few scholars, such as Smith-Rosenberg, took the arguments a step further, combing the records of the militant American Female Moral Reform Society to document middle-class white women's growing disenchantment with their circumscribed position in American society. Founded in New York in 1835 during the feverish aftermath of a half-decade of religious revivals, the society sought to redeem the city's growing ranks of prostitutes by preaching to them, praying with them, providing safe shelter for the repentent, and even publishing the names of customers caught in raids. For Smith-Rosenberg, the campaigns were an early index of women's rage over their limited options. As she explains (1985, p. 124), "Much of the Society's rhetorical onslaught upon the male's lack of sexual accountability served as a screen for a more general—and less socially acceptable—resentment of masculine social preeminence." In effect, the moral reform movement was an early chapter in women's revolt against patriarchy.

One legacy of the close connection between the rise of women's studies and the women's movement has been an ongoing interest in "separatist" groups (segregated by gender), ranging from abolitionist auxiliaries to social settlements, where women worked together to achieve their charitable or social aims. Although sensitive to the importance of race and ethnicity, Scott's *Natural Allies* (1991) and Evans's *Born for Liberty* (1989) exemplify the continuing emphasis on sisterhood and separatism. For Evans, separate-sex voluntary associations served as the opening wedge through which all women—black or white, immigrant or WASP—entered the country's democratic political culture; Scott emphasizes the efficacy of the associations as "early warning systems" that identified emerging social ills.

By the early 1980s, Marxist analysis had also begun to color feminist research, introducing a new emphasis on the fissures that separated women's groups from each other and from their professed constituencies. To Hewitt, feminist historians initially focused on:

the parallels in the establishment of women's spheres across classes, races, and ethnic groups and have as-

20

serted certain commonalities among them, assuming their common origin in the modernization of society during the nineteenth century. A closer examination now reveals that no such universal sisterhood existed, and in fact that the development of a sense of community among various classes of women served as a barrier to an all-embracing bond of womanhood. Finally, it is now clear that privileged women were willing to wield their sex-specific influence in ways that, intentionally or unintentionally, exploited other women in the name of "true womanhood" [1985, p. 315].

Kraditor was one of the first historians to sound a dissonant note in her *Ideas of the Woman Suffrage Movement* (1965). In addition to charting the movement's successes, Kraditor explores its darker side, including the racism and nativism exploited by some suffragists in order to win support for the female franchise in Southern states and the heavily immigrant industrial cities of the North.

Hewitt sharpens the emphasis on class divisions in *Women's Activism and Social Change* (1984), exploring different types of female-sponsored voluntary activity in the "burnt-over district" around Rochester, New York, during the nineteenth century. Hewitt's intricately detailed book traces three genres of women's groups: charities begun by the wives of prominent businessmen; reform groups created by middle-class perfectionists who spearheaded temperance campaigns and other religiously inspired initiatives for individual salvation; and "ultraist" groups, such as abolitionists, founded by radicals who tended to be among the more marginal elements of local society. Rather than gender-based imperatives, class considerations reign supreme in Hewitt's depiction of voluntarism in Rochester, as female activists aligned their interests and activities with their husbands' enthusiasms and economic pursuits.

Stansell took the theme of divisiveness still further in her 1986 study, *City of Women*. Concentrating on the years before the Civil War, Stansell shifts the line of sight to New York and to the interaction between female managers of charities and antivice reformers and the women they sought to serve. Far from understanding their constituents or finding ways to realistically meet their needs, the women in Stansell's book sentimentalized the plight of the poor, using urban slums as a mirror of everything the middle class was not. Thus, notes Stansell (1986, p. 37), "These genteel women were finding their own voice and articulating their own importance" rather than genuinely aiding the poor. "There was little in their language . . . that could help laboring women, whose identities were rooted outside the sphere of religion and the home." In effect, the cultural clashes inherent in charitable and reform activities provided the sounding board not for the beginnings of feminist sisterhood but for the consolidation of the bourgeoisie.

Although a few scholars have examined the efforts of women who sought to carve careers in male-dominated fields—such as Morantz-Sanchez's work (1985) on doctors, Rossiter's on scientists (1982), and Rosenberg's on social scientists (1982)—most historical literature has continued to concentrate on separatist social reform movements and nonprofit organizations.

In *Women's Culture* (1992), I sought to widen the analytical discourse by examining the strengths and weaknesses of three types of philanthropic strategies that women employed between 1830 and the eve of the Great Depression: separatism, assimilationism (that is, work within male-controlled institutions), and the efforts of highly individualistic women who created philanthropic ventures.

Separatist organizations allowed women to achieve a variety of important aims, from launching local charities and national reforms to enabling them to leverage constitutional change in an era in which they lacked the vote. Most were fueled by modest donations and heavy infusions of volunteer time. But crusades that succeeded by dint of numbers often proved impotent in changing the policies of the kinds of heavily endowed "legitimating institutions" created by such wealthy male patrons as John D. Rockefeller and Andrew Carnegie in the decades after the Civil War. These male-controlled foundations, museums, research universities, and think tanks tended to be national in aspiration, professionally staffed, generously endowed, and hierarchically structured, following the emerging model of the modern corporation. These were the institutions that set the canon in education, art, and policy making. They were also keystones in the emerging edifice of the American establishment of male policy makers and elites, organizations that used their prominence and wealth, and the legitimacy that both bestowed, in order to shape the course of professionalization in fields as diverse as medicine, curatorial work, science, and social science research.

Women played a limited role in these legitimating institutions, often handing over significant donations to the stewardship of male trustees. While women helped to build important national institutional resources, they garnered little in return, which had profound implications for women's ability to create and maintain professional gains. Insulated from popular pressures by endowments and private nonprofit status, many male-controlled legitimating institutions were impervious to reform, developing an array of policies and procedures that ultimately trivialized women's accomplishments in a variety of professions.

As women began to inherit substantial fortunes after the turn of the century, a few venturesome individuals, such as museum founders Isabella Stewart Gardner and Gertrude Vanderbilt Whitney, began to create alternative institutions of their own. The Gardner and Whitney museums were smaller than their male-dominated counterparts and more specialized in their aims. But they reflected a genre of female philanthropy previously neglected by historians. And they introduced the theme of money, a subject on which most historical works about women are silent. The feminist legacy of such individualistic patrons is more spotty than that of earlier, separatist groups. Created in the early twentieth century when the equation between female philanthropy and feminist aims was weakening, the theme of women helping women was no longer an inevitable part of the patrons' agenda. But because these women had the potential to promote change on a new scale through their sizable donations, their achievements (and shortcomings) merit further study.

Political and Economic Power

The second theme emerging in the historical literature on women and philanthropy consists of the ways in which women have exercised public power through their donations, voluntarism, and social reform. Certainly, power was not an unfamiliar theme to the first generation of feminist scholars, who defined the field. Indeed, much of their writing concentrated on voluntary associations precisely because of the obvious kinds of power that participation in such groups accorded: the power to work outside the home, to move freely about the city (even to the point of sacking brothels), the power to challenge male hegemonies, and the power to create a room of their own in a political arena that sought to exclude them.

However, in recent years, a number of works have begun to explore the more elusive forms of power that participation in the organizations allowed, including political and economic prerogatives that were traditionally regarded as falling beyond the grasp of middle-class Victorian women. A 1987 conference hosted by the Center for the Study of Philanthropy of the City University of New York set the stage for some discussions by emphasizing that the common denominator for women's donations, voluntarism, and social reform is the extent to which the activities have historically enabled women to exercise authority in societies intent upon rendering them powerless.

The themes are explored in the book that emerged from the conference, *Lady Bountiful Revisited* (McCarthy, 1990a).

For example, under the English common-law doctrine of *femme couverte,* married women were unable to own or transfer property in their own right. Until the passage of married women's property acts beginning in the mid-nineteenth century, the majority of American women legally controlled neither their dowries, their inheritances, nor their earnings (if they could find a remunerative job). In many states, a woman's signature on a contract was invalid. But gathered in a chartered charity or reform group, the same women could raise and invest money, buy property, and assume fiscal responsibility for organizational management (McCarthy, 1990b).

Since then, historians have begun to explore other, less obvious themes. Ginzberg's 1990 study, *Women and the Work of Benevolence* (see also Baker, 1984) examines the ways in which participation in antebellum charities provided an entree to the realms of politics and finance. According to the dictates of the Victorian cult of the lady, women—especially middle- and upper-class women—were expected to remain aloof from the brutish scramble for political influence and economic gain. But women's voluntary organizations habitually "lobbied for new laws, sought appropriations for their organizations, and argued for changes in their own status—in short, they worked hard to influence the leadership of local, state, and national governments" (Ginzberg, 1990, p. 69).

Nor were their activities a one-sided exchange. Savvy social hostesses used their influence and their salons to win contacts and backing for the politicians who supported the women's institutions. In effect, they played an important role of political brokering. And they did it by camouflaging their activities in the self-effacing language of charity and service that fills the pages of the annual reports of their organizations. As Ginzberg (1990, p. 65) points out, "For women involved in building charitable organizations, the rhetoric of female benevolence concealed authority that they wielded in the distribution of resources and services in their communities."

Unfortunately, such rhetoric could be a double-edged sword, opening new areas of activity while maintaining stereotypes of feminine inabilities to deal effectively with economic concerns. Ginzberg touches on some economic functions of nineteenth-century women's organizations, from fundraising to investments; *Women's Culture* (McCarthy, 1992) traces others. During the Civil War, the Sanitary Commission systematized the local activities detailed by Ginzberg into regional and national networks for the collection and distribution of donated goods. Afterward, some of the more enterprising women's organizations coupled the techniques with an emerging national network of female institutions—women's clubs, social settlements, decorative art societies, even missionary groups—to forge a national subterranean economy for the collection and sale of women's goods (McCarthy, 1992, chap. 3).

Societies for decorative art are a case in point. The first decorative art society was founded in 1876, in the wake of the Philadelphia Centennial Exposition. Within a decade, chapters were operating across the United States. The

movement's goal was twofold: to help impoverished women to find employment through the sale of elaborate em-
broideries and other decorative artifacts crafted in their
homes and to upgrade American household taste. To these
ends, local chapters created salesrooms, put together travel-
ing exhibitions, and arranged for consignments to be mar-
keted through women's groups in other towns.

Other types of organizations became involved as well,
selling lace produced by women on Indian reservations
through networks of female missionary societies and Appalachian quilts through exhibitions arranged along a national circuit of social settlements and women's clubs. By
1900, some decorative arts chapters and Women's Exchanges were tallying annual revenues around the $50,000
mark, a considerable sum. And most profits were generated without working capital, part of a twilight economy
of quasicommercial nonprofit entrepreneurship at which
women proved increasingly adept.

And yet they won and maintained the right to pursue
the activities by emphasizing not their successes but their
annual shortfalls and the continual need to subsidize their
activities through charity events. To ensure the success of
their charitable goals, they kept profits and commissions
to a minimum, skillfully obscuring the breadth of their
commercial achievements from their male contemporaries.
In the process, they rhetorically fed the patriarchal prejudices that historically undervalued women's work.

Two recent historical works, one a history, the other
historical sociology, have begun to explore the complex
interrelationships that linked female professionalism, pol-

itics, and the emerging welfare state. Muncy's *Creating a Female Dominion in American Reform* (1991) underscores the different prospects and pressures that shaped professional alternatives for middle-class male and female managerial elites over the first third of the twentieth century.

Unlike the men who held appointments in such bastions of masculine largesse as the great research universities, medical schools, and research institutes, aspiring women professionals tended to launch their public careers from such female-controlled organizations as social settlements. Because the women's institutions often had limited budgets, "the incomes of female professionals, unlike those of men in law, medicine or business, consequently came not from a fee-paying client but from wealthy benefactors" (Muncy, 1991, p. xiii). Dependence on women donors reinforced the emphasis on service and self-sacrifice, because "the true object of the patronage of elite women was to aid the downtrodden—not just to subsidize individual careers" (p. 36). As a result, professional women were often compelled to model their professional demeanor on Victorian assumptions about women's nature. As Muncy explains, the "prescriptions for female behavior directly contradicted the solidifying requirements of professional conduct: lingering 19th century feminine ideals urged women toward passivity, humility and self-sacrifice, while professionalism demanded activity, confidence, and self-assertion" (p. xiii). In effect, funding patterns that were different for women had profound implications for the contours of female professionalism.

Moreover, while male managerial elites moved through

philanthropically supported networks that linked government, business, and academe, many prominent female
policy makers followed career paths that led from social
settlements to government slots created and maintained
through the lobbying activities of national women's groups.
Muncy's description of the changing fortunes of the United
States Children's Bureau provides a fascinating illustration
of the ways in which men and women used their different philanthropic styles to wield professional authority in
American society. Ironically, although women's groups became "the leading proponents of an American welfare
state" in the 1910s, they ultimately lost control of their political fiefdoms after passage of the Nineteenth Amendment
in 1920 reduced their lobbying clout by revealing that female voters would not vote as a gender bloc (Muncy, 1991,
p. 108; for male managerial elites, see Karl and Katz, 1981).

Skocpol's book, *Protecting Soldiers and Mothers* (1992),
provides a similar analysis of the political impact of women's voluntary associations. Echoing a theme from *Lady
Bountiful,* Skocpol notes that organizations such as the
National Federation of Women's Clubs, the Women's Christian Temperance Union, and the National Congress of
Mothers constituted a three-tiered system that paralleled
the work of local, state, and national governments. Because
nonprofits were seen as less corrupt and self-interested
than government bodies, women were able to foster the
passage of social legislation in ways that government could
not, ultimately laying the foundations for the modern
American welfare state.

The programs they created focused on the needs of

women and children. Backed by women's groups and the Children's Bureau, mothers' pensions were enacted into law in forty states by 1920, and the Sheppard-Towner Infancy and Maternity Protection Act was passed by Congress the following year. As the nation's first federally sponsored social welfare program, Sheppard-Towner established government-funded clinics to distribute health information designed to reduce infant mortality rates. According to Skocpol, the efforts constituted a unique pattern among the welfare states of the world, because they were created and implemented primarily by women for women through a blend of public and private initiatives.

They also represented the triumph of gender considerations over class. While trade unions played a pivotal role in the rise of many Western European welfare states, women's voluntary groups were far more influential in this area in the United States. As Skocpol (1992, p. 528) explains, "Around the turn of the twentieth century, U.S. social politics stood out in cross national terms because it was more focused on solidarities of gender than on solidarities of economic class position." Women played this extraordinary role before they had the vote. Far from being politically peripheral, women's philanthropic activities and the public-private partnerships they created are coming to be viewed as examples of the unique way in which the United States dealt with welfare issues.

Historians and Practitioners

Skocpol's analysis brings the interpretive framework full circle, from depicting women's philanthropic activities as

31

a response to patriarchal discrimination to their role as central institutions in the American political arena. Yet as scholars continue to debate the relative importance of gender, class, and voluntarism in the historical record, other questions remain unanswered, including an array of issues of vital concern to contemporary practitioners within the nonprofit sector.

Many of the issues are raised in the other chapters of this book. However, it would be useful to consider the extent to which the contemporary questions and criticisms posed by a distinguished array of scholars and activists relate to the developing historical literature on women and philanthropy. Stated more bluntly, is there common ground for the concerns of scholars and practitioners?

One line of discussion focuses on race. According to this line of argument, although rhetorical emphasis on gender, class, and race has been strong, most research to date has focused on the efforts of white, American-born, middle- and upper-class women. Despite a few promising beginnings, more attention should be devoted to donations, voluntarism, and organizational entrepreneurship among Asian Americans, Hispanics, and African Americans. African-American philanthropy is a particularly compelling topic, one that could be traced in part through church records. How did black and white philanthropy differ over time? How have volunteer activities changed, and when did African-American entrepreneurs and performers begin to donate money as well as time within their communities? (See, for example, Hine, 1990.)

Boards are another surprisingly neglected area. When

and why do class and race as well as gender begin to have policy implications for the development of nonprofit organizations? Most historical literature has tended to concentrate on administrators and policy makers rather than on the interactions among board members. Class differences, including the scope and nature of working-class organizations, have barely been addressed. Differences among ethnic organizations also remain something of a terra incognita, a surprising lacuna given the current fascination with multiculturalism (see, for example, Hewitt, 1990; and Diner, 1983).

Even the notion of parallel power structures merits further consideration in light of contemporary trends. How have separatist organizations evolved since passage of the Nineteenth Amendment shattered the solidarity of Victorian women's culture in 1920? Do separatist institutions still confer benefits denied by mixed-gender groups? Has their efficacy varied over time? Do they still provide parallel power structures—alternatives to male-dominated cultures—today?

The place of female trustees and policy makers within male-controlled institutions has received even less attention. How and when were women recruited and promoted, and what, if any, difference did their appointments make? What sorts of constraints hampered them from playing more significant roles?

Surprisingly little work has been devoted to the role of women donors. Yet this issue is of growing importance, particularly because many women now control substantial salaries as well as inheritances. Although a great deal of attention has been devoted to women's roles in hosting fundraising benefits of various sorts, almost no historical research has focused on their roles in raising money from individuals. Were some groups or types of initiatives particularly successful in raising money? If so, why, and what lessons might these activities hold for contemporary fundraisers? At this point, we simply do not know.

How have notions of sisterhood shaped nonprofit hiring and firing practices? How willing have women of one ethnic group been to hire workers from another? How willing have they been to promote other women to managerial positions? How active have they been in forwarding women's professional interests within traditionally male-dominated institutions? To what extent have male and/or female trustees contributed to the wage gap for male and female workers in the nonprofit sector?

Conclusion

Since the late 1960s, feminist historians have begun to change our view not only of women's activities in different eras but also of the scope and nature of American democracy. If only the political record is examined for the first half of the country's history, the notion of American democracy is little more than a sham. Women, the poor, American Indians, and African Americans were all excluded from direct political action for part or all of the nineteenth century. Within this milieu, philanthropy and nonprofit organizations played an exceedingly important role, allowing disfranchised groups to participate in local and national policy-making debates. They enabled some women to wield economic prerogatives as well, forging national quasicommercial marketing networks that paralleled the more visible business activities of men under the cloak of nonprofit entrepreneurship. They provided a modicum of power in an otherwise discriminatory world. In the process, the study of women's nonprofit activities is beginning to provide a missing piece of the mosaic, a key to understanding the history of American society in ways that give new scope and meaning to the term *democracy*. The next challenge will be to strengthen the analytical bridges between past and present, activism and academe, moving beyond the sisterly rhetoric of earlier feminist campaigns to lend historical perspectives to a growing array of contemporary concerns.

References

Baker, P. "The Domestication of Politics: Women and American Political Society, 1780–1920." *American Historical Review,* 1984, *89,* 640–647.

Berg, B. *The Remembered Gate: Origins of American Feminism: The Woman and the City, 1800–1860.* New York: Oxford University Press, 1978.

Cott, N. F. *The Bonds of Womanhood: "Women's Sphere" in New England, 1780–1835.* New Haven, Conn.: Yale University Press, 1977.

Diner, H. R. *Erin's Daughters in America: Irish Immigrant Women in the Nineteenth Century.* Baltimore: Johns Hopkins University Press, 1983.

Evans, S. M. *Born for Liberty: A History of Women in America.* New York: The Free Press, 1989.

Flexner, E. *Century of Struggle: The Women's Rights Movement in the United States.* Cambridge, Mass.: Harvard University Press, 1959.

Ginzberg, L. D. *Women and the Work of Benevolence: Morality, Politics, and Class in the Nineteenth Century United States.* New Haven, Conn.: Yale University Press, 1990.

Hewitt, N. A. *Women's Activism and Social Change: Rochester, New York, 1822–1872.* Ithaca, N.Y.: Cornell University Press, 1984.

Hewitt, N. A. "Beyond the Search for Sisterhood: American Women's History in the 1980s." *Social History,* 1985, *10*(3), 299–321.

Hewitt, N. A. "Charity or Mutual Aid?: Two Perspectives on Latin Women's Philanthropy in Tampa, Florida." In K. D. McCarthy (ed.), *Lady Bountiful Revisited: Women, Philanthropy, and Power.* New Brunswick, N.J.: Rutgers University Press, 1990.

Hine, D. C. "'We Specialize in the Wholly Impossible': The Philanthropic Work of Black Women." In K. D. McCarthy (ed.), *Lady Bountiful Revisited: Women, Philanthropy, and Power.* New Brunswick, N.J.: Rutgers University Press, 1990.

Karl, B. D., and Katz, S. N. "The American Philanthropic Foundation and the Public Sphere, 1890–1930." *Minerva,* 1981, *19,* 236–270.

Kraditor, A. *The Ideas of the Woman Suffrage Movement.* New York: Columbia University Press, 1965.

McCarthy, K. D. (ed.). *Lady Bountiful Revisited: Women, Philanthropy, and Power.* New Brunswick, N.J.: Rutgers University Press, 1990a.

McCarthy, K. D. "Parallel Power Structures: Women and the Voluntary Sphere." In K. D. McCarthy (ed.), *Lady Bountiful Revisited: Women, Philanthropy, and Power.* New Brunswick, N.J.: Rutgers University Press, 1990b.

McCarthy, K. D. *Women's Culture: American Philanthropy and Art, 1830–1930.* Chicago: University of Chicago Press, 1992.

Morantz-Sanchez, R. M. *Sympathy and Science: Women Physicians in American Medicine.* New York: Oxford University Press, 1985.

Muncy, R. *Creating a Female Dominion in American Reform, 1890–1935.* New York: Oxford University Press, 1991.

Rosenberg, R. *Beyond Separate Spheres: Intellectual Roots of Modern Feminism.* New Haven, Conn.: Yale University Press, 1982.

Rossiter, M. W. *Women Scientists in America: Struggles and Strategies to 1940.* Baltimore: Johns Hopkins University Press, 1982.

Scott, A. F. *The Southern Lady: From Pedestal to Politics, 1830–1930.* Chicago: University of Chicago Press, 1970.

Scott, A. F. *Natural Allies: Women's Associations in American History.* Urbana: University of Illinois Press, 1991.

Skocpol, T. *Protecting Soldiers and Mothers: The Political Origins of Social Policy in the United States.* Cambridge, Mass.: Harvard University Press, 1992.

Smith-Rosenberg, C. "Beauty, the Beast, and the Militant Woman: A Case Study in Sex Roles and Social Stress in Jacksonian America." In C. Smith-Rosenberg, *Disorderly Conduct: Visions of Gender in Victorian America.* New York: Knopf, 1985.

Stansell, C. *City of Women: Sex and Class in New York, 1789–1860.* New York: Knopf, 1986.

Welter, B. "The Cult of True Womanhood, 1820–1860." *American Quarterly,* 1966, *18,* 151–174.

2

Women in the Nonprofit Labor Market

Anne E. Preston

The nonprofit sector has historically been an important employer of women. The period of 1969 to 1991, however, brought significant changes to women in the labor market and to the nonprofit sector. This chapter analyzes the evolving labor market status of women in the nonprofit sector against the backdrop of accelerating labor force participation of women, evolving legislation designed to increase educational and labor market opportunities for women, and a maturing women's movement.

While the labor force participation of women, and married women in particular, had been increasing for much of the twentieth century (Goldin, 1990), the passage of the Civil Rights Act of 1964 opened job opportunities for women that until then had been virtually closed. The act required that employers give nondiscriminatory treatment to men and women in the areas of hiring, promotion, and other conditions of employment. The Civil Rights Act of 1964 and the Equal Pay Act of 1963 began a series of legislative efforts that attempted to institutionalize equal treatment of men and women in various forums. While women still have not attained parity with men in many arenas, the effects of the legislation were probably accelerated by the women's movement of the late 1960s and beyond, which made women more aware of and vocal about their rights and opportunities.

Goldin (1990) notes that the social change of the 1960s may have contributed to the upward shift and changing nature of the supply of women to the labor force since that time. Not only were more women looking for work but they began investing more heavily in their own education and skills. The decade between 1961 and 1971 saw an acceleration of the steadily increasing percentage of women graduating from college, and by 1981, 50 percent of all college degrees were earned by women. In addition, women entered occupations previously reserved for well-educated men. By 1986, women accounted for 15 percent of all lawyers and 17 percent of all physicians (Goldin, 1990). The increase in educational attainment and occupational prestige of women began to translate into higher wages only in the 1980s, as women's wages, still roughly 30 percent lower than men's wages, increased relative to men's wages during the decade (Bound and Johnson, 1992).

From 1969 to 1990, the nonprofit sector grew in both revenue and employment (Hodgkinson and Weitzman,

1989). The role of the government in meeting basic welfare needs was already well established by the end of the 1960s. The growth of the role of government in the areas of welfare and health during the 1960s produced increases in funding for nonprofit firms that often provided the services needed at a local level (Salamon, 1987). The social movements of the 1960s also called for new nonprofit organizations to facilitate the changes that were being sought, and some of the new nonprofit organizations dealt exclusively with women's issues.

The nonprofit sector, dominated by educational, health, and social welfare organizations, has historically been an important employer of women. Estimates reveal that women account for two thirds to three fourths of the employees of the nonprofit sector (Preston, 1990b). Because much of the high representation of women in the sector is the result of occupational distribution in nonprofit organizations (Preston, 1990a), the increasing opportunities available to women in traditionally male occupations could threaten the supply of talented women for the nonprofit sector. However, at the same time, the nonprofit sector provides such nonpecuniary characteristics as job satisfaction, interesting work, and skill development, which are perceived as less prevalent in the private sector and also may be relatively more attractive to women (Mirvis and Hackett, 1983; Preston, 1990a).

The remainder of the chapter analyzes how women in the nonprofit sector have fared during a period of enormous growth in both the nonprofit sector and in employment opportunities for American women. The general thesis is

41

that as women made important inroads in the professional occupations of the for-profit sector during the 1970s and 1980s, they also continued to enter the nonprofit sector in increasing numbers. Wages of women in the nonprofit sector relative to wages of women in the for-profit sector declined during the 1970s but then held ground during the 1980s. Wages of nonprofit women have increased relative to wages of women employed by government, and as of 1991, the average nonprofit woman earned a higher hourly wage than her government counterpart. The occupational and educational distributions of men and women in the nonprofit sector have been converging over time, but there is evidence that women still lag in the attainment of managerial positions. Similarly, while wages of men and women in the nonprofit sector are approximately equal, wages of managerial women are more than 20 percent below wages of managerial men. Finally, while the changing occupational distributions of women of color have somewhat mirrored those of white women, the wages of women of color still lag behind the wages of white women, and that lag is most pronounced in the nonprofit sector. (The chapter follows the experience of black women, rather than the broader group of women of color, because this is the only racial or ethnic group consistently defined in the data throughout the period.)

Data

To investigate the changes in employment patterns of nonprofit women during the period from 1969 to the present, I use data from the Current Population Surveys (CPS) conducted by the U.S. Bureau of the Census. The Current Population Surveys are extensive monthly household surveys that were first conducted in 1968 and since have been conducted yearly. The surveys include questions about demographic characteristics and current work situations. My analyses are conducted on the May 1969 CPS, the May 1973 CPS, the May 1981 CPS, and the 1991 Annual Merged CPS Sample, a sample that merged data on different individuals interviewed in different months of 1991.

There is evidence that many changes in labor market outcomes for women spurred by the legislation and social movements of the 1960s did not become evident until the 1970s. Goldin (1990) shows that the white-collar distribution of women was relatively constant between 1930 and 1970, and the increase in the professional orientation of American women was first observed in the 1970s. Therefore, the data presented in this chapter more generally describe the changes in labor market status of women since the late 1960s.

The CPS does not ask workers whether they work for a nonprofit or for-profit firm. Therefore, I use an industry-based definition of *nonprofit status*. Within various industries, at least 60 percent of employees work for a nonprofit firm. The industries include hospitals, health services, elementary and secondary schools, colleges and universities, libraries, museums, art galleries, zoos, religious organizations, welfare services, residential welfare facilities, and nonprofit membership organizations. While some employees within these industries are employed by for-profit organizations, rough calculations for the period of the late

1970s and early 1980s reveal that only 9 percent of the workers classified as nonprofit are really for profit under the industry definition (Preston, 1989).

Several industries house a small but significant number of nonprofit employees. In 1981, these industries included radio and television broadcasting; security, commodity brokerage, and investment companies; commercial research, development, and testing labs; lodging places except hotels and motels; theaters and motion picture houses; miscellaneous entertainment and recreation services; educational services; convalescent institutions; legal services; and miscellaneous professional and related services. These are classified as "mixed" industries. The remaining industries are classified as private for-profit.

The analysis focuses on white-collar workers because the vast majority of nonprofit workers are white collar. White collar is an occupational categorization that includes professional and technical workers, managers and administrators, sales workers, and clerical workers. White-collar occupations include jobs with relatively high levels of education, prestige, and pay. Therefore, women's progress in these occupations signals real progress in the labor market. Because the Census Bureau altered occupational definitions slightly during the period of analysis to accommodate the changing technology of the work place, I used a bridging process described in Appendix A to ensure consistency of occupational classifications during the time period.

Occupational Distributions in 1969

While women were 43.6 percent of the white-collar work force in 1969, women were predominantly employed in clerical or sales occupations, and female professionals were likely to work in occupations traditionally reserved for women.

The relatively high representation of women in white-collar jobs in 1969 was the result of the large number of white-collar women in clerical and sales jobs (67.8 percent). Only 24.7 percent of white-collar women worked as professionals, and a mere 7.5 percent held managerial positions. The figures stand in contrast to the figures for their male counterparts. In 1969, 35.1 percent of white-collar men were professionals and 35.7 percent were managers.

Furthermore, the vast majority of those women who had achieved professional status were employed in "female" occupations: 43.6 percent were elementary and secondary school teachers and 16.9 percent were nurses (Table 2.1). Women were also highly represented in such professional positions as music teachers, social workers, and dental or medical technicians. Few of the traditionally male-dominated professions such as engineering, law, and medicine employed more than a handful of women. However, 3.6 percent of the female professionals were employed as accountants and auditors, and 1.2 percent were employed as editors or reporters.

Just as more recent estimates document the large number of women in the nonprofit and government sectors, in 1969 professional women were overrepresented in the nonprofit and government sectors. However, managerial women were underrepresented in these sectors.

Sectoral distributions of white-collar workers in 1969 (Figure 2.1) reveal that 6.6 percent of the white-collar workers held jobs in the nonprofit sector and 22.2 percent held

**Table 2.1. Changes in the Occupational Distribution
of Professional Women by Percentage in
Selected Occupations, 1969–1991.**

	1969	*1991*
Accountants and auditors	3.6	7.4
Registered nurses	16.9	15.6
Teachers (except college and university)	43.6	30.2
Technicians, health related*	4.0	7.3
Technicians, others	2.3	1.3
Lawyers and judges	0.1	1.3
Engineers	0.3	1.3
College professors	2.2	3.1
Computer systems analysts and scientists	**	2.2
Editors and reporters	1.2	1.4
Social workers	3.1	4.1
Social scientists	0.6	3.0
Natural scientists	0.3	1.2
Doctors	0.9	1.2

*The types of health-related technicians expanded rapidly during the time period.
**While there was no comparable occupational classification in 1969, there was a computer programmer classification, which employed 0.28 percent of professional women.

jobs in federal, state, or local government. However, the percentages understate the representation of women, and professional women in particular, in the nonprofit and government sectors. Twenty-two percent of professional women worked in the nonprofit sector and 59 percent worked in the government sector. The overrepresentation of professional women was especially striking for black women: 74.6 percent of black professional women worked for government, and 17.1 percent of black professional women worked in the nonprofit sector. The relatively low representation of professional women (19 percent) and black professional women (8.3 percent) in the for-profit sector was not a result of the occupational distribution within the for-profit sector: more than 60 percent of male professionals were employed in the for-profit sector. Rather, professional opportunities in the for-profit sector were not open to women.

The large difference in percentages of women and men holding management jobs implies that managerial opportunities were also generally closed to women. However, the situation was especially serious for nonprofit and government women. Women in managerial positions were underrepresented in these sectors—4.1 and 12.7 percent of managerial women were employed in the nonprofit and government sectors, respectively (Figure 2.1). Therefore, generally, the professional jobs held by women in the non-profit and government sectors did not lead to managerial positions. Black managerial women, on the other hand, who made up only 3.3 percent of all managerial women, were much more likely to be employed in the government (37.9 percent) than their white counterparts. Black women clearly had little access to managerial jobs, and their lack of access was striking, especially in the nonprofit and for-profit sectors.

In 1969, there were no signals from employment data of the imminent increases in the number of professional women and professional for-profit women in particular.

As pointed out earlier, the 1970s and 1980s were a time of increasing professional opportunities for women. Goldin (1990) notes that many of the new opportunities occurred in male-dominated occupations. Furthermore, the sheer magnitude of the increased numbers makes it necessary to conclude that much of the increase in professional opportunities came in the for-profit sector, the dominant sector in the U.S. economy. However, an examination of the sectoral distributions of young women in 1969 reveals that their labor market choices followed the choices of their predecessors.

The sectoral distributions of young, inexperienced white-collar women were not significantly different from the distributions of all white-collar women. Focusing the analysis on white-collar women whose years of calculated experience (age minus years of education minus five) were fewer than six permits the examination of the occupational distribution of a group of women who entered the labor force at the time of or after passage of the Civil Rights Act. Figure 2.2 shows the sectoral distribution of these women. Their sectoral distribution is similar to that for the complete sample of women displayed in Figure 2.1; 10 percent of the younger women were employed by the nonprofit sector and 28 percent were employed by the government. The stability of sectoral distributions extends to professional women. About 23 percent and 61 percent of the young professionals were employed in the nonprofit and government sectors, respectively. Young professional women had not yet found opportunities in the for-profit sector.

While the nonprofit and government sectors provided opportunities to educated women that were not available in the for-profit sector, opportunities for nonprofit women still lagged behind those for nonprofit men, and opportunities for black nonprofit women lagged behind those of all nonprofit women combined.

Figure 2.1. Sectoral Distributions of Selected White-Collar Labor Forces, 1969.

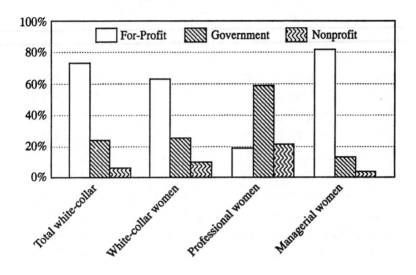

Figure 2.2. Sectoral Distributions of Inexperienced, Female White-Collar Workers, 1969.

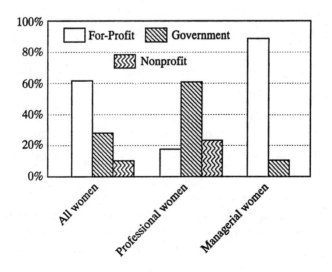

As Table 2.2 shows, women in the nonprofit and government sectors achieved levels of education and occupational status well above their for-profit counterparts. Women in the nonprofit sector had 0.5 fewer years of education than white-collar women in the government sector but 1.8 more years of education than white-collar women in the for-profit sector. While roughly 60 percent of nonprofit and government white-collar women were in either managerial or professional jobs, only 16.5 percent of white-collar for-profit women occupied these jobs. The one striking difference between nonprofit women and women employed by government was the extent of part-time activity. A female white-collar employee in the nonprofit sector was almost twice as likely to work part time as a female white-collar employee in the government sector (Table 2.2).

In 1969, within the government sector, the black woman's educational and occupational distributions were virtually identical to those of all women. However, within the nonprofit sector, black women had on average one full year less education than all women, and roughly 10 percent more black women than all women were in the less prestigious clerical and sales occupations (see Tables 2.2 and 2.3).

Within the nonprofit sector, women lagged behind men in educational attainment and occupational status. Nonprofit men, who made up slightly more than one third of the nonprofit labor force, had on average two more years of education than nonprofit women. Furthermore, nonprofit men were overrepresented in the professional and managerial occupations of the nonprofit sector: only 6.5

Table 2.2. Education and Occupational Distribution of Nonprofit, For-Profit, and Government Women and Nonprofit Men, 1969–1991

	Nonprofit Women	For-Profit Women	Government Women	Nonprofit Men
1969				
Years of education	14.7	12.9	15.2	16.8
Percentage of				
Professional	56.8	5.8	53.4	79.4
Managerial	3.3	10.7	3.5	14.1
Clerical and sales	39.9	83.5	43.1	6.5
Part-time	18.2	13.2	9.4	4.4
1981				
Years of education	15.1	13.7	15.4	16.9
Percentage of				
Professional	56.8	9.9	48.8	73.5
Managerial	6.6	13.6	6.3	17.7
Clerical and sales	36.6	76.5	44.9	8.8
Part-time	27.1	26.7	17.7	11.5
1991				
Years of education	15.6	14.2	15.7	16.9
Percentage of				
Professional	57.9	11.9	48.6	69.1
Managerial	12.1	15.9	10.8	20.4
Clerical and sales	30.0	72.2	40.6	10.5
Part-time	23.0	22.4	14.9	11.8
1991, Inexperienced				
Years of education	15.9	14.2	15.8	16.1
Percentage of				
Professional	60.9	10.3	51.5	64.2
Managerial	5.8	7.5	4.1	9.2
Clerical and sales	33.3	82.2	44.4	26.6

**Table 2.3. Education and Occupational
Distribution of Black Women, 1969–1991.**

	All White-Collar Women	Nonprofit Women	Government Women
1969			
Years of education	14.0	13.7	15.1
Percentage of			
Professional	31.4	49.1	50.0
Managerial	3.7	2.5	3.1
Clerical and sales	64.9	48.4	46.9
1981			
Years of education	14.4	14.1	14.9
Percentage of			
Professional	29.5	52.2	41.9
Managerial	7.5	6.2	6.1
Clerical and sales	63.0	41.6	52.0
1991			
Years of education	13.7	14.0	14.3
Percentage of			
Professional	26.2	48.3	40.0
Managerial	10.3	10.8	11.0
Clerical and sales	63.5	40.9	49.0

percent of these men were not employed in managerial or professional jobs (Table 2.2).

Changing Occupational Patterns by Sector: 1969–1991

Since 1969, the percentage of white-collar workers who are women has steadily increased, and the percentage of white-collar workers who are employed by nonprofit firms has steadily increased.

By 1981, women were 53 percent of the white-collar labor force, and in 1991, they were almost 56 percent of the white-collar labor force (Figure 2.3). The relative growth of women in the white-collar sector was especially striking in the professional and managerial jobs. Figure 2.4 shows that by 1991, women held almost 50 percent of professional jobs, and Figure 2.5 shows that women's representation in managerial occupations more than doubled from 1981 to 1991. Figures 2.3 to 2.5 also show that black women increased their representation significantly in the white-collar sector, especially in managerial occupations, where the percentage of managerial jobs held by black women increased from 0.5 percent in 1969 to 2.5 percent in 1991.

At the same time, the nonprofit sector was growing rapidly. According to the industrial definition of nonprofit sector used in this chapter, employees in the nonprofit sector increased from 6.6 percent of the white-collar labor force in 1969 to 8.8 percent in 1981 and to 10.8 percent in 1991 (Figure 2.6). As relative employment in the nonprofit sector was growing, relative employment in the government sector was decreasing. By 1991, government employees accounted for only 19 percent of the white-collar labor force.

Between 1969 and 1991, there was a large increase in the percentage of professional women who found employment in the for-profit sector and a somewhat smaller, although still sizable, increase in the percentage of professional women who found employment in the nonprofit sector.

The striking change in the sectoral distribution of professional women over the twenty-two-year period is displayed in Figure 2.7. The percentage of professional women employed in the nonprofit sector increased from 22 percent

**Figure 2.3. Gender Representation,
White-Collar Labor Force, 1969–1991.**

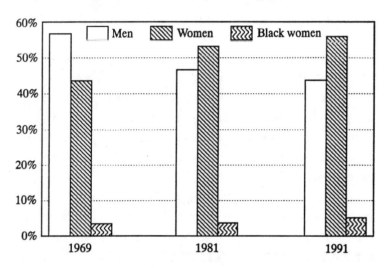

**Figure 2.4. Gender Representation,
Professional Occupations, 1969–1991.**

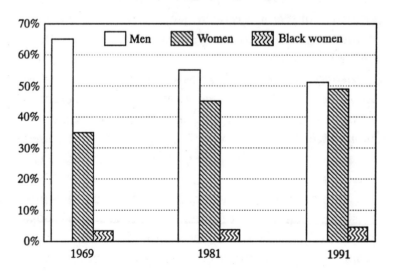

**Figure 2.5. Gender Representation,
Managerial Occupations, 1969–1991.**

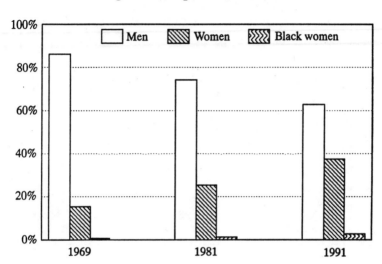

to 29.9 percent, a 35 percent increase. At the same time, there was a 36 percent decline in the percentage of professional women in the government sector, from 59 percent to 38.1 percent. Probably most important, professional opportunities in the for-profit sector were becoming accessible to women. The percentage of professional women in the for-profit sector increased from 19 to 32 percent, increasing the relative representation of professional women in the for-profit sector by more than two thirds. Furthermore, by 1991, almost 40 percent of young, inexperienced professional women were employed in the for-profit sector. Clearly, the change in the sectoral distribution of professional women is still in process.

As the for-profit sector opened its doors to professional women, the variety of professional jobs held by women

Figure 2.6. Sectoral Distribution,
Total White-Collar Labor Force, 1969–1991.

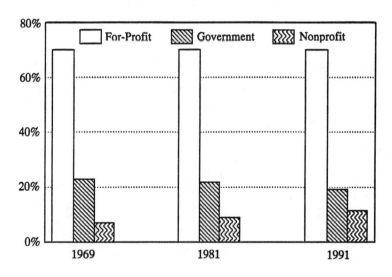

Figure 2.7. Sectoral Distribution,
Professional Women, 1969–1991.

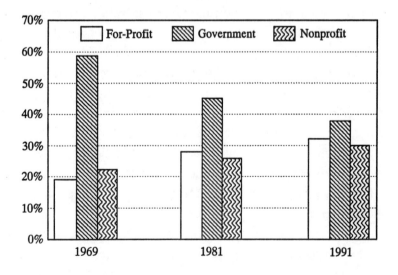

**Figure 2.8. Sectoral Distribution,
Managerial Women, 1969–1991.**

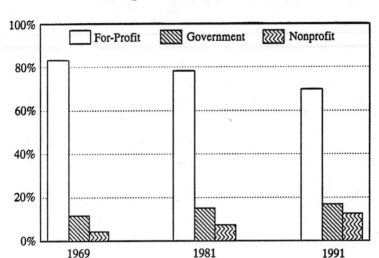

increased dramatically. In 1969, teaching and nursing accounted for more than 60 percent of all professional jobs held by women. By 1991, these occupations constituted only slightly more than 45 percent of all professional jobs held by women. The percentage of professional women working as lawyers or judges increased from 0.14 in 1969 to 1.32 in 1991. Similarly, while only 0.3 percent of all professional women were engineers in 1969, 1.34 percent were employed as engineers in 1991. (See Table 2.1 for more information on the changes in occupational distribution of professional women.) The percentage increases may mask the true gains in representation that women have made, because while the percentages were increasing, the absolute number of women in the professional occupations was increasing rapidly as well. From 1970 to 1990, the number of women employed in professional occupations increased from 3.5 million to well over 8.5 million.

During the period of 1969 to 1991, the managerial opportunities available to nonprofit women also increased.

As the for-profit sector increased its employment of women in professional positions, the nonprofit and government sectors increased their employment of women in managerial jobs (see Figure 2.8). The percentage of managerial women employed in the nonprofit sector increased from 4.1 percent in 1969 to 12.7 percent in 1991, a 210 percent growth in relative percentages. While such progress is undeniable, the 12.7 percent figure is still relatively low, even in a sector that has a small management component. According to Table 2.2, in 1991, 20 percent of nonprofit men were managers while only 12.1 percent of nonprofit women were managers.

By 1991, the educational and occupational distributions of nonprofit men and nonprofit women were approaching equality.

In 1991, women were roughly three quarters of the employees of the nonprofit sector. Focusing on men and women with five or fewer years of experience, inexperienced nonprofit women had, on average, only 0.2 fewer years of education than inexperienced nonprofit men (Table 2.2). Similarly, the male and female occupational distributions for the inexperienced workers were much more similar than they had been in previous years. By 1991, the nonprofit sector offered young women favorable occupational opportunities, not only in comparison to the opportunities offered by the other sectors but also in comparison to the opportunities offered to men in the non-profit sector.

In 1991, black professional and managerial women continued to find a majority of their opportunities in the government and nonprofit sectors, but within the government and nonprofit sectors, black women had lost ground relative to all women.

While professional opportunities for black women in the for-profit sector increased during the time period, by 1991 only 22.7 percent of black professional women were employed in the for-profit sector. Fifty-one percent of black professional women held government jobs and 26.3 percent held nonprofit jobs. Similarly, black managerial women were overrepresented in the government sector (35.7 percent) and underrepresented in the for-profit sector (49.9 percent).

Within the government sector, the approximate parity in education and occupational locus between black and all women eroded between 1969 and 1991. By 1991, in both the nonprofit and government sectors, black women had approximately 1.5 fewer years of education than all women, and 10 percent more black women than all women held the less prestigious clerical and sales jobs.

Sectoral Wage and Salary Comparisons, 1973–1991

Between 1973 and 1991, nonprofit women were increasingly working in jobs with higher skill and responsibility levels. However, it is also important to determine how relative wages were changing during the period. It has been well documented that the nonprofit sector is a low-paying sector (Mirvis and Hackett, 1983; Weisbrod, 1983; and Preston, 1989). Furthermore, studies that track the wage differential over time have revealed that the wages of nonprofit women relative to women employed in the for-profit sector have been declining in recent years (Preston, 1990a). In order to estimate wage differentials, I use a wage regression methodology that allows a comparison of wages for individuals with similar levels of education and experience. A similar methodology was used by Bound and Johnson (1992) to show that women's wages, which were 67.5 percent of men's wages in 1973, increased to 75.6 percent of men's wages in 1988. Roughly three quarters of the increase occurred in the 1980s.

The Current Population Survey of the Census Bureau began asking questions about wages and salary in 1968, but the early surveys allowed only categorical answers rather than exact monetary amounts. Therefore, I begin the wage analysis in 1973, the first year that wages and salaries were reported in dollars. The sample that I use excludes self-employed workers, because I am only interested in wage and salaried workers, and the income of self-employed people can deviate significantly from week to week and month to month. To ensure clean comparisons of wages and salaries of nonprofit, for-profit, and government workers, I also exclude all workers who are employed in the mixed industries, industries in which there is a small but significant representation of nonprofit workers.

While the wages of nonprofit women were declining relative to wages of for-profit women until 1981, they held their ground during the remainder of the 1980s.

The nonprofit wage differential for all full-time workers was −13.5 percent in 1973. While it increased in magnitude to −16.6 percent in 1981, it fell back to −13 percent in 1991. Much of the reduction in the magnitude of the negative nonprofit wage differential between 1981 and 1991 was the result of the reduction in the magnitude of the negative male wage differential from −30.5 percent in 1981 to −25 percent in 1991. Figure 2.9 presents nonprofit women's wages as a percentage of for-profit women's wages for all women and for professional women over the period. (A bar with height of 100 percent means that nonprofit women's wages are equal to for-profit women's wages, and a bar with a height of 90 percent means that nonprofit women's wages are 90 percent of for-profit women's wages.) The estimates provide new evidence that

**Figure 2.9. Nonprofit Women's Wages
as a Percentage of For-Profit Women's Wages, 1973–1991.**

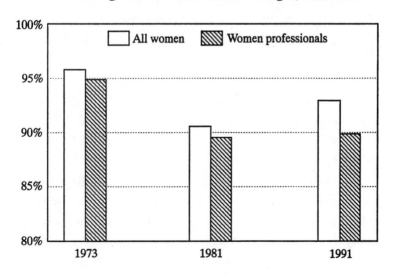

the magnitude of the negative wage differential between female nonprofit workers and female for-profit workers, which was increasing fairly steadily from 1973 to 1981, has been stable or even decreasing since that time. Nonprofit women's wages increased from 90.7 percent to 92.9 percent of for-profit women's wages from 1981 to 1991. I estimate (1990a) that the 7-percent differential between nonprofit and for-profit women's wages in 1991 was relatively constant in 1983 and 1985. Similarly, while nonprofit professional women's wages fell from 95 percent to slightly less than 90 percent of for-profit professional women's wages between 1973 and 1981, the 90-percent figure has remained relatively stable since 1981.

Interestingly, the analysis also reveals that, throughout the time period, the wage loss experienced by part-time nonprofit workers is less severe than the wage loss experienced by full-time nonprofit workers. In fact, by 1991, nonprofit part-time workers received a wage reduction no more severe than the wage reduction experienced by for-profit part-time workers. And female part-time workers in the nonprofit sector had wages 2 percent higher than female part-time workers' in the for-profit sector. The nonprofit sector has historically offered part-time opportunities to well-educated professional employees. The relatively high pay for part-time workers in the nonprofit sector may reflect the higher quality of part-time opportunities.

During the period of 1973 to 1991, the negative nonprofit-government wage differential decreased steadily, and by 1991, women in the nonprofit sector earned significantly higher wages than women in the government sector.

In order to estimate the nonprofit-government wage differential, the same regressions described earlier were estimated for a sample of nonprofit and government employees. The striking change in the female nonprofit-government wage differentials over the twenty-two-year period is displayed in Figure 2.10. Nonprofit women, who earned 94.6 percent of government women's wages in 1973, earned 101.2 percent of government women's wages in 1991. And by 1991, nonprofit female professionals were earning salaries 7.3 percent higher than comparable female government employees. The patterns extend to male employees as well. Male nonprofit employees, who earned salaries roughly 20.6 percent lower than salaries of government employees in 1973, earned salaries only 12.6 percent lower in 1991.

Figure 2.10. Nonprofit Women's Wages as a Percentage of Government Women's Wages, 1973–1991.

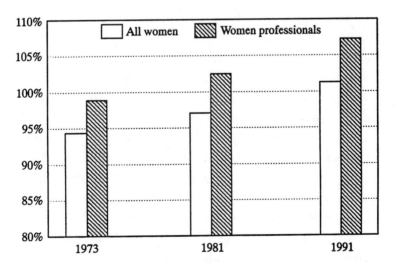

The figures for the general labor force show that wages of nonprofit men and women held ground relative to for-profit wages but increased relative to government wages during the 1980s. The specific patterns coincide with results of sectoral wage comparisons for scientists and engineers in the 1980s. Tracking a group of scientists and engineers from 1982 to 1989, I found (1993) that scientists and engineers in the nonprofit sector earned salaries roughly 14 percent lower than salaries of scientists and engineers in the for-profit sector during the complete period. However, nonprofit scientists and engineers who earned salaries roughly 3 percent below comparable government scientists' and engineers' in 1982 were earning salaries 9 percent higher than government employees' in 1989. Clearly, the pattern of retrenchment in the relative size of government employment has occurred in conjunction with a reduction in relative wage and salary growth. The government is becoming a less attractive place to work for many white-collar employees.

From 1973 to 1991, men and women in the nonprofit sector earned, on average, comparable salaries; however, some of the apparent equality was a result of the differing occupational distributions of nonprofit men and women.

Figure 2.11 presents female wages as a percentage of male wages in the nonprofit sector during the period of 1973 to 1991 for the three occupational categories. As I have noted previously (1990a), aggregate female wage differentials in the nonprofit sector are close to zero. The estimated female wage differential is small, at about −2 percent over the total period. The low wage differential

Figure 2.11. Nonprofit Women's Wages as a Percentage
of Men's Wages, 1973–1991.

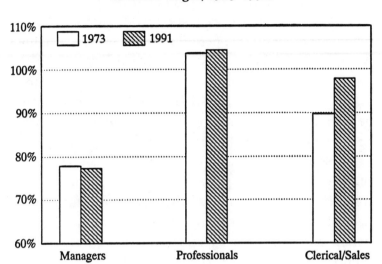

implies a much higher level of wage equality in the white-collar nonprofit sector than in the white-collar for-profit sector, where the female wage differential was approximately −18 percent in 1991.

The equality of wages across gender in the nonprofit sector, however, is not constant across occupational groups (see Figure 2.11). Within the managerial professions, women were paid wages roughly 22 percent lower than men's, perhaps because in the nonprofit sector men are employed in managerial positions with greater responsibility and prestige. In 1973 and 1981, female clerical and sales workers earned wages 10 to 20 percent lower than male clerical and sales workers' in the nonprofit sector. However, by 1991, the absolute value of the negative female wage differential for these occupations had declined to –3.3 percent, which is insignificantly different from zero.

In the professional occupations, on the other hand, women throughout the period were paid wages roughly 4 percent higher than men's. The positive female differential for professional nonprofit workers is the result of the differing occupational locus of professional men and women in the nonprofit sector. In 1973, roughly one third of male nonprofit employees were employed in the clergy or other types of religious work, and less than 2 percent of the women were employed in these occupations. While the percentage of nonprofit men employed in the clergy had declined to 15 percent by 1991, this low-paying occupation was still the occupation employing the greatest number of nonprofit men. When the 1991 nonprofit regressions were estimated by including a control for location in a religious occupation, the aggregate female differential grew from –2 percent to –8 percent. Within occupation, the male-female wage differentials for managerial and clerical occupations were unchanged. However, the female wage differential for professional nonprofit workers fell from positive 4 percent to negative 4 percent. While the negative female wage differential for professional nonprofit workers is statistically significant, its magnitude is still much lower than the magnitude of negative female wage differentials estimated elsewhere in the economy.

In order to determine whether female wage differentials are lower for newly employed workers, I reestimated the nonprofit wage regressions for inexperienced employees. Because there are few individuals in the sample of inexperienced nonprofit workers in the years 1973 and 1981, any estimated differences are at best preliminary. However, in both 1973 and 1981, the estimated female differential for inexperienced workers is positive. In 1991, inexperienced female nonprofit workers earned wages 7 percent higher than inexperienced male nonprofit workers'. Female professional workers earned wages 10 percent higher than male professional workers' and female managerial workers earned wages 12 percent lower than male managerial workers', a differential roughly one half the magnitude of the negative female wage differential for the total set of managerial workers in the nonprofit sector. These estimated differentials imply that the magnitude of the negative managerial female differential is falling for newly employed workers and that the complete wage distribution is becoming more equal. In some cases the inequality seems to be even reversing itself as women appear to earn a wage premium.

However, such a conclusion is premature. The earlier years, 1973 and 1981, also show a wage distribution in which newly employed nonprofit women earn a wage premium, although the estimates are not significant because of relatively small sample sizes. The pattern in which the female wage differential becomes more negative with a more experienced sample may be the result of higher levels of women than men leaving the labor force, not a changing wage distribution. There are several reasons for this. First, the age variable is a proxy for experience, because age minus years of education minus five gives potential years in the labor market for any respondent. If nonprofit women are more likely than men to take periods of unemployment for family or other considerations, the proxy for experience is likely to overestimate real experience to a greater extent for women than for men. Comparing men and women at the same age is really comparing men with higher levels of experience to women with lower levels of experience, and the gap in experience is likely to widen as the average age of the samples increase. The wage differentials are likely to reflect the differences in experience. At the same time, women may be less likely to climb the managerial ladder if they periodically leave the labor force. Therefore, managerial women may be employed in levels of managerial jobs lower than managerial men for reasons related to the differing career choices made by men and women in the nonprofit sector.

In my study of scientists and engineers between 1982 and 1989, I found that female scientists and engineers in the nonprofit sector are significantly more likely to leave the labor force than women in the government sector and slightly more likely to leave the labor force than women in the for-profit sector. In addition, female scientists and engineers in the nonprofit sector are significantly more likely than their male counterparts to leave the labor force. If labor force exit continues at a relatively higher rate for nonprofit women, the negative female wage differential for managers will probably persist, even in a sector in which wage gaps across gender are closing. However, one cannot ignore the fact that differing career choices may also be linked to discriminatory forces, if a lack of labor market opportunities open to women contributes to their decisions to interrupt work.

In 1991, black women's wages were below white women's wages, and the largest wage gap by race was in the nonprofit sector.

Figure 3.12 gives black women's wages as a percentage of white women's wages in the three sectors during the period of 1973 to 1981. In all three sectors, black women's wages as a percentage of white women's wages declined during the period. The decline was most abrupt for the nonprofit sector. In 1991, black women's salaries were less than 95 percent of white women's salaries in the nonprofit sector. By contrast, in government, black women earned salaries that were more than 98 percent of white women's salaries. Clearly, the statistics on black women show that, while black women have made progress in terms of representation in the white-collar sector, they have fallen behind

Figure 2.12. Black Women's Wages as a Percentage of White Women's Wages, 1973–1991.

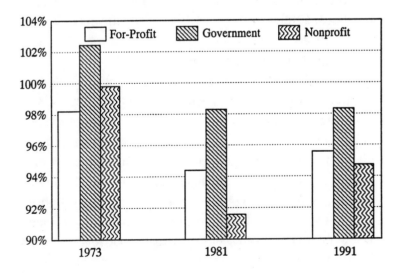

white women in terms of salaries. For-profit opportunities have not opened up to black women to the same extent as to white women, and within the nonprofit sector, black women's salaries continue to lag behind those of white women.

Conclusion

The 1970s and 1980s brought important and generally positive changes for women in the nonprofit sector. Opportunities for women in the nonprofit sector, already abundant before the Civil Rights Act was passed in 1964, increased. As the for-profit sector increased its relative employment of professional women by expanding opportunities available for women, so too did the nonprofit sector. Not only did more professional women find employment in the nonprofit sector but the percentage of nonprofit women in management jobs more than tripled as well. Furthermore, the educational level of nonprofit women increased by almost a full year on average. By 1991, the occupational distributions and educational levels of men and women entering the nonprofit sector were similar.

While the wages of women in the nonprofit sector fell relative to women in the for-profit sector from 1973 to 1981, new evidence reveals that wages of nonprofit women kept pace with wages of for-profit women during the 1980s. The new evidence is especially heartening to women in the nonprofit sector, because women's wages in general were gaining ground relative to men's wages throughout the 1980s. During the period of 1973 to 1991, women's wages in the nonprofit sector increased relative to women's wages in the government sector, and by 1991, the non-profit-government salary differential for women was 1.2 percent.

Throughout the period, the nonprofit wage distribution demonstrated a degree of gender equality not replicated elsewhere in the economy. On average, women's wages were 1 to 2 percent lower than men's wages; however, some of the apparent equality was the result of the large percentage of nonprofit men employed in the clergy. Controlling for the low pay of the clergy, women's wages were on average 8 percent lower than men's wages in the nonprofit sector, and nonprofit professional women earned wages 4 percent lower than nonprofit professional men's. The negative female wage differential for managers throughout the period may be exacerbated by labor force interruptions of nonprofit women.

The high degree of gender equality in salary and occupational attainment in the nonprofit sector, however, did not extend to racial equality. Within the nonprofit sector, black women had significantly lower levels of education, significantly lower wages, and a less prestigious occupational distribution than white women. In addition, the gaps in earnings and achievement increased between 1969 and 1991.

Throughout the period of analysis, the nonprofit sector has provided high-quality employment opportunities to talented, generally white, women. At the same time that these women were faced with an ever-increasing choice of employment options, they were increasingly turning to nonprofit employment. The success of the nonprofit sector in continuing to attract top-notch women needs to be further researched. But surely there are some obvious explanations.

First, as the for-profit sector was increasing its opportunities for women, the government sector was downsizing and reducing its employment opportunities. Second, the nonprofit sector greatly increased its management opportunities for women. Third, the nonprofit sector has a degree of flexibility that may not be present in other sectors. It has the highest percentage of part-time workers of the three sectors. Although in recent years part-time opportunities in the for-profit sector have increased to a level comparable to the nonprofit sector's, part-time female workers earn higher wages in the nonprofit sector than in the for-profit sector. The availability of part-time work is likely to be attractive for some women who are balancing family and work responsibilities. Furthermore, in 1991, 75 percent of the nonprofit work force was female. Therefore, it is likely that workplace policies in this sector are more favorable to working women than policies in the for-profit sector. Finally, occupational and wage distributions, which are approaching equality across genders, must be important drawing cards for women interested in the nonprofit sector.

Appendix A

In order to define an industry-based nonprofit sector, I first classify all individuals working for the federal, state, or local government as government employees. Second, all self-employed workers are classified as for-profit workers. The inclusion of self-employed workers in the occupational distributions is especially important, because female professional workers, especially in the 1960s, may have found self-employment a necessary option in a workplace that closed certain professional occupations to women. The remaining workers are classified as nonprofit if they work in an industry assigned three digits by the Standard Industrial Classification (SIC) in which at least 60 percent of all those employed are nonprofit workers. Rudney and Weitzman (1983) use the 1977 Census of Service Industries and annual Bureau of Labor Statistics employment data to construct indexes of nonprofit employment in three-digit SIC classifications for the years 1972 to 1982. By bridging the 1972 SIC code with the 1970 census industrial code (the industry classification used by the Census Bureau in the 1973–1981 CPS), I have identified the following industries as nonprofit: hospitals; health services; elementary and secondary schools; colleges and universities; libraries; museums, art galleries, and zoos; religious organizations; welfare services; residential welfare facilities; and nonprofit membership organizations.

A handful of other three-digit industries house a small but significant number of nonprofit employees. In 1981, these industries included radio and television broadcasting; security, commodity brokerage, and investment companies; commercial research, development, and testing labs; lodging places except hotels and motels; theaters and motion picture houses; miscellaneous entertainment and recreation services; educational services; convalescent institutions; legal services; and miscellaneous professional and related services. These industries are classified as "mixed" industries. Because of the relatively small number of nonprofit employees in many of these industries, the number of nonprofit employees in these industries is likely to be well below 10 percent.

The industrial coding scheme used by the Census has changed over time, and in order to deal with these changes, the industrial definitions used for the 1970 census are bridged to the 1960 industrial coding scheme, used for the 1969 Current Population Survey, and the 1980 industrial coding scheme, used for the 1991 Current Population Survey. (Priebe, Heinkel, and Greene [1972] define a bridge between the 1960 and 1970 Census codes.)

The 1960 industrial coding system is slightly less specific than the 1970 coding scheme; therefore, the mixed industries include all health services except hospitals, and the nonprofit industries do not include any specialized health services except hospitals. In addition, the set of mixed industries includes two more aggregated industries: miscellaneous business, which encompasses commercial research-and-development testing laboratories, and hotels and lodging places, which encompasses lodging places, except hotels. Therefore, in 1969, the set of "mixed" industries is disproportionately large. In 1981, the one important change in the definition of nonprofit industries is the inclusion of the newly created "noncommercial, educational, and scientific research" industry.

The employees in the mixed industries are added to the for-profit employees in the analyses of occupational distribution in Figures 2.1, 2.2 and 2.6 to 2.8 because, otherwise, the change in the size of these mixed indus-

74

tries due to definitional changes between 1969 and 1981 might skew the patterns of sectoral changes. In alternative analyses, the employees of these mixed industries are dropped from the samples to ensure cleaner comparisons of nonprofit and for-profit or government wages. The occupational codes also change slightly over the thirty-year period. For example, accountants and auditors are classified as professionals using the 1970 Census occupational codes and managers or administrators using the 1980 Census codes. However, I bridge the 1960 and 1980 occupational codes to the 1970 codes so that there is consistency throughout the period of analysis. Generally, the occupational bridging ensures consistency for the large group of occupations defined as professionals or managers. However, the number of three-digit occupational classifications increases from the 1960 census codes to the 1990 census codes.

Appendix B

In order to estimate wage differentials, I estimate a wage regression, where the natural logarithm of the hourly wage is the dependent variable. Salary measures are collected as hourly wage rates or weekly salaries when the individual is salaried. For salaried workers, the wage is calculated from the weekly salary divided by usual weekly hours. Independent variables include dummy variables for race, sex, professional occupation, managerial occupation, part-time status, union status, and residence in a metropolitan area. In addition, I include years of education as a measure of human capital and (age minus education minus five) and (age minus education minus five)^2 as proxies for experience.

In the first analysis, in which I estimate nonprofit/for-profit wage differentials, I estimate the wage regression on the sample of nonprofit and for-profit employees. Initially, I include a dummy variable for nonprofit status and a variable that interacts nonprofit status and part-time employment. Therefore, the reported wage differentials in Figures 2.9 to 2.12 relate to wage differentials for full-time workers. In order to estimate wage differentials for more specific samples, I reestimate the wage equations, including dummy variables representing the specific groups (for example, nonprofit females or nonprofit female professional employees). The wage differentials are estimated for 1973, 1981, and 1991.

References

Bound, J., and Johnson, G. "Changes in the Structure of Wages in the 1980's: An Evaluation of Alternative Explanations." *American Economic Review,* 1992, *82*(3), 371–393.

Goldin, C. *Understanding the Gender Gap: An Economic History of American Women.* New York: Oxford University Press, 1990.

Hodgkinson, V. A., and Weitzman, M. S. *Dimensions of the Independent Sector: A Statistical Profile.* Washington, D.C.: Independent Sector, 1989.

Mirvis, P. H., and Hackett, E. J. "Work and Workforce Characteristics in the Nonprofit Sector." *Monthly Labor Review,* April 1983, *106,* 3–12.

Preston, A. "The Nonprofit Worker in a For-Profit World." *Journal of Labor Economics,* 1989, 7(4), 438–463.

Preston, A. "Women in the White Collar Nonprofit Sector: The Best Option or the Only Option." *Review of Economics and Statistics,* 1990a, 72(4), 560–568.

Preston, A. "Changing Labor Market Patterns in the Nonprofit and For-Profit Sectors: Implications for Nonprofit Management." *Nonprofit Management and Leadership,* 1990b, 1(1) 15–28.

Preston, A. "The Market for Human Resources: Comparing Professional Career Paths in the Public, Private, and Nonprofit Sectors." In D. C. Hammack and D. R. Young (eds.), *Nonprofit Organizations in a Market Economy.* San Francisco: Jossey-Bass, 1993.

Priebe, J. A., Heinkel, J., and Greene, S. "1970 Occupation and Industry Classification Systems in Terms of Their 1960 Occupation and Industry Elements." Technical paper no. 26, U.S. Dept. of Commerce, 1972.

Rudney, G., and Weitzman, M. "Significance of Employment and Earnings in the Philanthropic Sector, 1972–1982." Working Paper no. 77, Program on Non-Profit Organizations, Institution for Social and Policy Studies, Yale University, 1983.

Salamon, L. M. "Partners in Public Service: The Scope and Theory of Government-Nonprofit Relations." In W. W. Powell (ed.), *The Nonprofit Sector: A Research Handbook.* New Haven, Conn.: Yale University Press, 1987.

Weisbrod, B. "Nonprofit and Proprietary Sector Behavior: Wage Differentials Among Lawyers." *Journal of Labor Economics,* July 1983, pp. 246–263.

3

Pay Equity
in Nonprofit Organizations:
Making Women's Work Visible

Ronnie J. Steinberg and Jerry A. Jacobs

Society has entrusted many vital functions to organiza
tions in the nonprofit sector: the health of citizens, the
care of children, the provision of aid to disaster victims,
the stewardship of the most esteemed cultural institutions,
and the maintenance of voluntary organizations that constitute much of the fabric of American communities. While
much of the work performed in nonprofit organizations
elicits the respect of the community, it does not yield
remuneration commensurate with the social importance
of the tasks and the skills of the service providers. This
chapter suggests that many tasks performed in nonprofit
settings are economically devalued in society because the
skills the jobs require are taken for granted and treated as
invisible. We believe this is the result, in no small part, of
the fact that the work is often performed by women and

that the skills and talents required of service workers are often assumed to be natural attributes of women, deserving no special compensation.

Ignoring Gender in Nonprofit Settings

It is remarkable how little has been written on the effect of gender metaphors, ideologies, and stereotypes on the character and composition of the nonprofit sector. The fact that most nonprofit sector workers are women and that most occupations within the sector have historically been staffed by women has been insufficiently studied. This oversight is as curious as would be studying ghettos without noticing the race or the ethnicity of the people who live in them.

One prominent, full-length study of the nonprofit sector, for example, mentions women in the most cursory way and rarely for more than a sentence or two at a time— only twice in the book does a discussion of women extend to two pages, although there are more than twenty index references to women's issues and organizations (O'Neill, 1989). The same pattern unfortunately also characterizes the authoritative *The Nonprofit Sector: A Research Handbook* (Powell, 1987), which treats women as virtually invisible. In the index, while there are five references to the women's movement and three references to women's organizations, there are not enough entries for *women* (and, of course, none for *gender*), nor is there an index entry for *wages* or *earnings.* The one table on wages, in Gabriel Rudney's chapter, combines the earnings of men and women in the nonprofit sector, in a remarkable break from long-standing statistical conventions. Even the U.S. Bureau of Labor Statistics, in its most routine report, distinguishes men's and women's earnings because they differ to such a large extent. Peter Dobkin Hall's historical overview of the nonprofit sector (Hall, 1987) is entirely consistent in maintaining women's invisibility. From Hall, the only conclusion possible is that the only role women played in the nonprofit sector was that by a widow (Margaret Olivia Slocum Sage, also known as Mrs. Russell Sage), who was disposing of her husband's estate. No mention is made of women's volunteer labor in maintaining a myriad of philanthropic organizations, of women who are paid staff members in nonprofit organizations, or even of such prominent leaders as Jane Addams of the settlement house movement. Hall's history encompasses only great men, great ideas (if penned by men), great legal precedents, great fortunes, and great checkbooks. It is no wonder that the foremost contemporary study of women volunteers is entitled *Invisible Careers* (Daniels, 1988).

Many organizational sociologists have been attracted to the study of nonprofit settings to test organizational theory. Because their principal concern has been in the relationship between organizations and their environment, they pay little attention to the gender of the actors. Labor economists examine the somewhat different issues of wage determination, primarily in comparison with for-profit firms. While the economists at least notice that women work in nonprofit settings and that the low wages of such workers are a concern that warrants careful examination, they hold that the nonprofit sector is of no distinct gender.

They attribute the low wages of workers in general in non-profits either to their low productivity or to their preferences to work in such jobs, assuming as well that ideologies and stereotypes about gender play no role in the wage-setting process.

Gender-neutral Explanations of the Nonprofit Sector

Anne Preston's research is perhaps the best that has been done on wage determination in the nonprofit sector within mainstream labor economics. Using data drawn from the large, reliable, and longitudinally consistent Current Population Survey, Preston finds only a small wage penalty for women working in the nonprofit sector. The penalty has increased gradually since the 1970s, from 3 to 7 percent for women overall and from 4 to 12 percent for women professionals. She also finds that men suffer a larger wage penalty than do women for working in the nonprofit sector. In discussing her findings, she offers a "labor donation" hypothesis, reasoning that employees trade money for the psychological benefits of performing socially beneficial work (Preston, 1989, p. 442; Preston, 1990a, p. 18).

The differential Preston finds probably is less a matter of the nonprofit status of an organization than it is the type of service provided and the occupations found in nonprofit settings. Much, if not all, of the differential probably would disappear if extremely detailed controls for occupation, job title, and organizational size were introduced to the analysis. Indeed, when occupation is controlled in a reasonably detailed way—as Preston was able to do for clerical workers—the sectoral differential essentially disappears. In her analysis, a significant wage differential remains only for the extremely heterogeneous managerial and professional categories. Had she been able to introduce detailed controls for occupation and for the gender composition of occupation among the managerial and professional workers in her sample, the differential she carefully documented likely would have been less. Sociological research on gender inequality in labor markets routinely introduces detailed measures of occupation and occupational gender composition, because there is substantial evidence that occupational segregation is a primary determinant of the gender gap in wages (for example, England, Farkas, Kilbourne, and Dou, 1988). Thus, the productivity and "labor donation" hypotheses might be moot, because little differential would remain.

However, assuming for the sake of argument that there is a nonprofit wage differential, consider the two leading explanations economists have considered—lower productivity and workers' preferences for socially beneficial work. Productivity in the service sector is notoriously hard to measure (Block, 1990; Kanter and Summers, 1987). Do social workers become twice as productive when their client loads are doubled? Do college professors teach more productively when their class size is increased by five or ten students? Clearly, the *quality* of the interaction is part of the service rendered, and measuring the number of interactions is insufficient to capture the productivity of services that typify much of the nonprofit sector.

But this is not the approach to productivity that labor

economists use. Instead, what they have in mind is that nonprofit workers have fewer skills and desirable work attributes. To her credit, Preston (1989) is rightly skeptical of the explanation, but without comprehensive measures in her data, she is unable to completely rule out the possibility. And what if wages in a sector were so low that it attracted workers that were somewhat less talented, on average, than those who sought more attractive jobs? Labor economists would consider the case closed, but we do not. For us, only half the story has been explored. For one thing, no one has examined why nonprofit groups are unable to offer more attractive wages to their best people in the first place. Instead, the analysis focuses only on the response of worker to jobs with unattractive compensation packages. The structure and character of the labor market is assumed; employee productivity and preferences are the object of scrutiny. For another, measures of productivity and of skill are socially constructed and reflect the distribution of power in the labor market (Block, 1990; Steinberg, 1990). Characteristics found in disproportionately high frequencies in female service work, such as the human relations skills associated with client work, psychosocial effort, and responsibility for clients' well-being, are notoriously absent from job evaluation systems used to build and legitimate compensation practices in all sectors of the economy (Steinberg and Walter, 1992).

The other leading explanation that labor economists seriously consider is that of preferences. This argument has two strands—compensating differentials and workers' preferences. The notion of compensating differentials considers the relationship between workplace amenities and compensation, holding that wage differentials among otherwise equivalent workers are typically offset by non-pecuniary rewards. In other words, some workers must be paid a wage premium for working in undesirable settings, while others accept lower wages in return for working in attractive, pleasant, or otherwise rewarding jobs. Applied to the nonprofit literature, the argument is that non-profits offer better working conditions to compensate for lower wages. The principal difficulty with the explanation, as with preference explanations in general, is the lack of evidence. Preston (1989, 1990a, 1990b) has creatively mined two sets of available data in this area, but she was able to identify only twenty-three women working in nonprofit settings in the 1977 Quality of Employment Survey and only fifty two in the 1980 Survey of Job Characteristics. In addition to the small sample size, Preston considered only a limited set of working conditions, finding that non-profit jobs have less repetition, more skills development, and more flexible schedules than for-profit jobs. Neither the sample size nor the range of job characteristics provide adequate information upon which to base valid conclusions about the nature of working conditions in the nonprofit sector. Moreover, what little evidence she has managed to provide does not make a compelling case in favor of the compensating differentials argument. By contrast, data from a survey specifically designed to capture a broad range of workplace conditions in a large government agency reveals that female-dominated occupations (many of which are also found in nonprofit settings) have about as many undesirable working conditions associated with them as do male-dominated occupations, including such characteristics as cleaning other people's dirt, working with difficult clients, and telling people things that they do not want to hear (Jacobs and Steinberg, 1990). The findings were confirmed in the results of focus group interviews involving nearly seventy-five registered nurses and allied health professionals in nonprofit hospitals and nursing homes conducted by Steinberg between 1990 and 1993.

A further difficulty with the compensating differentials thesis is that it fails to take into account the high rate of turnover in many nonprofit jobs. For example, recent data indicate that teachers in the United States have high rates of turnover, with nonprofit educational institutions experiencing twice the turnover rate of public schools (Choy, Medrich, and Henke, 1992). In another example, a study of registered nurses in Ontario, Canada, found that nurses were quitting hospitals because of the undesirable working conditions, excessive work load, and job stress (Armstrong, 1990). Armstrong's findings are consistent with the general literature on the shortage of registered nurses: plenty of nurses are graduating from schools and entering the nursing profession, but the way the work is organized leads to high exit rates, especially among hospital nurses. Turnover is especially problematic in the service sector, in that productivity is often enhanced as a function of an enduring relationship between the service provider and the recipient. For example, day-care centers with high turnover will not be as attractive to clients or as productive as, say, other centers with less turnover, other things being equal, because turnover undermines the relationship between teacher and student. If nonprofit jobs were so psychologically satisfying, why do workers leave so often? And, why have unionization rates among nonprofit workers been high relative to for-profit workers in the post–World War II period (Preston, 1989)? In all likelihood, the issue is not the desire of workers in nonprofits to make "labor donations" that keeps wages down but rather the inability of nonprofit organizations to raise their wages sufficiently to pay adequately for the work performed and thus to hold on to their valued and experienced employees.

One final wrinkle on the compensating differentials explanation is Preston's suggestion (1990b, p. 568) that "the low wages in the nonprofit sector relative to the for-profit sector are to some extent mitigated by the greater equality between male and female wages within the nonprofit sector." Here the suggestion is that greater gender equality in nonprofit settings is an attraction for women and substitutes for some of women's low wages. But no one has ever asked women whether they would prefer to work near men who earn relatively low wages (instead of making more money themselves). Furthermore, what little research there is on social comparisons in the workplace suggests that it is relatively rare for comparisons of wages to be made across gender-segregated occupations and job families (see Majors, 1989, for a summary of the research). Because the labor market is so segregated—at last count, more than 70 percent of women would have to change jobs to be distributed as men are (Tomaskovic-Devey,

1993)—it is highly unlikely that women in the nonprofit sector would compare themselves to men in different jobs and at different levels of the organization.

Another argument used by labor economists focuses more directly on employees' preferences and less on the attributes of the jobs. The argument suggests that nonprofit workers are willing to accept lower wages because they place such a high value on working in a socially beneficial setting. They make, in economists' terms, a labor donation. Unfortunately, this explanation falls short as well. First, the conclusion is inferred from discounting other explanations, not from direct evidence (see, for example, Preston, 1989). Second, in order to account for the concentration of women in the nonprofit sector, the argument would have to assume that women are less interested in money than men. Yet survey data suggest that working women rank income as high as do men on a list of factors in choosing a job (as reviewed in Jacobs and Steinberg, 1990; see also Schultz, 1990). Third, the preferences explanations in general assume more stability in preferences than actually exists. However, data on career aspirations show substantial inconsistency between individuals' preferences and jobs actually pursued—one study found that preference was a poor predictor of occupational behavior as little as ten years later (Jacobs, 1989). While no tests of the relationship have been specifically made among nonprofit workers, it is logical to assume that the finding would hold for these workers as well. Fourth, the preferences explanation does not account for the high turnover of workers in nonprofit settings.

Fifth, the approach ignores the relationship between opportunity and preferences. Preferences are not attributes that spring into individuals' heads at one moment and remain fixed forevermore. Rather, they are actively shaped and reshaped throughout prelabor market and labor market years by many factors and contingencies, a good many of which emerge from labor market experience (Gerson, 1985; Schultz, 1990). Those who work in historically female jobs and, by extension, in historically female sectors, typically do not "choose" to work for lower wages but are constrained to accept jobs that pay in terms of a wage structure that is related to gender and that devalues women (Reskin, personal communication to author, 1992).

Finally, on its face, the idea of a labor donation implies that nonprofit employees are passive and indifferent to the low wages that they receive relative to the work that they perform. Such explanations, based as they are on the logic of economic equations, are too far removed from actual labor relations and are out of touch with the significant organizing drives among allied health professionals and nurses in the hospital sector and among teachers and clerical workers at universities, to name only a few of the most visible efforts. Such initiatives by nonmanagerial workers in the nonprofit sector must be considered significant facets of nonprofit organizations in order to see their character realistically and to understand the everyday practices that sustain the lower wages of nonprofit-sector employees relative to their for-profit counterparts.

This discussion is designed to raise questions regarding the preferences and productivity explanations that have

89

been offered. To understand the wage differentials and labor market dynamics in the nonprofit sector, it is necessary to include an analysis of both supply and demand. A complete analysis requires an understanding of the nonprofit sector as a market also shaped by "historic customs, prejudices, and ideologies" (Feldberg, 1986, p. 171) and in which there is no pure "economics" free of gender hierarchies (Phillips and Taylor, 1980, pp. 80–81; Steinberg 1990, p. 454).

There is an alternative explanation of the low wages of the nonprofit sector, one that reflects the role of gender in mediating labor market transactions and in artificially depressing the wages of work historically performed by and associated with women. In other words, the low level of wages paid in this sector is, in no small part, a function not only of the devaluation of women's work in the sector but also the result of the devaluation of the nonprofit sector because it is heavily populated by women.

To our knowledge, this chapter represents the first attempt to develop an understanding of the ways in which gender informs the character and contours of the nonprofit sector. As such, we view our efforts as a starting point. We hope to stimulate further consideration of our thesis and further inquiry based on it. Let us turn, then, to a discussion of the gendered character of the nonprofit sector.

The Gendered Nature of the Nonprofit Sector

The discussion begins with a disclaimer and a definition. The role of gender varies within the nonprofit sector, a variation that this chapter provides insufficient space to explore systematically. For example, consider the four major industrial subsectors that constitute the nonprofit sector: health, education, social services, and religion. Some variations in the occupations are noteworthy. At one extreme, the occupational distributions for health and religion are characterized by a relatively small, male-dominated elite and a large pool of women at lower levels of the hierarchy. At the other extreme, social services offers a flatter distribution of occupations and an organizational hierarchy more thoroughly dominated by women. Education falls somewhere in between. This discussion of the gendered character of the nonprofit sector of necessity will be insufficiently attentive to variations among nonprofit settings.

In terms of defining the nonprofit sector, the issue of what constitutes the nonprofit sector and what distinguishes it from the for-profit sector has been one of the important issues about nonprofits addressed in the 1980s and 1990s. Does the legal form of the organization translate into a generic set of behaviors and characteristics (DiMaggio and Anheier, 1990, pp. 147–153; Clarke and Estes, 1992; Powell and Friedkin, 1987)? The consensus, at least among sociologists, is that "the quest . . . is problematic" and the differences are overrated (DiMaggio and Anheier, 1990, p. 149; Clarke and Estes, 1992). One difference that has been noted is that nonprofit organizations tend to be "service organizations" and "labor-intensive" (Rudney, 1987, p. 57). Of course, the distinctions are only tendencies and averages, in that an increasing number of for-profit firms provide labor-intensive services. Nonetheless, Rudney's characterization of the nonprofit sector as service oriented and labor-intensive is accurate, and we add to it the occupational distribution that includes a disproportionate number of historically female jobs. In other words, the typical nonprofit employee is a woman. Thus, here the legal status that privileges the nonprofit sector and that is so often used to define its parameters matters less than the nature of the product and its occupational composition.

Nonprofit organizations are "gendered" institutions. *Gender* means not only a social category used for making distinctions between men and women and between masculinity and femininity but also a basis by which people order their "activities, practices, and social structures in terms of differentiations between women and men" (Acker, 1992, p. 567). Gender is not only the basis upon which society creates distinctions among people, ideas, and symbols but also an extremely significant basis upon which society creates systems of domination and subordination, of high and low valuation, of power and powerlessness.

At the level of the individual, as suggested by West and Zimmerman (1987), gender is an ongoing accomplishment of constructing an appropriate identity that involves engaging in appropriate behavior and demeanor for varying interactions and institutional settings (Acker, 1992, p. 568). Even at the institutional level, it starts with appropriate male and female behavior and interaction between individuals as they conduct their everyday business in organizations. But it goes beyond this. For an organization to function smoothly, it is necessary to maintain appropriate images of gender relations. For example, priests are men and nuns are women. Their relationship within the organization is interdependent and hierarchical in predictable and rule-bound ways. Financial officers tend to be men. A woman who is a financial officer must, in some way, smooth over her exceptionalism.

Thus, gender not only is constructed within institutions as a process of ongoing social interaction it is also a property of institutions in that "gender is present in the processes, practices, images and ideologies, and distributions of power in the various sectors of social life" (Acker, 1992, p. 567). In most organizations, there is what Acker has called a "gender understructure" that encompasses both "overt decisions and procedures" and "the construction of images, symbols, and ideologies that justify, explain, and give legitimacy to institutions" (p. 568). But to suggest that institutional arrangements, apart from the individuals that constitute institutions, are gendered is not to suggest that gender is a passive or fixed entity. It is created and maintained both by everyday social interaction and by past practices and policies that represent the culmination of previous decisions and compromises, much of it gender neutral in appearance. Indeed, the appearance of neutrality gives the policies and practices much of their force.

Gender ideologies and processes are apparent in the nonprofit sector along a number of dimensions. Four manifestations of the gendered character of the nonprofit

93

sector are examined here: the sex of the typical worker, the character of jobs and occupations, the hierarchies within the nonprofit sector, and the metaphors that stereotype the nonprofit sector as a whole. All contribute to the subordination of the nonprofit sector relative to the for-profit sector and to the devaluation of the work performed within its parameters.

At the simplest level, the nonprofit sector is gendered in that the overwhelming majority of its workers are female. In 1987, 68.3 percent of all nonprofit employees were female, with the heaviest concentration in health care (Hodgkinson and Weitzman, 1989, p. 148). Indeed, the typical nonprofit worker is not a philanthropist, board member, or foundation executive, as might be inferred from the disproportionate attention given to women who hold these positions, even in the academic literature that does address women in the nonprofit sector (Ostrander, 1984; Daniels, 1988; Odendahl, 1990). Nor is she likely to be a minister, physician, lawyer, or school administrator, although women are moving into such occupations in unprecedented numbers. Instead, if she is a professional, she is likely to be a nurse, social worker, teacher, or librarian. If not, she is likely to be a clerical worker, housekeeper, or food service worker.

A second way the nonprofit sector is gendered is that it is characterized by organizations in which a small male elite holds the power and sets the agenda for an overwhelmingly female pool of employees and volunteers. McCarthy (1991) has noted this phenomenon in American philanthropy and art, and Wallace (1992; see also Barthel,

1992) has noted the phenomenon in religion, suggesting that it is a "system in which male gender is the necessary (but not sufficient) characteristic of those who assume top leadership positions" (as quoted in Lummis, 1992, p. 581). At the same time, perhaps with the exception of religious institutions, where male leadership is divinely sanctioned (Schneiders, 1991, as cited in Lummis, 1992, p. 582), women appear to be having a relatively easier time moving into positions of leadership in nonprofit organizations than in for-profit organizations.

In certain respects, women are breaking down barriers as they enter historically male professions and nonprofit managerial positions such as hospital and school administration. Yet even here, the gendered character of the sector can, in part, explain their success. As Shaffer (1980) has shown for the manufacturing sector, it is easier for women to enter managerial jobs in organizations in which a large number of women already work. So, given the large numbers of women who already work in the nonprofit sector, it is easier for women to "fit," even in new organizational schemes. The explanation is also consistent with economist Barbara Bergmann's "segregation code" (1986, pp. 114–116). Based on her investigation of several corporations, Bergmann noted a pattern consistent with a taboo on women supervising men. Thus, it is easier for women to enter professional and managerial jobs in sectors in which they will predominately supervise women.

One remarkable paradox of nonprofits, then, is that, even as women enter the professional and managerial ranks, a male-dominated hierachy represents to society a type of work overwhelmingly populated by women. Further research on how male elites are able to define and advance the female-typed work of the nonprofits would be helpful. One consequence, for the managers, of working in a feminized sector is the devaluation of wages paid for their positions relative to such positions in for-profit organizations. As Treiman and Hartmann (1981, p. 28) note in a book published by the National Academy of Sciences, *Women, Work, and Wages,* "The more an occupation is dominated by women, the less it pays." By extension, the more an occupation is embedded in a set of occupations dominated by women, the lower the entire wage structure. The pattern and the explanation remain untested.

Third, the nonprofit sector is also gendered in the distribution of *occupations* found within it. As Acker has argued, the construct of a job implies a particular relationship to home life and work life and thus a gender division of labor. Is there an expectation, built into the design of the job, for example, that the incumbent's primary time and emotional commitment is to home and family or to the workplace? Is there the expectation, to cite another example, that the incumbent's primary commitment to the family is as breadwinner or as care giver? The gender division of labor is not just distributed among individuals, where, on average, men primarily assume the role of breadwinners and women, on average, the role of care givers. Independent of the gender of the actual incumbent, ideas, stereotypes, and assumptions premised on the gender division of labor are embedded in how jobs are designed, in which people are selected to fill positions, in what is noticed about job content, and in the structure of compensation (Steinberg, 1992, p. 387). As soon as one gender or the other predominates in a position, the process of gender stereotyping begins (Reskin and Roos, 1990).

Both managers and nurses are, for instance, expected to work overtime if necessary. Yet the symbols, ideologies, and images invoked to justify the overtime expected in each case varies in ways that implicate the gender of the typical incumbent. For managers, their primary commitment to the work organization as a leader is taken for granted. Pointing to a "masculine ethic," Kanter (1977) describes management work as involving a tough-minded orientation to problem solving and to the commitment, as a leader, to be there to get the job done whenever necessary. A nurse, on the other hand, works overtime, not for the benefit of the organization but for the benefit of the client. The nurse's ethical responsibility to the client is invoked. The nurse's care-giving responsibilities are implicated. These are seemingly "natural" extensions of the gender division of labor and grow out of the nurse's role as nurturer.

Indeed, images of the registered nurse are replete with gender stereotypes. In focus groups conducted by one of the authors to determine the content of nursing work, one nurse, a man, said that it would be necessary to change the title of the job and the rate of pay to interest more men in the field. Images of nursing are rooted in nineteenth-century assumptions about voluntarism and charity and in the cult of domesticity that suggested that women should engage in good works (Melosh, 1982; Remick,

97

1984). They are rooted in "naturalism," the assumption that the nurturing and care-giving roles associated with nursing are natural extensions of feminine family roles. Nursing was subject to what has been called the *Nightingale ideology*, which stresses the importance of "character" in the development of a good nurse (Gray, 1989, p. 139). Nursing, according to historian Susan Reverby (1987), was not only a livelihood but a badge of virtue.

The image of nursing as grounded in good character and charitable impulses continues today, despite increasingly sophisticated medical technology, medical specialization, the increasing seriousness of patients' conditions in hospitals, and the emphasis on technical training and credentials in nursing. Even in the nineteenth century, the emphasis on virtue blocked out the professional ambitions underlying Florence Nightingale's reform of nursing. According to Growe, "a division of labour based on gender presented no ideological problems for women living in nineteenth-century England; . . . there was little overlap between the medical arena, under the exclusive rule of men, and the *separate but equal* department of nursing services, governed by women. . . . The essence of Nightingale's nursing reform was to take all power over nursing out of the hands of male physicians and administrators and put it into the hands of one female trained head. . . . Nightingale . . . did not foresee her two-stream separate-but-equal hierarchy collapsing into one" (1991, pp. 47, 50).

Linking the skills and responsibilities of nursing to voluntarism confuses job content with the stereotypical attributes of the typical incumbent. Because inherent attributes are not seen as acquired skills (at least in women), women are not seen as needing compensation for the work. Because women's work is not seen as productive, it is seen as requiring few skills. As Remick also points out (1984, p. 90), voluntarism is embedded in the wage structure of nurses in that "rewards for nurses were to come in the form of good feelings for having been helpful." By associating content with the characteristics of the gender of the incumbent, that content is rendered noncompensable. Doing so ignores job requirements that include sophisticated knowledge of complex technical, communication, and human relations skills. As a result, nurses are compensated unfairly.

A fourth way in which the nonprofit sector is gendered involves the images, stereotypes, ideologies, and metaphors used to describe the work and the values invoked to justify its low wage structure relative to the for-profit sector. The dimension involves a comparison of the nonprofit sector with the for-profit sector. It concerns as well metaphorically invoking the gender division of labor, in which the for-profit sector is the sphere of production of commodities and material goods and the nonprofit sector is the sphere of "reproduction"; previously unpaid work has been shifted to paid work but continues to be viewed as less productive and as supportive of the sphere of production. The fact that it is now paid service work does not render it any less gendered in its origins and its valuation. As Acker (1992, p. 567) puts it, "In industrial capitalist societies, production is privileged over reproduction. Business and industry are seen as essential and the source of well-being and wealth, while children, child care, elder care, and education are viewed as secondary and wealth consuming."

Thus, relative to the for-profit sector, the images associated with the nonprofit sector project a feminine cast. The missions of nonprofit organizations are "soft"—encompassing the provision of services, a preoccupation with moral and ethical concerns, producing beauty, helping people. They must, at the very least, give the appearance that such hard-nosed concerns as making money are secondary to service provision or to the maintenance of cultural and moral standards.

By contrast, the image of the businessman and the stereotypes associated with the role conjure associations with masculinity. Kanter (1977) refers to the for-profit manager as a tough-minded problem solver, a subordinator of emotional involvement to task accomplishment, and an abstract reasoner. The business leader is regularly referred to in popular periodicals in terms characterized by Connell (1987) as "hegemonic masculinity"—as Acker says, "aggressive, goal oriented, competitive, efficient, but rarely as supportive, kind, and caring" (1992, p. 568). In compensation systems, the stereotypes translate into skills and become the universal and seemingly gender-neutral standard against which all work is assessed and valued for the purposes of compensation (Steinberg, April 1990). Accordingly, women in health care who must use extensive psychosocial skills, and men and women religious workers, who routinely show great empathy and understanding, score lower when evaluated against the business standards,

100

thus justifying their lower pay. If added to this is an ideology in which making money is subordinate to doing good, the result is little public support when, for example, nurses go out on strike for higher wages and thus abandon their clients.

Further, the values used to describe the nonprofit sector—"voluntarism, pluralism, altruism" (DiMaggio and Anheier, 1990, p. 153)—are also associated with the feminine. So is a concern with charity, service, and good works (Daniels, 1992). A significant portion of nonprofit work is still carried out by volunteers. Wuthnow (1991) found that 45 percent of those he surveyed work as volunteers for about five hours a week. But amazing as it may seem, Wuthnow fails to mention that the majority of those who perform service-oriented volunteer work are women. Moreover, men and women who participate in voluntary groups do so in different types of voluntary groups (Smith-Lovin and McPherson, 1986).

Because gendered ideologies and processes are most effective in maintaining the subordination of the feminine when they are invisible (Acker, 1989; Steinberg, 1990; Steinberg, 1992), it is difficult to illustrate how they operate in everyday social practices in the absence of conflict. (For a similar argument about power, see Lukes, 1974, and Gaventa, 1980.) It is easier, however, to uncover the empirical examples of the gendered character of everyday practices when they are challenged in public settings.

As a society, Americans appear to value culturally activities associated with the nonprofit sector when they are performed as unpaid labor by volunteers who are members of a community. As a society, Americans also view such activities, historically and culturally, as associated with women, who have freed men to pursue economic gain for themselves and their families. In other words, the activities are regarded as socially productive but not necessarily as economically productive, both because of where they have been performed and because of who performs them. Not surprisingly, then, when these activities become paid work, those who perform the work are paid relatively low wages.

Gender and Wage Determination in the Nonprofit Sector

The cost of labor is by far the major expense for nonprofit organizations, which are labor-intensive organizations. In 1987, labor costs were 53.1 percent of total costs, down slightly from 58 percent in 1980 (Rudney, 1987; Hodgkinson and Weitzman, 1989, p. 1). If nonprofit organizations had to pay the average wage of men in the for-profit sector, they would have dramatically higher wage costs. The labor-intensive character of nonprofit organizations has made it difficult for them to contain costs. Yet cost containment is crucial, because the fees they charge rarely cover the cost of services (Kanter and Summers, 1987; Powell and Friedkin, 1987).

There are several additional incentives for keeping labor costs down: greater discretion over where to spend excess funds, less need to raise money, and higher relative salaries for management. Preston has noted, for example, that in the nonprofit sector, "Profits can be earned, however, they may not be distributed to those in control [as profits]" (Preston, 1989, p. 441). "Managers may," she continues, "have a certain amount of discretion over where profits are channeled in the organization." The multiple motivations for cost containment result in opposition to labor's demands every bit as forceful as in the for-profit sector. In the area of labor relations, then, distinction between nonprofit and for-profit firms tends to be overrated. Indeed, one of us has found, in fifteen years of direct experience in assisting in struggles to gain higher wages for nurses, clerical workers, teachers, and other incumbents of historically female occupations, that the efforts of women workers to revalue their work is met with staunch, and often effective, resistance. At best, the wage adjustments received fall far short of what the wages would be if the content of the work was valued at the rate paid for jobs held by white men (Steinberg, 1991). In this respect, there is a commonality in the experiences of the for-profit and nonprofit sectors.

Moreover, in recent years, nonprofit organizations have increasingly borrowed their compensation practices from those developed for for-profit firms. The very practices they are borrowing are replete with assumptions about gender.

A Case Study of Pay Equity in a Nonprofit Setting

On the surface, the case of the Ontario Nurses Association (ONA) and three nonprofit hospitals in Ontario, Canada—North York, Women's College, and Sunnybrook—might seem to be a routine labor-management conflict over wages. (Steinberg, the senior author of this chapter, served as a consultant to the ONA in this case.) The ONA, an amalgamated union representing more than thirty-five thousand hospital workers, bargained for higher wages for its nurses, while the Ontario Hospital Association (OHA), the centralized association representing these three as well as more than 100 additional nonprofit hospitals, claimed that the nurses were being paid according to the recommendations of an independent consulting group of compensation professionals. A closer examination, however, reveals that the central issue was the value of professional service work traditionally performed by women and the ability of traditional job evaluation systems imported from for-profit companies to capture the range and complexity of nurses' work.

Most large organizations employ standardized systems for evaluating the contributions jobs make to the overall performance of the organization. While economists maintain that the market sets wages for jobs, most organizations prescribe specific salary ranges for jobs that reflect both external market competitiveness and internal equity vis-à-vis other jobs within the organization. The job evaluation systems helped give impetus to the movement for comparable worth, which maintains that such systems need to be purged of gender bias. Comparable worth holds that jobs of equal contribution to the organization should be paid the same amount.

Comparable worth policies are more comprehensive in the Canadian province of Ontario than in the United

States, because specific legislation prohibits wage discrimination on the basis of sex and because that legislation requires firms to be proactive in demonstrating that their pay systems are free of gender bias. Thus, in Ontario, government action helped to disseminate the practice of job evaluation to the nonprofit sector. This legislation prompted OHA to solicit the services of a management consulting firm to implement a hospitalwide job evaluation exercise for use among all its member hospitals. The OHA unilaterally chose a job evaluation system—the Stevenson, Kellogg, Ernst, and Whinney (SKEW) system—although the legislation explicitly required joint selection of an evaluation system when employees were represented by unions. Subsequent to its selection of the system, OHA convinced several unions to agree to use it, making some cosmetic changes to its structure. One union, ONA, refused. ONA feared that the system would undervalue the historically female professional, clinical, and service-provider jobs in the hospital setting.

The complaint of ONA, beyond the bad-faith bargaining engaged in by the hospital association, was that OHA had sought a dated system drenched with gender bias in the guise of ridding gender inequity from hospital compensation. The bias would mean that key skills, responsibilities, and undesirable features of the work of jobs represented by ONA would be overlooked and thus not compensated relative to the content of hospital administrative and managerial work. ONA based these conclusions on its own assessment and assessments by expert consultants of SKEW in light of a growing body of scholarship on gender bias in job evaluation (see Steinberg, April 1990, for a discussion of the literature and a fuller discussion of the difficulties with the system).

Sexist assumptions about gender and the labor market were built into job evaluation systems, in large measure because they were the predominant views of the appropriate role of women in the labor market during the 1940s and 1950s, when most of the current systems in use were developed. Detailed historical research has shown the essential continuity of the systems over time, despite the occasional rephrasing of the concepts and measures (Steinberg, 1992). The early job evaluation systems chose factors and factor weights to best reproduce an existing wage hierarchy, including lower wages for historically female work (Treiman, 1979; Schwab, 1985). This method of constructing job evaluations assured that characteristics differentially associated with historically female jobs would *not* be treated as valuable.

So the issue in the Ontario controversy centered on the value placed on different types of work and the range of skills compensated. Job evaluation rates each job on a number of content dimensions. Each dimension is given a weight, and the scores of each job are totaled. The points allotted to each job are then used to allocate compensation to each job evaluated. The pay of jobs not included in the evaluation is pegged to those in the system. Any skill or responsibility not covered is not compensated. Thus, making a case for including in job evaluations the broadest range of skills and responsibilities becomes of paramount concern in arguing for higher points and thus higher wages. Not surprisingly, the union made the case that the SKEW system ignored important responsibilities and skills performed by nurses. They argued for more attention to such often-ignored skills as human relations, communication, specific task capabilities, and record keeping. Moreover, the union maintained that there was little recognition of the work hazards common in the hospital setting: needle sticks, the risk of infection, and the exposure to dangerous and infected substances. Traditional job evaluations focus on the undesirable working conditions generally associated with blue-collar, male-dominated occupations, if they acknowledge working conditions at all, and consequently the working conditions that women confront on the job rarely factor into their compensation (Jacobs and Steinberg, 1990).

Perhaps the most limiting factor in the SKEW system was the great emphasis placed on supervisory responsibility. No professional job can get more than five points for responsibility (on a scale of one to eight) unless the position includes management skills. It is particularly ironic that in a hospital setting, job evaluation tends to emphasize formal responsibility over actual responsibility. Thus, if a nurse must decide to initiate a life-saving procedure, the ultimate formal responsibility lies with a doctor who might not be present, yet most job evaluation systems give responsibility points to the doctor and not the nurse. The SKEW system also rates nurses low on initiative (because of the formal responsibility of the doctor), on effect of results (because the consequences of error are not associated with financial solvency but only with life or death), and moderately low on technical skills (because of nursing's traditional association with vocational education).

The managerial bias reflects the fact that job evaluation systems were designed to measure managerial positions in private-sector manufacturing jobs or in other for-profit administrative contexts (Shils, 1972). In a review of the most widely used evaluation systems on the contemporary market, Treiman and Hartmann (1981) observe a lack of fit between the categories of work on which job evaluation systems were developed and the types of technical and service-provider work characteristic of the labor market in the late twentieth century.

Fourth, in unilaterally carrying out the actual evaluation of jobs at North York Hospital, only managerial employees were involved. Ironically, but not surprisingly, management rated its own jobs higher than did the consultant who rated the same jobs. Management also rated the nursing jobs consistently lower than the consultants did. This illustrates that, in conducting a pay equity study initiated to redress the legislatively recognized undervaluation of female wages, management attempted to SKEW the compensation system further in its favor, perhaps as a way to rectify the historical erosion of management salaries vis-à-vis professional jobs during the 1970s and 1980s.

Negotiations broke down, and a case was pressed against the three representative hospitals of OHA before the Ontario Pay Equity Tribunal, an administrative court established by the legislation, in late 1989. After almost two years of testimony (with more than fifty days of testimony just by experts presented by ONA), the tribunal found in favor of the nurses' union, tracing in a detailed fifty-eight-page majority decision the ways in which the SKEW system was not inclusive of the content of the job of registered nurse. The tribunal required that a system value work in relation to the *mission* or *objective* of the organization, in this case in relation to the obligation of a hospital to provide patients with high quality and technically competent care. It further required the parties, on the basis of its detailed guidelines about the inadequacies of SKEW, to return to the bargaining table, jointly decide on an evaluation system, and determine how undervalued the work of a registered nurse was.

Although the parties were required to offer a modified job evaluation system within sixty days, only ONA did so. OHA responded with some hand-edited, cosmetic changes to its system. Thus began about ten months of deliberations between OHA and ONA, both of which signed a memorandum of agreement on June 3, 1993. The agreement covers not only the three hospitals against which the case was originally brought but also more than 100 other hospitals represented by OHA. It provides a wage increase of $1.13 per hour for all registered nurses, phased in until January 1, 1996. It also provides a retroactive payment of $4,100 to registered nurses for the period of 1990 to 1993, during which the dispute was being resolved, to be paid in three sequential pay periods.

While the adjustments seem high, they must be assessed in the context of what was traded to obtain them. First, neither OHA or ONA would agree to a joint system of job evaluation, regardless of the tribunal's order. Instead, each evaluated a set of agreed-upon jobs, using a joint questionnaire for collecting information about job content but using different evaluation systems. Second, each came to the table with a different male job that it found to be equivalent to registered nurse. ONA selected a middle-level administrative job in the hope of establishing a precedent that registered nurse positions are comparable in hospitals to certain middle-management positions. OHA came to the table with a male professional position—senior dialysis technician—for basing wage adjustments. In negotiation, OHA would not budge, and the professional position selected was the male job. Thus, no precedent was set by any Ontario nonprofit hospital in relation to the value of historically female professional, clinical, and service-provider work and its comparison to managerial work.

The actual wage adjustments also fell far short of what the nurses would have received if their salaries were fully adjusted, even to the level of the professional comparison agreed upon in collective bargaining. The difference in pay was $12,000 per year, about five times the amount that actual adjustment of $1.13 per hour will yield. And $4,100 in back pay falls far short of the $36,000 in lost wages found to obtain for registered nurses on the basis of a jointly agreed-upon male comparison. Thus, in every respect, the outcome was highly imbalanced in favor of hospital management.

One final piece of information is worth noting. The case took more than two years to complete and then almost another year to negotiate. It cost each party almost

$2 million. Yet both sides did not suffer the same financial burden in taking the case through extensive deliberations. The provincial government of Canada provides OHA with $3 million per year simply to engage in its labor relations activities. OHA used a portion of that money on this case. By contrast, ONA relied solely on its budget, generated from members' dues. Not surprising, its members were concerned about the amount of money being poured into this and a number of other cases for which no adjustments had been obtained. The distribution of power was clearly on the side of the nonprofit employer. And, ironically, the provincial government funded only one side—the employer—in its appearance before the government's conflict resolution body—in a case in which the employer was attempting to contest and narrow the meaning of the most important piece of equity legislation passed on behalf of women workers.

The case study of conflict over the level of wages paid to registered nurses and, by extension, to other allied health professionals in three nonprofit hospitals in Ontario, Canada, illustrates that women workers do not passively accept their low wages as a labor donation, that nonprofit managers resist efforts by women workers to improve their wages and are willing to invest significant resources to deter their efforts, and that gender is implicated in the methods used to evaluate and devalue nursing, despite the appearance of gender neutrality. Even as the nurses won some critical victories, the final settlement in wages fell far short of the salary paid for performing a comparable male job involving equivalent work.

To dampen the claims of registered nurses and defeat their wage initiatives, hospital management (the positions of which were often filled by women) drew upon systems of job evaluation developed for use in the for-profit sector. The systems emphasized as valuable job content typically found in historically male managerial jobs. The same systems ignored, among other dimensions of work, the skills and responsibilities associated with historically female, client-oriented service-provider and clerical work. The hospitals and nurses fought about the use of the systems at the bargaining table and in the courts. There was also an ideological struggle over what was an appropriate system for evaluating client-oriented service provision. The conflict was never resolved.

Conclusion

This chapter attempted to trace the implications of the inattentiveness of scholarship on the nonprofit sector to issues of gender. Many studies ignore gender entirely, while others maintain that gender-neutral principles account for low wages in the nonprofit sector. In criticizing the gender neutrality of the accounts, the chapter paid particular attention to the theories that attribute the low pay of jobs in the nonprofit sector to productivity differences or the preferences of women.

Gender must be understood as integral to the formation and definition of much of the nonprofit sector. The preliminary thesis is that there are four manifestations of gendering of the nonprofit sector: the sex of the typical worker, the character of jobs and occupations, the hierar-

112

chies within the nonprofit sector, and the metaphors that stereotype the nonprofit sector as a whole. The undervaluation of female work is not unique to the nonprofit sector but rather is endemic in the economy as a whole. The low wages of work performed by women are crucial to the viability of the nonprofit sector, where labor costs are a leading budget item.

Finally, the hospital wage conflict illustrated the importance of maintaining the invisibility of the undervaluation of women's work in order to maintain the low wages paid a large group of workers. The case illustrates the ways that power and ideology maintain the gender gap in wages within nonprofit settings.

The seemingly neutral compensation practices borrowed from the for-profit sector and introduced to the nonprofit sector maintain the power of the small elite of historically male managerial positions and maintain the undervaluation of the overwhelming majority of historically female positions that constitute the essential character and work performed in the nonprofit sector. The compensation practices thus simultaneously maintain the dominance of for-profit production standards over nonprofit reproduction values. They also maintain the fiction that historically male jobs are more skilled, more responsible, and thus more productive than historically female clinical service and clerical jobs. The ostensibly objective compensation procedure maintains sector and gender subordination. As Acker noted, "Understanding how the appearance of gender neutrality is maintained in the face of overwhelming evidence of gendered structures is an important part of analyzing gendered institutions. One conceptual mechanism is the positing of an abstract, general human being, individual, or worker who apparently has no gender" (Acker, 1992, p. 568). Moreover, because so many of the abstract general human beings are women in the nonprofit sector, the tactics have serious and differentially deleterious consequences for women.

References

Acker, J. *Doing Comparable Worth.* Philadelphia: Temple University Press, 1989.

Acker, J. "From Sex Roles to Gendered Institutions." *Contemporary Sociology,* 1992, *21,* 565–568.

Armstrong, P. *Vital Signs: Nursing Work in Transition.* Unpublished manuscript, 1990.

Barthel, D. "They Also Gave: Women, Men, and Museums." *Contemporary Sociology,* 1992, *21,* 587–589.

Bergmann, B. R. *The Economic Emergence of Women.* New York: Basic Books, 1986.

Block, F. *Post-Industrial Possibilities.* Berkeley: University of California Press, 1990.

Choy, S., Medrich, E., and Henke, R. *Schools and Staffing in the United States: A Statistical Profile, 1987–88.* Washington, D.C.: U.S. Department of Education, 1992.

Clarke, L., and Estes, C. "Sociological and Economic Theories of Markets and Nonprofits: Evidence from Home Health Organizations." *American Journal of Sociology,* 1992, *97,* 945–969.

Connell, R. W. *Gender and Power.* Stanford: Stanford University Press, 1987.

Daniels, A. *Invisible Careers: Women Civic Leaders from the Volunteer World.* Chicago: University of Chicago Press, 1988.

Daniels, A. "Women Philanthropists in the Community." Paper presented at the conference "Women, Power, and Status in the Nonprofit Sector," Menlo Park, Calif., November 15–18, 1992.

DiMaggio, P., and Anheier, H. "The Sociology of Nonprofit Organizations and Sectors." In W. R. Scott and J. Blake (eds.), *Annual Review of Sociology,* 1990, *16,* 137–169.

England, P., Farkas, G., Kilbourne, B., and Dou, T. "Explaining Occupational Sex Segregation and Wages: Findings from a Model with Fixed Effects." *American Sociological Review,* 1988, *53,* 544–558.

Feldberg, R. "Comparable Worth: Toward Theory and Practice in the United States." In B. Gelpi, N. C. Harstock, C. C. Novak, and M. H. Strober (eds.), *Women and Poverty.* Chicago: University of Chicago Press, 1986.

Gaventa, J. *Power and Powerlessness: Quiescence and Rebellion in an Appalachian Valley.* Oxford: Clarendon, 1980.

Gerson, J. *Hard Choices: How Women Decide About Work, Career, and Motherhood.* Berkeley: University of California Press, 1985.

Gray, D. "Militancy, Unionism and Gender Ideology." *Work and Occupations,* 1989, *16,* 137–152.

Growe, S. *Who Cares: The Crisis in Canadian Nursing.* Toronto: McLelland and Stewart, 1991.

Hall, P. D. "A Historical Overview of the Private Nonprofit Sector." In W. W. Powell (ed.), *The Nonprofit Sector:*

A Research Handbook. New Haven, Conn.: Yale University Press, 1987.

Hodgkinson, V., and Weitzman, M. *Dimensions of the Independent Sector: A Statistical Profile.* (3rd ed.) Washington, D.C.: Independent Sector, 1989.

Jacobs, J. A. *Revolving Doors: Sex Segregation and Women's Careers.* Palo Alto, Calif.: Stanford University Press, 1989.

Jacobs, J. A., and Steinberg, R. "Compensating Differentials and the Male-Female Wage Gap: Evidence from the New York State Comparable Worth Study." *Social Forces,* 1990, *69,* 439–468.

Kanter, R. M. *Men and Women of the Corporation.* New York: Basic Books, 1977.

Kanter, R. M., and Summers, D. "Doing Well While Doing Good: Dilemmas of Performance Measurement in Nonprofit Organizations and the Need for a Multiple-Constituency Approach." In W. W. Powell (ed.), *The Nonprofit Sector: A Research Handbook.* New Haven, Conn.: Yale University Press, 1987.

Lukes, S. *Power: A Radical View.* London: Macmillan, 1974.

Lummis, A. "Women in Patriarchal Religious Institutions." *Contemporary Sociology,* 1992, *21,* 581–584.

McCarthy, K. *Women's Culture: American Philanthropy and Art, 1830–1930.* Chicago: University of Chicago Press, 1991.

Majors, B. "Gender Differences in Comparisons and Entitlement: Implications for Comparable Worth." *Journal of Social Issues,* 1989, *45*(4), 99–115.

Melosh, B. *The Physician's Hand.* Philadelphia: Temple University Press, 1982.

Odendahl, T. *Charity Begins at Home: Generosity and Self-interest Among the Philanthropic Elite.* New York: Basic Books, 1990.

O'Neill, M. *The Third America: The Emergence of the Nonprofit Sector in the United States.* San Francisco: Jossey-Bass, 1989.

Ostrander, S. *Women of the Upper Class.* Philadelphia: Temple University Press, 1984.

Phillips, A., and Taylor, B. "Sex and Skill: Notes Toward a Feminist Economics." *Feminist Review,* 1980, *6,* 79–88.

Powell, W. W. (ed.), *The Nonprofit Sector: A Research Handbook.* New Haven, Conn.: Yale University Press, 1987.

Powell, W. W., and Friedkin, R. "Organizational Change in Nonprofit Organizations." In W. W. Powell (ed.), *The Nonprofit Sector: A Research Handbook.* New Haven, Conn.: Yale University Press, 1987.

Preston, A. "The Nonprofit Worker in a For-Profit World." *Journal of Labor Economics,* 1989, *7,* 438–463.

Preston, A. "Changing Labor Market Patterns in the Nonprofit and For-Profit Sectors: Implications for Nonprofit Management." *Nonprofit Management and Leadership,* 1990a, *1*(1), 15–28.

Preston, A. "Women in the White-Collar Nonprofit Sector: The Best Option or the Only Option?" *Review of Economics and Statistics,* 1990b, *72*(4), 560–568.

Remick, H. "Dilemmas of Implementation: The Case of Nursing." In H. Remick (ed.), *Comparable Worth and Wage Discrimination.* Philadelphia: Temple University Press, 1984.

Reskin, B. F., and Roos, P. *Job Queues, Gender Queue: Explaining Women's Inroads into Male Occupations.* Philadelphia: Temple University Press, 1990.

Reverby, S. *Ordered to Care: The Dilemma of American Nursing, 1850–1945.* Cambridge, England: Cambridge University Press, 1987.

Rudney, G. "The Scope and Dimensions of Nonprofit Activity." In W. W. Powell (ed.), *The Nonprofit Sector: A Research Handbook.* New Haven, Conn.: Yale University Press, 1987.

Schneiders, S. *Beyond Patching: Faith and Feminism in the Catholic Church.* New York: Paulist Press, 1991.

Schultz, V. "Telling Stories About Women and Work: Judicial Interpretations of Sex Segregation in the Workplace in Title VII Cases Raising the Lack of Interest Argument." *Harvard Law Review,* 1990, *103,* 1749–1843.

Schwab, D. "Job Evaluation Research and Research Needs." In H. Hartmann (ed.), *Comparable Worth: New Directions for Research.* Washington, D.C.: National Academy Press, 1985.

Shaffer, R. "Improving Job Opportunities for Women from a U.S. Corporate Perspective." In R. Steinberg-Ratner (ed.), *Equal Employment Policy for Women.* Philadelphia: Temple University Press, 1980.

Shils, E. "Developing a Perspective on Job Measurement."

In M. Rock (ed.), *Handbook of Wage and Salary Administration.* New York: McGraw-Hill, 1972.

Smith-Lovin, L., and McPherson, M. "Sex Segregation in Voluntary Associations." *American Sociological Review,* 1986, *51,* 61–79.

Steinberg, R. "Report on Gender Neutrality in the Stevenson, Kellogg, Ernst, and Whinney Job Evaluation System." Paper prepared for the Ontario Nurses Association, April 1990.

Steinberg, R. "The Social Construction of Skill: Gender, Power and Comparable Worth." *Work and Occupations,* 1990, *17,* 449–482.

Steinberg, R. "Job Evaluation and Managerial Control: The Politics of Techniques and the Techniques of Politics." In J. Fudge and P. McDermott (eds.), *Just Wages: A Feminist Assessment of Pay Equity.* Toronto: University of Toronto Press, 1991.

Steinberg, R. "Gendered Instructions: Cultural Lag and Gender Bias in the Hay System of Job Evaluation." *Work and Occupations,* 1992, *19,* 387–423.

Steinberg, R., and Walter, W. L. "Making Women's Work Visible, The Case of Nursing: First Steps in the Design of a Gender-Neutral Job Comparison System." Paper presented at the Third Women's Policy Research Conference, Institute for Women's Policy Research, Washington, D.C., May 15–16, 1992.

Tomaskovic-Devey, D. *Gender and Racial Inequality at Work: The Sources and Consequences of Job Segregation.* Ithaca, N.Y.: ILR Press, 1993.

Treiman, D. *Job Evaluation: An Analytic Review.* Washington, D.C.: National Academy of Sciences, National Research Council, 1979.

Treiman, D., and Hartmann, H. *Women, Work, and Wages: Equal Pay for Jobs of Equal Value.* Washington, D.C.: National Academy Press, 1981.

Wallace, R. *They Call Her Pastor.* Albany: State University of New York Press, 1992.

West, C., and Zimmerman, D. H. "Doing Gender." *Gender and Society,* 1987, *1,* (2), 125–151.

Williams, C. "The Glass Escalator: Hidden Advantages for Men in the 'Female' Professions." *Social Problems,* 1982, *9,* 253–267.

Wuthnow, R. *Acts of Compassion: Caring for Others and Helping Ourselves.* Princeton, N.J.: Princeton University Press, 1991.

4

The Occupational Structure of Nonprofit Industries: Implications for Women

Lynn C. Burbridge

According to 1990 census figures, women constitute 65 percent of the paid labor force in the nonprofit sector. Because so many of the activities associated with the nonprofit sector are in the area of health and human services, it should come as no surprise that women are so important to nonprofits. About 75 percent of the jobs in the health and human services industries are in such female-intensive occupations as teaching, nursing and other health care work, social work, day care, and administrative support. The growth in the nonprofit sector in recent decades—in concert with the overall expansion of the service sector—has contributed to the demand for women in the service-oriented occupations and to the sharp increase of women in the labor market over the past forty years.

While considerable research has focused on women as

volunteers, activists, and philanthropists in the nonprofit sector, there is a dearth of information on women who are paid for their work in the nonprofit sector, apart from biographies of stellar women in the field and papers by Preston (1985a, 1985b), who also appears in this book. Derrickson's extensive bibliography of literature on the nonprofit sector (1989) shows little information on the subject. One explanation may be the lack of data specifically differentiating between those working in nonprofit and for-profit firms and agencies. Many studies, for example, have focused on women in service occupations in general; few have examined differences in the career paths of women working for nonprofits and those in for-profit or government agencies. Yet the sheer magnitude of women's contribution to the nonprofit sector requires more attention than the few studies now available.

The approach in this chapter focuses on the macroeconomic, structural, and historical factors determining the importance of the nonprofit sector to women's employment. As such, it complements two other chapters in this book: one by Anne Preston focusing on the status and characteristics of women in the nonprofit sector and one by Ronnie Steinberg and Jerry Jacobs that examines issues affecting women in the sector. The three chapters provide different approaches for exploring similar issues.

Women in the Nonprofit Sector: An Overview

Women have been involved in the nonprofit sector from its beginnings in this country. They founded some of the first charities, settlement houses, and philanthropic efforts. Katz (1986) makes a strong case that women played a critical role in the formation of the nonprofit sector in the United States—particularly as it related to charity work, social welfare programs, and advocacy for the poor. He also argues that the development of the social welfare system is inextricably linked to the development of feminism in this country, because many important female social reformers were feminists as well. The irony, of course, was that when many programs designed and run by women obtained social respectability, they were taken over by men. In addition, women were often denied access to paid jobs within the new agencies, although their volunteer labor was always of great importance, making them "the shock troops of charity" (Katz, 1986, p. 64).

The role of women in charity work should not be romanticized. For many middle-class and upper-class women, charity work was the only arena within which they could attain power and prestige, as other areas of civil life were closed to them (Katz, 1986). Despite their involvement in public service, however, many—including the more militant feminists—maintained the class and racial prejudices of the dominant society (Katz, 1986; Davis, 1981). As a result of the indifference, hostility, and paternalism of the dominant society, people of color formed their own mutual aid and social service agencies, which—not surprisingly—depended greatly on the work and leadership of women. The commitment of African-American women and Latinas to social service and advocacy for their people has been ably documented (Bonilla-Santiago, 1993;

Carson, 1987; Gallegos and O'Neill, 1991; Giddings, 1984; Hine, 1990; Neverdon-Morton, 1989; Salem, 1990; Sterling, 1984). Their involvement remains clear today in the heavy concentration of professional women of color in government and nonprofit employment (Preston, Chapter Two).

Less is known about Asian-American and Native American women, because the literature is sparse. It does appear, however, that professional Native American women rely as heavily on government employment as African-American women, suggesting similar reasons for their nonprofit employment (U.S. Bureau of the Census, 1984). Asian-American women appear to be more similar to white women in their reliance on government employment, but they have a very different history: until the end of World War II, most were not permitted to immigrate to the United States to join the Asian men who came to work and who were forced to live in "bachelor societies" (Karnow and Yoshihara, 1992). How this affected the development and characteristics of nonprofits operating in the Asian community would be an interesting question to research.

Beginning with the New Deal in the 1930s, society realized that the government had to assume more responsibility for the activities carried out in the nonprofit sector. The expansion of the welfare state opened many opportunities for paid employment for women in those fields where they previously had served as volunteers (Ginzberg, Hiestand, and Reubens, 1965). The growth in demand for services was not confined to the welfare state but was a general phenomenon of the post–World War II experience in the United States and in other advanced industrial societies (Stanback, Bearse, Noyelle, and Karasek, 1981). In addition, the increasing labor force participation of women led to increased demand for services that had primarily been provided in the household—such as day care and food preparation—resulting in the encroachment of the market in the household sphere (Wolfe, 1989). Women mostly filled these jobs as well.

The government sector, the nonprofit sector, and the for-profit sector gained significant numbers of female employees as a result of the transformation. One would expect the nonprofit sector to be particularly reliant on women, if for no other reason than that it is dominated by health and human services, which represent 62 percent of total revenues in the sector (Hodgkinson, Weitzman, Toppe, and Noga, 1992). The reliance on the two fields, by definition, suggests high employment levels for women.

The Occupational Structure of Nonprofit Industries

While relatively little research has focused on women in paid jobs in the nonprofit sector, those who have examined the issue hypothesize that women gravitate to the sector because it provides a variety of nonfinancial rewards that compensate for its lower salaries. Preston (1985b) cites evidence from a survey that women are attracted by the nonpecuniary aspects of nonprofit employment. Young (1984) and Majone (1980) suggest that people would not enter the nonprofit sector were it not for nonpecuniary rewards such as greater job satisfaction.

While there is no reason to discount these analyses, in a broader context it must be emphasized that most people make an *occupational* choice first, to be a teacher or a nurse or a social worker; the choice of sector is often secondary or, at most, jointly decided with the choice of occupation. If women are more likely to work in the industries and occupations that predominate in the nonprofit sector, they will be concentrated in the sector because of its occupational structure, regardless of their preferences.

Table 4.1 provides selected statistics on women in health services, legal services, educational services, and social services, industries within which there is considerable nonprofit employment. Column one shows the percentage of women in the various industries in 1980. Social services (77 percent female) and health services (76 percent female) were particularly dominated by women. More dramatic statistics were found for various industry subcategories. Under social services, child day-care services were 94 percent female; under health services, nursing and personal care facilities were 87 percent female. Thus, estimates showing high percentages of women in nonprofits (Hodgkinson, Weitzman, Toppe, and Noga, 1992) are perfectly in line with the characteristics of the industries that predominate in the nonprofit sector.

Columns two and three of Table 4.1 explore the occupational structure of the industries. They provide the percentages of jobs in these industries that in 1980 were in female-intensive occupations, defined as occupations that are more than 50 percent female. (Because women are 45 percent of the labor force, these are occupations

Table 4.1. Selected Statistics for Selected Industries, 1980.

	Percent Female	Percent of All Jobs in Female-intensive Occupations	Percent of Jobs Held by Women in Female-intensive Occupations
Total	42.64	37.60	68.95
Health services	76.20	75.82	88.35
Hospitals	76.63	78.55	88.63
Nursing & personal care facilities	87.31	86.78	91.31
Legal services	51.26	41.54	77.92
Educational services	65.00	69.74	83.24
Social services	76.97	75.38	82.84
Child day-care services	93.80	86.47	88.57
Residential care facilities	64.54	72.74	81.99
Museums, art galleries & zoos	52.91	43.31	60.29
Religious organizations	42.82	35.25	70.98
Membership organizations	53.90	47.11	68.42

Source: U.S. Bureau of the Census, 1984.

that draw disproportionately on women.) More than 75 percent of jobs in health and human services were in female-intensive occupations in 1980. From 80 to 90 percent of jobs held specifically by women in health and human services were in female-intensive occupations.

Thus, the route women take into the industries, and ultimately into the nonprofit sector, comes by way of traditionally female occupations. Similar findings are apparent for educational services. And while in legal services only 42 percent of all jobs in 1980 were in female-intensive occupations, 78 percent of women in legal services were in female-intensive fields.

The actual occupations defined as female-intensive can be grouped into six categories. First are the professional and technical occupations, primarily in care-giving or helping fields: nurses, dieticians, health therapists, teachers, counselors, librarians, social and recreation workers, religious workers (nonclergy), and health technicians. Second are administrative support occupations: secretaries, receptionists, computer operators, and records processors. Third are service occupations such as food preparation workers, personal service workers, and health service workers. Fourth, the field of retail sales is dominated by women. Fifth, textile workers and production inspectors are the two blue-collar fields dominated by women. And finally, only three managerial fields are dominated by women: underwriters, managers in medicine and health, and an amorphous category of "managers, not elsewhere specified." Occupations in the first three categories bring the most women into the nonprofit sector.

Further, a more stringent definition of female-intensive occupations—those in which 65 percent employed in the field are women—produces similar results. The percentages presented in columns two and three in Table 4.1 change only by one or two percentage points. The managerial occupations drop out, however, because women dominated these fields by a narrow margin.

The importance of examining the interface between occupations and industries is further illuminated in Table 4.2. The table examines employment in three service industries (health, education, and social services) by race, sex, and occupation in 1980. Some figures are quite remarkable. Eight percent of white male managers, 44 percent of white male professionals, 14 percent of white male technicians, 7 percent of white male administrative support workers, and 19 percent of white male service workers could be found in health, education, and social services. Contrast this with black women: 27 percent of black female managers, 85 percent of black female professionals, 72 percent of black female technicians, 17 percent of black female administrative support personnel, and 47 percent of black female service workers were employed in the three industries. While the differences between white males and black females were the most significant, white and Hispanic women also depended heavily on these industries. But black female managers and service workers were more heavily dependent on these industries (with differences in the range of ten percentage points) than their white and Hispanic counterparts. While black males' dependence on the industries fell between that found for

Table 4.2. Percent of Total Employed by Race, Sex, and Occupation in Health, Education, and Social Services.

Occupation	Black Females	Hispanic Females	White Females	Black Males	Hispanic Males	White Males
Total	35.28	23.30	28.93	12.44	7.78	9.44
Executive, administrative, managerial	27.40	17.48	17.83	18.04	9.04	8.26
Professional specialty	85.29	78.88	80.75	58.35	47.51	43.65
Technician and related support	72.37	60.39	64.37	25.24	19.47	13.68
Sales	2.86	1.62	1.54	1.03	.56	.48
Administrative support	17.31	23.19	20.65	9.84	8.78	6.63
Service	47.46	38.66	38.60	29.76	19.18	18.65
Other	4.59	2.11	4.75	2.57	1.68	1.86

Note: The "other" category includes precision, production, and craft occupations; operators, laborers, and handlers; and farming, fishing, and forestry occupations.

Source: U.S. Bureau of the Census (1984).

white males and for all women, Hispanic males appeared to be more like white males. It should be noted, however, that there is considerable variability among Hispanics; there may be significant cultural differences among Mexican Americans, Puerto Ricans, Cuban Americans, and Hispanics whose ancestors are from other Central and South American countries.

Despite these results, it should also be noted that there are indications that women do better in these industries, even when they are *not* in female-intensive occupations. Table 4.3 examines occupations with low proportions of women in 1980, 35 percent or less. It focuses on management, professional, and technical fields in which the overall representation of women has traditionally been low. Nevertheless, health services, legal services, educational services, and social services employed women in these occupations to a much greater extent than they were employed in the labor market overall. For example, women represented 14 percent of lawyers and judges overall but 46 percent of lawyers and judges in social services. Women were 5 percent of all engineers but 40 percent of engineers in social services. Table 4.3 presents many examples that suggest that the four service industries employed women in many occupations to a much larger extent than they were employed in the labor market overall. Important research questions include why these industries are more receptive to women in fields with relatively low percentages of women, and to what extent employment practices in the nonprofit sector (in comparison with the government and for-profit sectors) contribute to the greater receptivity to women in these occupations.

Table 4.3. Selected Occupations with Low Percentages of Women, 1980.

	All Industries	Health Services	Legal Services	Education Services	Social Services
Total	42.64	76.20	51.26	65.00	76.97
Managerial occupations					
Financial managers	31.24	39.93	48.32	35.47	39.86
Purchasing managers	21.15	37.12	23.81	24.57	26.67
Managers, marketing, advertising, & public relations	17.40	38.65	68.52	45.24	48.85
Management analysts	25.13	62.17	18.07	48.09	53.21
Business and promotion agents	32.86	70.97		51.44	53.46
Inspectors and compliance officers	17.27	20.80	49.63	42.22	40.73
Professionals					
Architects	8.20	13.65	8.26	17.01	22.05
Engineers	4.57	12.20	3.43	8.98	39.62
Surveyors	3.65	41.86		57.52	43.55
Mathematical and computer scientists	25.95	45.29	50.00	35.06	58.90
Natural scientists	19.64	41.47	16.19	27.56	38.49
Pharmacists	23.87	38.02	35.29	50.54	39.05
Lawyers and judges	13.78	22.15	11.23	28.58	45.96
Technicians					
Engineering and related technologists	16.45	47.10	18.24	37.91	50.48
Science technicians	30.73	53.27	36.36	46.27	45.00
Technicians, except health, engineering, and science	31.43	54.70	75.35	38.06	57.90

Source: U.S. Bureau of the Census (1984).

What the three tables clearly demonstrate is the importance of examining the overall industrial and occupational context within which the nonprofit sector exists. Unfortunately, few studies have examined the nonprofit sector from this perspective, making it difficult to identify how the sector may be different from government and private-sector agencies also operating within this context, particularly with respect to the employment of women.

Implications of Occupational Structure

Discussing the disproportionate presence of women in the nonprofit sector as a function of their segregation in specific occupations begs the questions of why they are concentrated in these fields in the first place and what the segregation may imply for women's employment in the nonprofit sector. One argument is that women have been tracked into certain jobs because of discrimination. This crowding of women in a relatively small number of fields results in a depression of productivity and wages in the fields (Bergmann, 1980). Another argument is that women have based their choices of certain occupations on their current and anticipated investments in education, training, and work experience. According to this view, women want less demanding occupations that tend to offer lower wages, given their current or planned child-rearing and family responsibilities (Polocheck, 1979; O'Neill, 1983). The difficulty is that it is still a "chicken or egg" argument: Do women choose these jobs because they want to be able to interrupt their careers for child-rearing responsibilities, or do they experience frequent interruptions because of the nature of the jobs they are in (Gronau, 1982)?

These arguments have implications for nonprofit employment. If women do seek such jobs to better balance work and family needs, are nonprofits more accommodating than government or for-profits? If women are being discriminated against, is that more or less likely to occur in the nonprofit sector? In other words, can these arguments, as they have been defined in the literature on occupational segregation, be specifically applied to nonprofits?

While economists have examined the issue of discrimination versus choice, occupational psychologists have taken a different tack, focusing on women's feelings about traditionally female jobs. The primary focus in the literature has been on women in care-giving occupations such as nurses, social workers, and day-care workers. It appears from the literature that even if women do choose care-giving jobs, they become increasingly dissatisfied. Studies of nurses, social workers, and day-care workers find that while many enjoy the helping aspects of their jobs, 40 to 60 percent indicate that they consider their occupation temporary or that they desire to find other employment (Whitebook, Howes, and Phillips, 1989; Jayaratne and Chess, 1984; Brabson, Jones, and Jayaratne, 1991; Fimian, Fastenau, and Thomas, 1988). High turnover because of burnout is a number one concern in the literature about teachers, nurses, social workers, and day-care workers, with actual turnover rates estimated to be as high as 30 to 50 percent (Blegen and Mueller, 1987; Cherniss, 1980; Whitebook, Howes, and Phillips, 1989). Unfortunately, little information is available on where women go when they leave these jobs.

Many reasons have been given for women's dissatisfaction, but most center on pay, benefits, and working conditions.

Pay and Benefits

Women in traditionally female jobs are generally dissatisfied with their pay. Even top-level administrators make less than they might in other arenas. According to Young (1984), salaries of executive directors of nonprofit social service agencies averaged about $32,000 in the early 1980s. Day-care directors made $13,000 to $24,000 (Whitebook, Howes, and Phillips, 1989), with the high end of the range representing those with some postgraduate education. Further, Whitebook, Howes, and Phillips (1989) also note that many day-care workers made poverty-level wages, even when working full time.

According to Feldberg (1992), nurses have been so distressed about their earnings, given their training and expertise, that they have brought more comparable worth cases to court than any other profession (Feldberg, 1992). Yet nurses are better off than many other health care workers. Home health aides, the fastest-growing health occupation, make poverty-level wages, which has contributed to critical shortages of workers in some areas (Burbridge, 1993).

As is the case for all employees, access to benefits depends on standing in the occupational hierarchy. Women in the low-paying occupations—such as day-care workers and home health aides—often receive no health benefits (Whitebook, Howes, and Phillips, 1989; Burbridge,

1993), a phenomenon that is not without irony, because the same women who are providing care for others often do not have access to care for themselves or their families. Many women in traditionally female jobs also encounter difficulties in obtaining full-time work, which usually also means few or no benefits (see, for example, Marshall, Barnett, Baruch, and Pleck, 1991).

In addition, many of these fields offer few opportunities for advancement. Thus, many women do not see options for upgrading their position (Marshall, Barnett, Baruch, and Pleck, 1991). In some cases, the lack of promotional opportunities reflects the relatively flat job structure in many fields (for example, see Feldman, Sapienza, and Kane, 1990). In other cases, women encounter discrimination in seeking higher-level administrative jobs. This is of some concern, because the availability of promotional opportunities is often a key predictor of job satisfaction (Jayaratne and Chess, 1984).

Working Conditions

The literature on traditionally female occupations raises several issues about working conditions. The issues of work load, role conflict, and decision authority occur repeatedly in the literature on a variety of occupations. Heavy work load, increased paperwork, and insufficient time to complete tasks are constant complaints among health and social workers (Cherniss, 1980; Jayaratne and Chess, 1984; Jones, 1988; Marshall, Barnett, Baruch, and Pleck, 1991). In addition, there are indications that work loads are increasing, because budget cutbacks have hit all care-giving fields. Not only has this resulted in higher caseloads for existing staff but caseloads that are increasingly comprised of the most difficult cases—the sickest patients (Feldberg, 1992) or clients who are most likely to be in crisis (Kimmich, 1985).

A related issue is role conflict—workers torn between the demands of care giving and meeting the bureaucratic requirements of their agency. Sometimes, the needs of clients seem to be in conflict with agency rules and regulations (Brabson, Jones, and Jayaratne, 1991; Cherniss, 1980; Abel and Nelson, 1990). Care givers also feel a lack of decision authority as agencies become more formalized and more subject to government regulation and as jobs become more routine and monotonous (Cherniss, 1980; Feldberg, 1992; Jayaratne and Chess, 1984; Jones, 1988; Maraldo, 1988, Marshall, Barnett, Baruch, and Pleck, 1991).

Not only care givers suffer in this situation; so do their clients and families. Marshall and Barnett (1991) cite concerns of care givers that their children may suffer as a result of their jobs, particularly among those in lower-paying jobs who occasionally have to work double shifts. Schorr (1988) has noted that those programs that have been most successful in delivering services to clients are those that provide staff with flexibility and involve them in decision making and those jobs in which care givers can work with a mix of clients rather than only the most difficult cases.

Finally, less skilled women in low-paying jobs and women of color also note issues of discrimination based on race or class (Brabson, Jones, and Jayaratne, 1991; Feldman, Sapienza, and Kane, 1990; Marshall and Barnett, 1991).

Discrimination can be exhibited both by supervisors and by clients. Thus, the less skilled women and women of color experience lack of respect for who they are, coupled with the lack of respect often shown toward care givers in general.

Unfortunately, the literature offers little that distinguishes between the employment practices of nonprofits and those of government and for-profits. In her examination of the day-care industry, Preston (1985a) suggests that the compensation differentials between nonprofit and for-profit day-care centers are not significant when the centers are allowed to compete on an equal basis. Young (1984) found some differences between nonprofit and other agencies in compensation and in other personnel matters but no clear patterns: there seems to be considerable variation by industry. This suggests that it may not be useful to look at nonprofits as a homogeneous group of agencies, which, of course, they are not. Unfortunately, Young's study was not structured in a way that makes it possible to draw specific implications for women.

Unlike the Preston and Young studies of compensation, which found little or inconsistent evidence of major differences, another report ("More Generous Fringe Benefits," 1990) suggests that nonprofits may be lagging behind other kinds of agencies in the provision of employee benefits. Obviously, more research is needed to provide a complete picture of differences in employment practices of the nonprofit, government, and for-profit sectors. Where there is a particular concern about the effect of such policies on women, the studies should focus on the kinds of jobs within the nonprofit sector in which women are concentrated.

Finally, employment practices develop in a larger context. What nonprofits can or will do depends on the resources that are available to them, which, in turn, depend on a variety of economic and political factors.

Trends and Prospects

The chapter began with a discussion of the growth in the nonprofit sector as part of a general expansion of the service sector. There has been a tremendous growth in demand for service workers and, as a result, a tremendous growth in demand for female labor. The other side of the story has been the declining importance of manufacturing in modern Western societies. This has resulted in declining real wages of men and—as a result—declining real family income, despite gains made by women (Levy, 1988). Thus, women face increasing pressures to contribute to family income by increasing their time in the formal labor market. Because past political and economic trends have played a key role in increasing the pressures, it is interesting to assess the political and economic trends that will affect women working in this sector in the future.

Five political and economic trends seem to be particularly relevant to the nonprofit sector and to the employment of women within it. First is the tremendous growth in government expenditures for health and human services—as provided by the government or via nonprofit intermediaries (Salamon, 1992). Second, the increased government spending has meant increased government regulation in health and human services, affecting government and nongovernment agencies alike. Third is a growing countertrend to reduce government expenditures for ideological reasons and because of a seemingly insurmountable federal budget deficit. Fourth, nonprofits are facing increased competition from for-profit agencies that have been entering the health and human services field in significant numbers since the early 1970s. Finally, the service sector faces continuing problems with productivity growth; almost by definition it is labor-intensive, with serious limitations on how production can be increased by adding capital or by taking advantage of higher returns to scale (Baumol and Bowen, 1966).

Most nonprofits have been affected by these different factors in one way or another, although their effect has varied. The health and social services fields, on which this chapter focuses considerable attention, are excellent examples.

Health has been the biggest beneficiary of growth in government. Between 1977 and 1989, government spending for health increased 81 percent, and revenues of nonprofits in the health field grew 92 percent, representing the biggest share of nonprofit growth, 60 percent (Salamon, 1992). In 1989, government expenditures represented 36 percent of revenues in the health field (Hodgkinson, Weitzman, Toppe, and Noga, 1992, p. 147). But with the aging of the population and citizen demands for a more comprehensive, national health system, the proportion can only rise. With the growth has come increasing regulation, however, usually with respect to the Medicare and Medicaid programs and increasingly with a focus on cost containment.

Nonprofit health agencies have also faced increased

competition from for-profit providers. Some feel that whatever distinctiveness nonprofit hospitals may have had in the past will be blurred as they are forced to compete with for-profit hospitals and acute care facilities for paying customers (Netting, McMurtry, Kettner, and Jones-McClintic, 1990; Ferris and Graddy, 1989; Hansmann, 1989). And while rising health care costs can be explained in part by the increased use of expensive procedures and inefficient management, there are real limits to productivity increases in the field, given its reliance on hands-on services from health care providers and public concerns about improving the quality of care.

Social services have been hardest hit by the countertrend to reduce government expenditures (O'Neill, 1989; Salamon, 1982). From 1977 to 1989, government spending for social services declined 19 percent. Nevertheless, revenues of nonprofit social services agencies grew by 62 percent during the period, and the agencies are still heavily dependent on government expenditures, which represent 42 percent of revenues received by them (Salamon, 1992). The resilience of social service nonprofits, despite severe cuts, reflects the important need that the agencies fill, particularly with respect to poor and disenfranchised populations.

Nonprofit social service agencies have also been subject to increased regulation and to the limitations imposed by performance-based contracting (Terrell and Kramer, 1984). They face increased competition from for-profit agencies in such areas as day care and residential care facilities. And here too, productivity increases are difficult to measure and may even be resisted by those who feel that their primary goal should be the provision of high-quality services.

What do these developments suggest for the employment of women in the nonprofit sector? First, opportunities for women in the health field will continue to increase. This is suggested by the Bureau of Labor Statistics's occupational projections to 2000 (Table 4.4). All health fields are expected to grow more rapidly than overall occupational growth and more rapidly than other female-intensive occupations.

Table 4.4 also provides verification for another trend that may be developing: an increasing emphasis on lower-paying jobs. Spiraling health costs and slow productivity growth, government cost-containment strategies, and a continuing backlash in regard to government spending encourage the use of cheap labor. The number of less skilled health workers—home health aides, licensed practical nurses, and nursing and psychiatric aides—is expected to grow more than the number of registered nurses. The lowest-paying health occupation—home health aide—is one of the fastest-growing occupations in the country.

Third, the increasing participation of women in the labor market will increase the need for child-care workers and other service personnel. According to Table 4.4, child-care workers and preschool teachers are expected to experience more rapid rates of growth than other teaching professions.

Fourth, some fields may experience wage growth in response to labor shortages, but this will be uneven. There is some evidence, for example, that nurses' wages have increased in response to such a shortage (Feldberg, 1992). But those in low-skilled service and administrative support occupations will have greater difficulty increasing their earnings, particularly if, as Reich (1991) has argued, the decline of the manufacturing sector increases the number of workers competing for service jobs. Further, while productivity increases are difficult, computer and information technology will provide some growth opportunities in this sector ("Why Non-Profits Should Gear Up," 1993). This may have a disparate effect on nonprofit workers if their jobs are changed or eliminated by new technologies.

Fifth, care givers may face continuing pressure to increase their work loads and to balance the needs of their clients with mounting government regulation and funding cutbacks. The increasing wages of nurses must be balanced against the increasing responsibilities they have undertaken in response to recent Medicare regulations (Feldberg, 1992). Further, recent health care reform proposals suggest that nurses may take on even more responsibility ("White House Health Plan," 1993). While many proposals suggest a long-deserved recognition of the important role of nurses in hospitals, the advantage to nurses of the proposals will depend on their effect on work loads and compensation levels. And while there is general agreement that health care reform is essential, the effect on health care workers will depend on how hospitals and other health agencies respond to any federal proposal to change how they do business.

Social and human service workers have experienced

Table 4.4. Occupational Employment in 1988, Projected Occupational Employment for 2000, Growth and Rate of Change (Numbers in Thousands).

Occupations	1988	2000	Numerical Growth	Percentage of Change
All occupations	118,104	136,211	18,107	15.3
Education/child-care occupations				
Child-care workers	670	856	185	27.8
Librarians, archivists, and related workers	159	176	17	10.7
Library assistants	105	111	6	5.7
Teachers:				
Special education	275	317	42	15.3
Preschool	238	309	71	29.8
Kindergarten/elementary	1,359	1,567	208	15.3
Secondary	1,164	1,388	224	19.2
Teachers' aides	682	827	145	21.3

Health occupations

Dental assistants	166	197	31	18.7
Dental hygienists	91	107	16	17.6
Dieticians and nutritionists	40	51	11	27.5
Homemaker–home health aides	327	535	208	63.6
Licensed practical nurses	626	855	229	36.6
Nursing and psychiatric aides	1,298	1,703	405	31.2
Registered nurses	1,577	2,190	613	38.9
Therapists (occupational, physical, respiratory, etc.)	256	367	111	43.4

Social service occupations

Human service workers	118	171	53	44.9
Social workers	385	495	110	28.6
Welfare eligibility workers	91	102	11	12.1

Other Female–intensive occupations

Cosmetologists and related workers	649	731	82	12.6
File clerks	263	290	27	10.3
Flight attendants	88	123	35	39.8
Secretaries, stenographers, and typists	4,517	4,991	474	10.5

Source: U.S. Department of Labor, Bureau of Labor Statistics, *Outlook 2000*, Bulletin 2352. Washington, D.C.: Government Printing Office, 1990.

increasing work loads with the budget cuts of the 1980s and 1990s, first at the federal and more recently at the state and local levels. And although the Clinton administration is more sympathetic to social programs, the federal deficit will limit how much relief social service workers get. In addition, those social programs funded by the government have also been subject to a variety of rules in terms of how much can be spent on administration, what services can be provided, and what reporting requirements are necessary.

Finally, there will be a great deal of uncertainty. The country is in the midst of an ongoing debate about the need for health and human services, how much should be spent on these services, and who should pay for them. A change in administration—whether on the federal, state, or local government levels—can result in a total revision of priorities. This can have severe repercussions for women in careers in the government and nonprofit sectors, if for no other reason than that women rely more heavily on these sectors for employment than do men (Abramovitz, 1988).

Conclusion

It is clear that the demand for women in the service sector will continue, particularly in health fields. This may prove to be a bitter pill, however, because economic and political pressures may work to keep wages down and work loads up. Further, there is little doubt that the nonprofit sector will be affected by the trends; those fields in which women predominate are heavily reliant on government support and are subject to increasing government regulation. This does not mean that government regulation is bad per se, but it may limit the ways in which nonprofits can innovate to take some pressure off their care givers.

The most obvious implication for future research is to examine how nonprofits cope in light of the overall trends. For example, while research has focused on nonprofits versus other sectors, more research is needed on women in nonprofits in the context of occupational segregation. Is there more or less occupational segregation in the nonprofit sector? Do women have more opportunities to move from traditionally female jobs to administrative or managerial jobs in the nonprofit sector?

Many important questions can be raised about compensation and benefits in the nonprofit sector compared with other fields, as well as about other employment practices and the overall work environment. Do women in the nonprofit sector experience less role conflict? Are they given more decision authority? Is there more or less job dissatisfaction and turnover among women in the nonprofit sector? Have nonprofits done a better job of handling the stress and discrimination experienced by care givers? Are they better at helping workers balance the demands of work and family? If so, what are some of the more successful models?

With respect to government regulation and budget cutbacks, it would be useful to know how the careers of women in nonprofits have been affected relative to the careers of women in other sectors. Have nonprofits done a better job of shielding workers from the more negative consequences of the trends? The effects of privatization and productivity also can be examined in regard to women's careers in these sectors.

Finally, differences within the nonprofit sector may be considerable. For example, day-care centers, hospitals, social service agencies, legal aid societies, and regional theaters are different in their employment practices and the effect they may have on women. What are the commonalities and differences in the various kinds of nonprofits and what explains them? The data also indicate significant differences by race and ethnicity in the dependence of women on service industries. What are the commonalities and differences for women workers in the nonprofit sector, and what explains them?

Those who have worked for nonprofit organizations or who have studied them know that they are filled with people who have found ways around all kinds of barriers, such as budget shortfalls or difficult regulations. But surmounting barriers takes much work and imagination and an understanding of the context surrounding nonprofits. A concerted effort to address the issues affecting women working in the nonprofit sector demands an understanding of the issues that they face, some of which have been presented in this chapter.

References

Abel, E. K., and Nelson, M. K. *Circles of Care: Work and Identity in Women's Lives.* Albany: State University of New York Press, 1990.

Abramovitz, M. *Regulating the Lives of Women: Social Welfare Policy from Colonial Times to the Present.* Boston: South End Press, 1988.

Baumol, W. J., and Bowen, W. G. *Performing Arts: The*

Economic Dilemma. New York: Twentieth Century Fund, 1966.

Bergmann, B. "Occupational Segregation Wages and Profits When Employers Discriminate by Race or Sex." In A. Amsden (ed.), *The Economics of Women and Work.* New York: St. Martin's Press, 1980.

Blegen, M. A., and Mueller, C. W. "Nurses' Job Satisfaction: A Longitudinal Analysis." *Research in Nursing & Health,* 1987, *10,* 227–237.

Bonilla-Santiago, G. *Breaking Ground and Barriers: Hispanic Women Developing Effective Leadership.* San Diego: Marin Publications, 1993.

Brabson, H. V., Jones, C. A., and Jayaratne, S. "Perceptions of Emotional Support, Stress, and Strain Among African-American Human Service Workers." *Journal of Multicultural Social Work,* 1991, *1*(3), 77–101.

Burbridge, L. "The Labor Market for Home Care Workers: Demand, Supply, and Institutional Barriers." *The Gerontologist,* 1993, *33*(1), 41–46.

Carson, E. "The Contemporary Charitable Giving and Voluntarism of Black Women." Paper prepared for the Center for the Study of Philanthropy, Conference on Women and Philanthropy: Past, Present, and Future, City University of New York, June 17–18, 1987.

Cherniss, C. *Staff Burnout: Job Stress in the Human Services.* Newbury Park, Calif.: Sage, 1980.

Davis, A. Y. *Women, Race, and Class.* New York: Vintage, 1981.

Derrickson, M. C. *The Literature of the Nonprofit Sector: A Bibliography with Abstracts.* New York: Foundation Center, 1989.

Feldberg, R. "Comparable Worth and Nurses in the United States." In P. Kahn and E. Meehan (eds.), *Equal Value/Comparable Worth in Britain and the United States.* London: Macmillan, 1992.

Feldman, P., Sapienza, A. M., and Kane, N. M. *Who Cares for Them? Workers, Work Life Problems and Reforms in the Home Care Industry.* New York: Greenwood, 1990.

Ferris, J. M., and Graddy, E. "Fading Distinctions Among the Nonprofit, Government, and For-Profit Sectors." In V. A. Hodgkinson, R. W. Lyman, and Associates (eds.), *The Future of the Nonprofit Sector: Challenges, Changes, and Policy Considerations.* San Francisco: Jossey-Bass, 1989.

Fimian, M. J., Fastenau, P. S., Thomas, J. A. "Stress in Nursing and Intentions of Leaving the Profession." *Psychological Reports,* 1988, *62,* 499–506.

Gallegos, H. E., and O'Neill, M. (eds.). *Hispanics and the Nonprofit Sector.* New York: Foundation Center, 1991.

Giddings, P. *When and Where I Enter: The Impact of Black Women on Race and Sex in America.* New York: Bantam Books, 1984.

Ginzberg, E., Hiestand, D. L., and Reubens, B. G. *The Pluralistic Economy.* New York: McGraw-Hill, 1965.

Gronau, R. "Sex-related Wage Differentials and Women's Interrupted Labor Careers—The Chicken or the Egg." National Bureau of Economic Research Working Paper No. 1002. Cambridge, Mass.: National Bureau of Economic Research, 1982.

Hall, C. "More Generous Fringe Benefits: One Way for Non-Profits to Compete for Employees." *Chronicle of Philanthropy,* October, 16, 1990, p. 28.

Hansmann, H. "The Two Nonprofit Sectors: Fee for Service Versus Donative Organizations." In V. A. Hodgkinson, R. W. Lyman, and Associates (eds.), *The Future of the Nonprofit Sector: Challenges, Changes, and Policy Considerations.* San Francisco: Jossey-Bass, 1989.

Hine, D. C. (ed.). *Black Women in United States History.* New York: Carlson, 1990.

Hodgkinson, V. A., Weitzman, M. S., Toppe, C. M., and Noga, S. M. *The Nonprofit Almanac, 1992–1993: Dimensions of the Independent Sector.* San Francisco. Jossey-Bass, 1992.

Jayaratne, S., and Chess, W. A. "Job Satisfaction, Burnout and Turnover: A National Study." *Social Work,* 1984, *29,* 448–453.

Jones, P. A. "The Home Care Personnel Shortage Crisis: Preliminary Results of a NAHC Survey." *Caring,* May 1988, pp. 6–9.

Karnow, S., and Yoshihara, N. *Asian Americans in Transition.* New York: Asia Society, 1992.

Katz, M. B. *In the Shadow of the Poorhouse: A Social History of Welfare in America.* New York: Basic Books, 1986.

Kimmich, M. H. *America's Children: Who Cares? Growing Needs and Declining Assistance in the Reagan Era.* Washington, D.C.: Urban Institute, 1985.

Levy, F. *Dollars and Dreams: The Changing American Income Distribution.* New York: W. W. Norton, 1988.

Majone, G. "Professionalism and Non-Profit Organizations." Program on Non-Profit Organizations Working Paper No. 24. New Haven, Conn.: Yale University, Program on Non-Profit Organizations, Institution for Social and Policy Studies, 1980.

Maraldo, P. J. "Nursing Supply Crisis: How Does Home Care Compare to Other Sectors?" *Caring,* May 1988, pp. 10–14.

Marshall, N. L., and Barnett, R. C. "Race, Class and Multiple Role Strains and Gains Among Women Employed in the Service Sector." *Women and Health,* 1991, *17*(4), 1–19.

Marshall, N. L., Barnett, R. C., Baruch, G. K., and Pleck, J. H. "More Than a Job: Women and Stress in Caregiving Occupations." In H. Z. Lopata and J. A. Levy (eds.), *Current Research on Occupations and Professions: A Research Annual* (Vol. 6) Greenwich, Conn.: JAI Press, 1991.

Netting, E. F., McMurtry, S. L., Kettner, P. M., and Jones-McClintic, S. "Privatization and Its Impact on Nonprofit Service Providers." *Nonprofit and Voluntary Sector Quarterly,* 1990, *19*(1), 33–46.

Neuffer, E. "White House Health Plan Would Stress Nurses' Role." *Boston Globe,* April 8, 1993, p. 1.

Neustadt, R. M. "Why Non-Profits Should Gear up for 'Information Superhighways'." *Chronicle of Philanthropy,* April 20, 1993, pp. 42–43.

Neverdon-Morton, C. *Afro-American Women of the South*

and the Advancement of the Race, 1895–1925. Knoxville: University of Tennessee Press, 1989.

O'Neill, J. *The Determinants of Wage Effects of Occupational Segregation.* Washington, D.C.: Urban Institute, 1983.

O'Neill, M. *The Third America: The Emergence of the Nonprofit Sector in the United States.* San Francisco: Jossey-Bass, 1989.

Polocheck, S. W. "Occupational Segregation Among Women: Theory, Evidence, and Prognosis." In C. B. Lloyd, E. S. Andrews, and C. L. Gilroy (eds.), *Women in the Labor Market.* New York: Columbia University Press, 1979.

Preston, A. E. "Compensation Differentials in the Non-Profit Sector: An Application to the Day Care Industry." Program on Non-Profit Organizations Working Paper No. 99. New Haven, Conn.: Yale University, Program on Non-Profit Organizations, Institution for Social and Policy Studies, 1985a.

Preston, A. E. "Women in the White Collar Non-Profit Sector: The Best Option or the Only Option?" Program on Non-Profit Organizations Working Paper No. 101. New Haven, Conn.: Yale University, Program on Non-Profit Organizations, Institution for Social and Policy Studies, 1985b.

Reich, R. B. *The Work of Nations: Preparing Ourselves for 21st Century Capitalism.* New York: Knopf, 1991.

Salamon, L. M. "The Nonprofit Sector." In J. L. Palmer and I. V. Sawhill (eds.), *The Reagan Experiment.* Washington, D.C.: Urban Institute, 1982.

Salamon, L. M. *America's Nonprofit Sector: A Primer.* New York: Foundation Center, 1992.

Salem, D. *To Better Our World: Black Women in Organized Reform, 1890–1920.* New York: Carlson, 1990.

Schorr, L. B. *Within Our Reach: Breaking the Cycle of Disadvantage.* New York: Doubleday, 1988.

Stanback, T. M., Bearse, P. J., Noyelle, T. J., and Karasek, R. A. *Services: The Economy.* Totowa, N.J.: Allanheld, Osmun, 1981.

Sterling, D. *We Are Your Sisters: Black Women in the Nineteenth Century.* New York: W. W. Norton, 1984.

Terrell, P., and Kramer, R. M. "Contracting with Non-Profits." *Public Welfare,* 1984, *42*(1) 31–37.

U.S. Bureau of the Census. *1980 Census of Population.* Vol. 2: *Subject Reports: Occupation by Industry.* Washington, D.C.: Government Printing Office, 1984.

U.S. Department of Labor, Bureau of Labor Statistics. *Outlook 2000, Bulletin 2352.* Washington, D.C.: Government Printing Office, 1990.

Whitebook, M., Howes, C., and Phillips, D. *Who Cares? Child Care Teachers and the Quality of Care in America, Final Report of the Child Care Staffing Study.* Oakland, Calif.: Child Care Employee Project, 1989.

Wolfe, A. *Whose Keeper? Social Science and Moral Obligation.* Berkeley: University of California Press, 1989.

Young, D. R. "Performance and Reward in Nonprofit Organizations: Evaluation, Compensation and Personnel Incentives." Program on Non-Profit Organizations Working Paper No. 79. New Haven, Conn.: Yale University, Program on Non-Profit Organizations, Institution for Social and Policy Studies, 1984.

5

Women,
Changing Demographics,
and the Redefinition of Power

Juanita Tamayo Lott

At first glance, associating power with women in the non-profit sector seems questionable. In all institutions that have been developed by and are dominated by men, women hold subordinate positions. This is true even in the family, where women's role is central (Acker, 1992, p. 567). Women in nonprofit organizations also are subordinate because of the relative position of the sector. First, *nonprofit* is an ambiguous concept, comparable to *nonwhite*, understood more by what it is not—not government and not the business sector—than by anything inherently distinctive. Second, alternate terms such as the *independent sector* or *the third sector* (O'Neill, 1989; Commission on Private Philanthropy, 1983) underscore a relative and secondary status. The term independent sector may be misleading in that the sector is dependent upon contributions and volunteers for its existence. The term third sector connotes sequence and may evoke comparisons with *Third World,* such as less-developed technology and lower economic status.

That women lack power in the nonprofit sector is further evidenced by the fact that their status and roles are virtually unscrutinized and undocumented despite their long intense involvement in philanthropy and voluntarism. Pioneering research tends to be selective, focusing on higher-status women (such as biographies of wealthy women philanthropists) or on readily available data (such as statistics on women in foundations, although foundations account for less than 5 percent of the revenue of the nonprofit sector). Research and statistics on the nonprofit sector itself have been generated only in recent years.

Nevertheless, the issue of women and power in the nonprofit sector is becoming more pressing. The sector has been viewed as the locus of social change and empowerment not found in the government and for-profit sectors (O'Connell, 1983). As government and corporate support decrease because of budget deficits, nonprofit organizations are expected to meet growing public needs (Murninghan, 1990, p. 1). The number of nonprofit organizations and the proportion of nonprofit sector employees, disproportionately female, continue to increase. In 1990, there were almost 1.4 million nonprofit organizations. Between 1977 and 1990, the independent sector (which consists of most but not all nonprofit organizations) increased its share of employment from 8.5 percent to 10.4 percent and increased its share of total national income from 5.8 percent to 6.8 percent. (Hodgkinson, Weitzman, Toppe, and Noga, 1992, p. 4). All these factors suggest the need to examine more closely the issue of women and power in the nonprofit sector.

Implications of Demographic Shifts

Two demographic shifts have implications for the roles of women and the redistribution of power in a heterogeneous society. The first is a shift from a male majority to a female majority. The shift was initially documented in the 1950 Census and has been maintained for each decade since, with women now constituting 51 to 52 percent of the American population (U.S. Bureau of the Census, 1987, p. 17; 1992b, p. 15).

The second shift has become apparent only in the last two decades but will continue for the foreseeable future. The shift is the result of relaxation of restrictive immigration policies as well as of differential fertility rates and age structure in various ethnic groups. This is the shift from a mainly white European population to a more heterogeneous population, including traditional racial and ethnic minorities—African Americans and native peoples—and more recently emerging populations—Latinos and Asian Americans. According to the most recent projections of the Census Bureau, the growth and diversity will continue.

The U.S. population is expected to increase from 255 million in 1990 to 383 million in 2050, an increase of 50 percent (U.S. Bureau of the Census, 1992a). The racial and ethnic composition of Americans is likely to change from 25 percent minority in 1992 to 50 percent minority in

157

2050. Specifically, in 1992, 1 percent of the American population were American Indians and Alaskan natives, 3 percent were Asian and Pacific Islanders, 12 percent were blacks, and 9 percent were Hispanics, with 75 percent non–Hispanic whites. By 2050, almost one of two Americans is expected to come from the four racial or ethnic minority groups. American Indians and Alaskan natives still are likely to constitute 1 percent. The Asian and Pacific Islander population is expected to almost quadruple, to 11 percent. The black population is likely to grow to 16 percent. The Hispanic population is to increase to 21 percent. Non–Hispanic whites are expected to decrease, to 52 percent.

The two shifts confirm a greater presence of women generally, a greater presence of people of color, and the need for additional recognition of the diversity of women by race, ethnicity, color, culture, and native origin. Unfortunately, the data on such diversity in the nonprofit sector are quite limited. For example, data on beneficiaries of philanthropic funds may not be available by gender and race, and what data exist are not encouraging. As recently as 1987, only 3.4 percent of foundation and corporate funding was identified as going specifically to women beneficiaries (Women and Foundations, 1992, p. 4). For Latino populations, the figure was 1.3 percent (Cortés, 1991, p. 145). Asian Americans and Pacific Islanders in Philanthropy (1992, p. 1) identified only one tenth of 1 percent of foundation and corporate philanthropy as targeted for Asian- and Pacific-American communities between 1983 and 1990. With respect to board membership, a 1989 survey of the top seventy-five community, corporate, and private foundation boards by Women and Foundations/Corporate Philanthropy (1992, p. 16) found, "Only 14 percent of the board members were people of color, 20 percent were women, and just 5 percent were women of color."

Larger proportions of women and people of color have not necessarily translated into increased power. Research on pay equity has demonstrated that occupations with disproportionately high numbers of women and people of color pay lower wages than occupations held disproportionately by white men. According to Hodgkinson, Weitzman, Toppe, and Noga, in the nonprofit sector, employees in the independent sector (which contained 93 percent of all nonprofit sector employment in 1990), have had lower average wages and salaries than employees in business or government: "Between 1982 and 1987, the average wages or salaries in the independent sector were 73 percent of the average of the other sectors, and by 1990, this average had increased to 74 percent" (1992, p. 8). At the same time, the independent sector employs a greater proportion of female and black employees: "Over two-thirds (69%) of the employees in the independent sector were female compared with 46 percent for all employees in 1990. Blacks made up 14 percent of all employees in the independent sector compared with 11 percent for all employees" (1992, p. 8). These proportions are also greater than the proportions of women and blacks in the general population.

The statistics illustrate that as women and people of

159

color become the majority of the American population, their access to power remains differential: an increase in numbers does not automatically lead to an increase in power. At the same time, the future viability of the nonprofit sector depends on the support and meaningful participation of women and people of color at all levels and in ways that reflect the needs of their communities. They compose not only the pool of future donors, volunteers, and clients but also the pool of paid staff, managers, and trustees.

The Nature of Nonprofit Work

Accommodating demographic changes would be challenging by itself for a stable nonprofit sector. However, the nature of nonprofit work is also changing. The work of nonprofit organizations can be divided into three sets: charitable works and mutual assistance, advocacy and social change, and creation of legitimating institutions. Philanthropy and voluntarism are the mechanisms for conducting such work. These activities have developed alongside the evolution of the American economy from an agricultural to an industrial society and most recently to a postindustrial information-and-service society. Charitable works and mutual assistance is the category most associated with the nonprofit sector: the majority of organizations fall in this category. Advocacy and social change are also generally associated with the nonprofit sector, although only a small number of organizations are in the category. Advocacy and social change are viewed as the unique functions of the sector that distinguish it from the private and government sectors. According to O'Neill (1989, p. 120), "The ultimate defining characteristic of the nonprofit sector is its ability to disregard political and economic mandates and march to a different drummer." Creation of legitimating institutions is becoming more prominent as such nonprofit entities as universities, major foundations, and hospitals approximate the bureaucratic structures and functions of big business and big government.

Before the Civil War, when American society was primarily agricultural, work associated with the nonprofit sector was carried out by voluntary bodies or associations. This was an era when men and women were responsible for both reproductive and productive work. Mutual assistance was given by neighbors and other community members, who shared common backgrounds and a moral sense of mutual obligation. Men and women were similarly involved in such work. According to McCarthy (1992, p. 4), "antebellum voluntary associations were precisely what that term implied—organizations built on the services of volunteers, coupled with fairly modest donations from a variety of sources. This was as true of national movements such as antislavery campaigns as it was of charitable institutions such as asylums."

With the industrial era and the growth of bureaucratic organizations, place of work and place of residence became distinct entities, and work became systematized and impersonal. Reproductive work became the primary responsibility of women, while productive work was for men. Nonprofit work reflected the changes in two ways. First, charitable works and reform causes, many initiated by women on a voluntary basis, were transformed into bureaucracies staffed by men on salary. Second, the nature of nonprofit work expanded beyond providing aid and care to defining standards and norms of culture. The less personal, more detached professional characterization was evident in the establishment of multipurpose museums and research universities, the primary purpose of which was to be " 'legitimating' institutions that sought to set national standards of professionalism and taste in a variety of fields" (McCarthy, 1992, p. 4). The new institutions were the domain of white men of privilege and power.

Today, in an information-and-service society in a global economy, the nature of nonprofit work continues to evolve according to the needs of various segments of a more heterogeneous American population and the resources available to the nonprofit sector. The three sets of nonprofit work—charitable works and mutual assistance, advocacy and social change, and creation of legitimating institutions—still characterize the nonprofit sector but have become more diverse and specialized as nonprofit activities and organizations grow. For example, the *National Taxonomy of Exempt Entities* classifies nonprofit organizations in twenty-six major categories. Within each group are as many as seventy-nine separate activities. Most major categories include nineteen activities (Hodgkinson, Weitzman, Toppe, and Noga, 1992, p. 593).

The three sets of work also are affected by the phenomenon of privatization, which was prompted by growing populations with greater needs, cuts in government and corporate funding, and such policies as the 1986 Tax Reform Act, which selectively inhibited charitable giving. The trends have increased the professionalization and commercialization of the nonprofit sector (Hansmann, 1989, p. 91). Many organizations have been forced to diversify their funding base, supplementing government and philanthropic support with membership dues, service fees, and products for sale. Such actions assume a clientele with income and may limit the participation of people most in need, including poor people, refugees and immigrants, children, and racial or ethnic minorities, who are disproportionately poor. The fact that such actions are more characteristic of the for-profit sector raises questions about the unique status of the nonprofit sector. According to Hodgkinson (1989, p. 10), "The potential impact of the movement of nonprofit services toward a market orientation is even farther reaching. It is causing a crisis in public confidence in service provision by government and the nonprofit sector; it is eroding our faith in mutual obligation to serve those suffering from poverty, hunger, lack of education, and lack of skills; and it is leading to the basic abrogation of social responsibility for government and by the nonprofit sector, particularly in its advocacy functions."

In a more competitive and commercial environment, nonprofit organizations and the people who maintain them are becoming more sophisticated and professional. The people who have been traditionally served by the nonprofit sector may be served less or not at all. What is unclear is to what extent such sophistication decreases, maintains, or reconfigures the stratification of power by gender, class, and race or ethnicity.

163

Expanding Roles of Women

A similar evolution of women's roles has accompanied the evolution of work in the nonprofit sector. Despite the diversity among women by race or ethnicity, class, and generation, the traditional image of women is overwhelmingly homogeneous. It is the image of the care giver that is based on women's reproductive role and that depicts women as supporting men and nurturing children. Such supportive images are so pervasive that they are often taken for granted and invisible. They are images that emphasize relational definitions (such as daughter, mother, wife), economic dependence (because "women's work" is unpaid), and invisibility. By contrast, the traditional image of men is that of leading and providing for women and dependents. The image is based on men's productive role and emphasizes visibility, independence, and economic power.

The images and roles of women and men have been reflected in the nonprofit sector. The most popular image of the sector—altruism and charitable works—is consistent with women's care-giving image. As voluntary and mutual assistance organizations were joined by less personal and more formal professional organizations, men's and women's roles became even more differentiated along lines of production and reproduction. Women's roles became restricted and even invisible. They were confined to being unpaid fundraisers and unseen voluntary or low-paid staff.

Female philanthropists of the nineteenth and early twentieth centuries were primarily white women of wealth whose primary objective was to support institutions, such as universities, research centers, and museums, that reflected the interests of their fathers, husbands, and sons and thus to maintain their class position. While the women supported activities related to women and girls, research suggests that levels of funding were in the thousands of dollars compared to millions of dollars for men's institutions (McCarthy, 1992). With respect to their roles as staff members, women not only were overrepresented in certain roles (volunteer, care giver) but they were and continue to be isolated in subsectors (education, health care, social services) that reinforce their traditional roles and are deemed of lesser value and provide lower remuneration (Burbridge, 1992). While the roles of support and service provider render a degree of invisibility, the historical role of women as clients and recipients of nonprofit services is even less visible and unknown.

Although traditional images suggest confined roles for women, in reality women in the voluntary sector have taken on a multiplicity of roles that both affirm and expand their care-giving images. The roles are based on various reasons for being involved in the nonprofit sector that in turn reflect their class, generation, and race or ethnicity. For example, for earlier generations of wealthy women, the roles of volunteer and philanthropist not only ensured the maintenance of their class positions but provided an avenue for fulfilling work in the public world (McCarthy, 1992; Odendahl and Youmans, 1992).

For working-class and middle-class women, participation in the nonprofit sector includes the role of staff member in paid jobs or voluntary experience leading to paid positions. For other women, nonprofit-sector work has provided roles as social reformers as they seek ways to improve the conditions of specific disadvantaged communities, including their own, or to address national issues of discrimination. Mainstream and feminist women's organizations are associated with such efforts. Less well known are mutual aid and community-based organizations that immigrant women and women of color developed to meet the needs of their communities, neither recognized nor served by dominant institutions (Jang, Lee, Morello-Frosch, and Pendleton, 1991). African-American women were involved in black philanthropic organizations such as church groups in the mid 1700s and also established black women's organizations related to charitable works and educational programs (Carson, 1987, p. 1).

Such roles for women are not merely care giving but are active and productive. They are the roles of "doers" who were able to exploit their traditional roles fully and move beyond them to leadership roles, both voluntary and remunerated. The roles are associated with a major image of the nonprofit sector—advocacy and social change. The image is related directly to power but has not automatically been associated with women, despite their involvement as leaders in major social movements such as abolition, temperance, and welfare reform.

In more recent times, traditional images and roles of women related to reproduction continue; they are, however, being questioned and supplemented with images of women in productive roles. Since the late 1960s, women have greatly increased their participation in higher education. The trend has been associated with unprecedented opportunities for productive and remunerated work for women, particularly in the professions. Their participation is well suited not only to an information-and-service society but also to an increasingly market-oriented nonprofit sector. While images of care giving and altruism continue, women can be found in a variety of roles, including paid staff, managers, donors, and trustees. The more diverse roles are assigned to women who are privileged in a nontraditional sense. They are a new generation of highly educated women with a salaried income rather than inherited wealth. The new generation includes women of color and white women who are the beneficiaries of affirmative action.

The Role of Women's Organizations

The role of women's organizations in redefining power for women in the nonprofit sector cannot be overlooked. While most such organizations are small in monetary terms, like their Hispanic, African-, and Asian-American counterparts, they provide vital leadership on issues directly affecting women. The issues include domestic violence, pay equity, and reproductive rights. Furthermore, women's organizations, particularly since the late 1960s, have provided women with opportunities to assume fully all functions of the nonprofit sector and all personnel positions, especially leadership positions.

The organizations are local, national, and international. Like other nonprofit organizations, they range from direct-service providers to education agencies and membership associations. They can be single issue or multiple issue agencies. They include organizations of women of color. Some have a long history, dating to the nineteenth century. For example, the American Association of University Women (1888), the National Council of Jewish Women (1893), and the National Association of Colored Women (1896) were established during the first wave of the women's movement. Others, such as the National Federation of Business and Professional Women's Clubs and the Women's International League for Peace and Freedom, were founded in the early twentieth century. Many have emerged since the 1960s with the second wave of the women's movement. At the national level, these include the National Organization for Women, the Mexican American Women's National Association, the National Institute for Women of Color, the Women's Legal Defense Fund, the National Women's Political Caucus, the National Coalition Against Domestic Violence, and the National Network of Women's Funds.

Women's organizations address power issues primarily in relationship to white men. In an investigation of nineteen national women's organizations working on public policy, Spalter-Roth and Schreiber state (1992, p. 29), "Although most of these organizations give at least lip service to combatting racism and homophobia, few offer a class analysis of the U.S. economic system. Most do not explicitly address the disparities among women and the ways in which class differences affect women; they are more likely to address the need for women's economic equity—equity relative to white men."

As women assume more expanded roles in women's organizations and other nonprofit entities, women can maintain power in a traditional sense—assuming roles and status equal to those of men in the nonprofit sector. Or, they can choose to recognize, address, and alleviate power differentials between women and not just between men and women. Women also have the option to change the status quo to be more inclusive and heterogeneous in terms of who serves and who is served by the nonprofit sector and in terms of who legitimates and what standards of power are legitimated.

Utility of Current Data

The phenomena of demographic shifts, the changing nature of nonprofit work, and the expanding roles of women are not well captured in current data. Only since the 1970s and 1980s have data on the nonprofit sector been collected and compiled systematically. Data on women (and other populations) in the sector are selective and fragmentary. In both instances, comparative baseline figures are often lacking.

A major difficulty in attempting to identify, compile, and analyze data on women and the nonprofit sector is the ambiguity and diversity of the sector. It can be conceptualized narrowly or broadly. It is readily and concretely personified with attributes of service and care, provided by voluntarism and philanthropy. The term *nonprofit,* however, is formal and legal. It is used by the Internal Revenue Service to designate tax-exempt status for organizations that engage in a range of broad and vague activities (Commission on Private Philanthropy, 1983, p. 301). Beyond the legal definition, the nonprofit sector does not have unique characteristics.

A wealth of information has been compiled and classified by Independent Sector in four biennial nonprofit almanacs. The data, however, focus not on the nonprofit sector but on the independent sector, the largest component of the nonprofit sector. The independent sector is more easily defined and consists primarily of organizations classified as 501(c)(3), including religious, charitable, scientific, literary, and educational organizations, contributions to which are tax deductible, and 501(c)(4) organizations, such as social welfare organizations, local employee associations, and civic leagues. In 1990, the independent sector comprised 71 percent of almost 1.4 million nonprofit-sector entities. It employed 92 percent of almost 16 million nonprofit-sector staff members. The nonprofit sector accounted for 11 percent of estimated employment, compared with 70.9 percent by the for-profit sector and 17.7 percent by government (Hodgkinson, Weitzman, Toppe, and Noga, 1992, pp. 23 and 29).

Because nonprofit organizations are further characterized by diversity, generalizations must be made with caution. They can range from numerous small local organizations that are staffed solely by volunteers to a few national institutions with full-time salaried employees and annual budgets well in excess of $10 million. While attention accrues to the better funded and larger organizations, it must be noted that "in 1989, over 70 percent (327,000) of the 460,000 501(c)(3) organizations, excluding religious independent organizations and foundations, had total revenue below $25,000, and therefore did not have to provide financial data to the Internal Revenue Service. . . . The independent sector is dominated by a large number of small organizations about which little is known" (Hodgkinson, Weitzman, Toppe, and Noga, 1992, p. 11).

Additionally, the almanac data are presented in terms of organizational rather than demographic characteristics. Personnel data are based on surveys by the U.S. Bureau of Labor Statistics and other estimates that provide basic numbers that confirm greater proportions of women and minority staff in the independent sector but concentrated in selected subsectors. For women in 1990, these were health services, social and legal services, and foundations (Hodgkinson, Weitzman, Toppe, and Noga, 1992, p. 116). Employment data are also provided by race but, unfortunately, not by race and gender, so differences between white women and minority women cannot be discerned. For the first time, the 1990 Census sample survey (one sixth of all U.S. households) asked a question about employment by type of sector. Overall, data on the status and role of women are not easily obtainable in current data on nonprofit organizations.

Data on women in the nonprofit sector have emerged and currently exist outside any compiled references on the sector. The research is found in separate disciplines with specific focuses. For example, McCarthy's historical research (1992) examines the philanthropic patterns of wealthy women. Daniels (1988) using sociological methods, and Odendahl (1990), with anthropological research, extend the work to contemporary women of wealth and privilege. Preston's work focuses on employees and compares labor market patterns of nonprofit and for-profit employees (1989, 1990a, 1990b). Studies by women's organizations emphasize the growing presence of women in philanthropic decision making in the foundation world and newly formed women's funds (Murninghan, 1990; Rose, 1992).

The preliminary picture gleaned from the diverse interdisciplinary data is that women are continuing in traditional roles in the nonprofit sector and increasing their involvement in areas in which they once were not present—boards of trustees, paid fundraising, and management. The progress, however, is mixed. Manifestations of power and progress are accompanied by persistent instances of diminished or absent power. While woman are becoming visible in leadership roles, Odendahl and Youmans observed, "The kinds of nonprofits where women usually hold leadership roles are assigned low status" (1992, p. 3). Gittell (1990) found consistent "token ratios" for women and people of color on foundation boards, regardless of type of foundation. The ratios were similar for college boards. In both cases, women sat in less than 25 percent of the boards' seats, and Asian, African, and Latino representatives held 6 percent. "The token ratio for all these groups is a depressing 9:1" (Gittell, 1990, p. 6). Mixer's work (1992, p. 34) reveals a "feminization of fundraising"—greater numbers of women are on staff as fundraisers, yet they continue to be paid salaries lower than male fundraisers', and men hold two thirds of the top development and advanced positions.

For comparisons over time, sector, and gender, Preston's analyses (1989, 1990a, 1990b, 1992) are pioneering and instructive. On the one hand, she finds two signs of progress—greater gender equality in wages in the nonprofit sector than in the private or government sectors and a tripling of managerial women in the nonprofit sector between 1969 and 1991; during the same period, managerial women in government increased by about one third and women managers in the for-profit sector actually declined. On the other hand, she notes that the general equality of wages by gender in the nonprofit sector did not apply to higher-level positions, as managerial women consistently were paid about 22 percent less than their male counterparts from 1973 to 1991. Additionally, men in nonprofit work earn less than men in for-profit work.

Like the nonprofit sector data, research on women in nonprofit work rarely differentiates women by race, except to note a lack of diversity. Such data are crucial, for the experience of the for-profit sector suggests differential access for white women and for minority women and men. In its review of the glass ceiling phenomenon, the U.S. Department of Labor found that "the highest placed woman generally was at a higher reporting level to the CEO than the highest placed minority in the majority of the companies" (1991, p. 14).

In summary, the progress of women in the nonprofit sector is not easily assessed with current data. Limited national and local data indicate a variety of participation, from none to small to parity. While current data provide preliminary information, they also suggest the need for research on the various roles of women. For example, with regard

173

to managers, how well do equal job titles translate into equal authority and equal compensation, especially in an era of greater responsibilities and organizational downsizing with a more diverse work force and more heterogeneous clients? With regard to staff, does nonprofit work offer opportunities for tenure and promotion, or does it promote a contingent work force? With regard to trustees and donors, to what extent do women moving into decision-making and legitimating roles reproduce traditional class and race distinctions? With regard to beneficiaries, are women given meaningful choices and services that effectively address their needs? What constitutes power for women in the nonprofit sector? Does it vary by roles for women, by types of nonprofit organization, and by the communities that nonprofit organizations serve?

Toward Redefinitions of Power

Exploratory data on women in the nonprofit sector suggest that women's attainment of power in a traditional sense—assuming roles and status equal to men's in the nonprofit sector—is a slow process. It is also problematic, for two reasons. First, the changing functions and greater responsibilities of a nonprofit sector that is serving a more heterogeneous population with more limited resources raise questions about women's ability to secure traditional power. The lower pay of female managers who replace male managers may be a symptom. Second, in a traditional distribution of power, women who are most like the power elite—upper-class, older, and white—would have greater opportunities and access to legitimating and decision-making roles than other women. At the other end of the continuum, lower-class, young, minority women who continue in traditional care-giving roles in sectors that are disproportionately staffed by women would have less access to power.

In a traditional distribution of power—dominance over subordination—power differentials would continue to exist between women. As a result, some women are beginning to have second thoughts about the attainment of traditional power (Murninghan, 1990). Women in traditional nonprofit organizations and in women's organizations, especially women's funds (Rose, 1992), speak instead of *empowerment,* redefining power as inclusive, consensual, and heterogeneous in terms of who serves and who is served. Such redefinition is not easy, existing more as an ideal than as a reality (Rose, 1992). However, such redefinition is necessary to be consistent with and representative of the values and life experiences of women and people of color, who have traditionally been excluded and assigned secondary status.

The redefinition of *philanthropist* to include people of more modest means is one example of redefining power. At one community foundation that decided to consider for board membership anyone who contributed a gift, whether $5 or $5 million, "the board was transformed from a white, monied, mostly male membership to one that included five women and six people of color" (Bonavoglia, 1991, p. 9). The women's funding movement goes further with "the idea that anyone can be a philanthropist—

that $1.00 is as important as $1,000. Giving is valued intrinsically, not merely for the dollar amount" (Murninghan, 1990, p. 13).

An even more nontraditional definition of philanthropist is the inclusion of recipients of nonprofit services in funding decisions. One of the primary objectives of the National Network of Women's Funds is to create organizations in which the beneficiaries (women themselves) have primary responsibility in the allocation of the philanthropic dollar. Decisions are made by those who receive and those who give (Messing, 1989, p. 10). Everyone is a giver and a receiver.

The women's funds have also redefined board composition by gender, class, and race to reflect the community being served. According to Carol Mollner, executive director of the National Network of Women's Funds, the majority of board members are women, with women of color accounting for more than 30 percent of the board.

The definition of women as donors and volunteers is similarly being expanded. In addition to privileged women who have used their wealth to maintain their positions while supporting good works, other women donors and volunteers are being recognized. These include women with earned, not inherited, incomes, many of whom entered the labor force in the second women's movement. Contributions of contemporary women are not insignificant. According to Mixer (1992, p. 2), in 1989, 78 percent of women as compared to 72 percent of men contributed money to nonprofits. While the dollar value contributed by women was about 60 percent of the dollar value for men (consistent with the overall wage gap between men and women), women's contributions totaled $25.9 billion. With such leverage, women of all incomes, not just wealthy women, have the opportunity to recommend how their contributions are allocated and their time spent.

The experience of racial or ethnic minority communities also supports an expanded definition of women as donors and volunteers. According to Carson (1990, p. 1), traditional black nonprofit organizations have seldom viewed donors, volunteers, and fundraisers as separate people; they encourage individuals to assume all roles. The use of multiple-yet-inclusive roles has been a common survival strategy for people of color. Such a strategy may be considered useful as women and people of color increase their presence among those who serve and are served by the nonprofit sector. Consideration of alternate philanthropic and service strategies is particularly relevant in major metropolitan areas such as Los Angeles, Chicago, and New York, where minority communities approach a third to two fifths of the population.

Conclusion

As the United States undergoes dramatic demographic changes, the nonprofit sector becomes more complex, and the roles of women and people of color expand, the concept of power is being questioned and redefined by women. Even as women move into roles from which they had been excluded or redefine the roles in nontraditional terms, women continue to serve disproportionately in traditional female roles in the nonprofit sector. Similarly, the nonprofit sector maintains its three sets of functions directed to the public good, even as it grapples with privatization issues.

Nevertheless, by modest yet different acts of redefining *donors, trustees, managers, paid staff, volunteers,* and *beneficiaries* in ways that are more inclusive and diverse, women are applying the social change nature of the nonprofit sector to the institution itself. Furthermore, they reaffirm the original mutual obligation ethos of the sector, which fosters self-sufficiency and independence. Finally, through entities such as the women's funds and community-based organizations, they have the potential to provide alternate legitimating institutions that are more representative of a diverse nation.

References

Acker, J. "From Sex Roles to Gendered Institutions." *Contemporary Sociology,* 1992, *21,* 565–569.

Asian Americans and Pacific Islanders in Philanthropy. *Invisible and in Need.* San Francisco: Asian Americans and Pacific Islanders in Philanthropy, 1992.

Bonavoglia, A. *Making a Difference: The Impact of Women's Philanthropy.* New York: Women and Foundations/Corporate Philanthropy, 1991.

Burbridge, L. C. "The Careers of Women in the Nonprofit Sector." Paper prepared for conference on Women, Power, and Status in the Nonprofit Sector, Menlo Park, California, November 15–18, 1992.

Carson, E. "The Contemporary Charitable Giving and Voluntarism of Black Women." Paper prepared for the Center for the Study of Philanthropy, Conference on Women and Philanthropy: Past, Present, and Future, City University of New York, June 17–18, 1987.

Carson, E. "Black Volunteers as Givers and Fundraisers." Paper prepared for the Center for the Study of Philanthropy, Conference on Volunteers and Fundraisers, City University of New York, November 14, 1990.

Commission on Private Philanthropy and Public Needs. "The Third Sector." In B. O'Connell (ed.), *America's Voluntary Spirit: A Book of Readings.* New York: Foundation Center, 1983.

Cortés, M. "Philanthropy and Latino Nonprofits: A Research Agenda." In H. E. Gallegos and M. O'Neill (eds.), *Hispanics and the Nonprofit Sector.* New York: Foundation Center, 1991.

Daniels, A. K. *Invisible Careers: Women Civic Leaders from the Volunteer World.* Chicago: University of Chicago Press, 1988.

Gittell, M. "The Mysterious 7:3: The Token Representation of Women on Foundation Boards." In Women and Foundations/Corporate Philanthropy, *Far from Done: The Challenge of Diversifying Philanthropic Leadership.* New York: Women and Foundations/Corporate Philanthropy, 1990.

Hansmann, H. "The Two Nonprofit Sectors: Fee for Service Versus Donative Organizations." In V. A. Hodgkinson and R. W. Lyman (eds.), *The Future of the Nonprofit Sector: Challenges, Changes, and Policy Considerations.* San Francisco: Jossey-Bass, 1989.

Hodgkinson, V. A., "Key Challenges Facing the Nonprofit

Sector." In V. A. Hodgkinson and R. W. Lyman (eds.), *The Future of the Nonprofit Sector: Challenges, Changes, and Policy Considerations.* San Francisco: Jossey-Bass, 1989.

Hodgkinson, V. A., Weitzman, M. S., Toppe, C. M., and Noga, S. M. *Nonprofit Almanac 1992–93; Dimensions of the Independent Sector.* San Francisco: Jossey-Bass, 1992.

Jang, D., Lee, D., Morrello-Frosch, R., and Pendleton, G. *Domestic Violence in Immigrant and Refugee Communities: Asserting the Rights of Battered Women.* San Francisco: Family Violence Prevention Fund, 1991.

Lott, J. "Do United States Racial/Ethnic Categories Still Fit?" *Population Today,* 1993, *21*(1), 6–9.

McCarthy, K. "Women, Professionalization, and Philanthropy." Paper prepared for Conference on Women, Power, and Status in the Nonprofit Sector, Menlo Park, California, November 15–18, 1992.

Messing, S. "Women's Funds Take Chances." *New Directions for Women,* November/December 1989, p. 10.

Mixer, J. "Women, Fundraising, and Philanthropy." Paper prepared for Conference on Women, Power, and Status in the Nonprofit Sector, Menlo Park, California, November 15–18, 1992.

Murninghan, M. *Women and Philanthropy: New Voices, New Visions.* Boston: Lighthouse Investment Group, 1990.

O'Connell, B. (ed.). *America's Voluntary Spirit: A Book of Readings.* New York: Foundation Center, 1983.

Odendahl, T. *Charity Begins at Home: Generosity and Self-interest Among the Philanthropic Elite.* New York: Basic Books, 1990.

Odendahl, T., and Youmans, S. "Toward Theory Concerning Women on Nonprofit Boards." Paper prepared for Conference on Women, Power, and Status in the Nonprofit Sector, Menlo Park, California, November 15–18, 1992.

O'Neill, M. *The Third America: The Emergence of the Nonprofit Sector in the United States.* San Francisco: Jossey-Bass, 1989.

Preston, A. "The Nonprofit Worker in a For-Profit World." *Journal of Labor Economics,* 1989, 7, 438–463.

Preston, A. "Changing Labor Market Patterns in the Nonprofit and For-Profit Sectors: Implications for Nonprofit Management." *Nonprofit Management and Leadership,* 1990a, 1(1), 15–28.

Preston, A. "Women in the White-Collar Nonprofit Sector: The Best Option or the Only Option?" *Review of Economics and Statistics,* 1990b, 72, 560–568.

Preston, A. "Labor Market Status of Women in the Nonprofit Sector, 1965–1991." Paper prepared for Conference on Women, Power, and Status in the Nonprofit Sector, Menlo Park, California, November 15–18, 1992.

Rose, M. S. "Philanthropy in a Different Voice: The Women's Fund." Paper prepared for the 1992 Annual Conference, Association for Research on Nonprofit Organizations and Voluntary Action (ARNOVA), Yale University, October 30–November 1, 1992.

Spalter-Roth, R., and Schreiber, R. "Gaining Power and Avoiding Co-optation: Women's Organizations in the Policy Making Process during the 1980s." Unpublished paper, Institute for Women's Policy Research, Washington, D.C., 1992.

U.S. Bureau of the Census. *Statistical Abstract of the United States, 1987.* Washington, D.C.: Government Printing Office, 1987.

U.S. Bureau of the Census. *Population Projections of the United States by Age, Sex, Race, and Hispanic Origin: 1992 to 2050.* Washington, D.C. Government Printing Office, 1992a.

U.S. Bureau of the Census. *Statistical Abstract of the United States, 1992.* Washington, D.C.: Government Printing Office, 1992b.

U.S. Department of Labor. *A Report on the Glass Ceiling Initiative.* Washington, D.C.: Government Printing Office, 1991.

Women and Foundations/Corporate Philanthropy. *Getting It Done: From Commitment to Action on Funding for Women and Girls.* New York: Women and Foundations/Corporate Philanthropy, 1992.

6

Women on Nonprofit Boards

Teresa Odendahl and Sabrina Youmans

Despite an increasing interest in the study of philanthropy and voluntarism, there is a striking lack of theory, and limited data and research, on women and nonprofit board membership. A slight majority (Hayghe, 1991, p. 17) of the more than 94 million adults who volunteer (Hodgkinson, Weitzman, Toppe, and Noga, 1992) are women. Yet few studies of nonprofit activities make distinctions on the basis of gender or between levels of volunteer involvement, for example, board service versus stuffing envelopes (Daniels, 1988; Jenner, 1982).

Detailed information or scholarship is also rare concerning women's participation as corporate directors (Ghiloni, 1986, 1987), although more is known about the limited numbers of women in high-ranking government posts (Karpilow and Brootkowski, 1989; Kleeman, 1987; Martin,

1989). Cross-comparisons of female trusteeship in the various sectors are virtually nonexistent. Gender, together with board membership, have not generally been considered salient focuses of study.

Boards and executive staff are responsible for governance and policy-making functions. By definition, a trustee is someone who holds the confidence, trust, and voice of the public. In recent years, more women have been brought on boards, sometimes specifically because women's voices are underrepresented. Such compensatory measures may have led to an insidious belief that women speak only for women and do not or cannot represent all humanity. There is a widely held assumption that men alone, and especially affluent white men, represent people or the public good. Upper-class women, however, have long been trustees of nonprofit organizations.

In addition to gender, class is a category little attended to by researchers. For example, wealthy women may serve on nonprofit boards primarily because of their class position, yet class privilege is rarely examined in connection with trusteeship. Class background has been used to study corporate directorship, leading to the suggestion that women and people of color become a "major challenge to [the] need for similarity and compatibility at the very top" (Zweigenhaft, 1987, p. 38). Class legitimation appears to be a major motivation for wealthy women's nonprofit board membership (Covelli, 1989; Ostrander, 1984; Odendahl, 1990).

The complicated intersection of gender and class is largely unexamined in the philanthropic literature. Only

3 to 4 percent more women than men regularly volunteer (Hodgkinson, Weitzman, and the Gallup Organization, 1992), yet men outnumber women on boards of directors. And there is evidence that the trustee roles of women and men vary, both on boards and by types of boards. For example, wealthy board women may be more involved with planning gala charity events than with making policy for prestigious organizations.

Women of all classes are more likely than men to perform clerical or direct service work as volunteers. Yet the distinctions are "problematic because a person can sit on a board and be a nonplayer at the same time that another person stuffs envelopes and indirectly contributes to saving the organization" (J. Saidel, personal communication to the author, 1992).

Board members are often considered to be of elite status (Baughman, 1987, pp. 9–19). Scholarly definitions of elites include being listed in the *Social Register,* membership in specific private clubs, and attendance at prestigious preparatory schools (Baltzell, 1958, 1964, 1979; Domhoff, 1967, 1970, 1980, 1983; Domhoff and Dye, 1987), but the concept of elitism may elude definition (Mills, 1956; Odendahl, 1990).

Both elite and other women have a socially inferior status in comparison with men, a situation that is generally assumed and rarely given critical attention. Regardless of class, the voluntary boards on which women hold leadership roles are often gender segregated. Except for national women's organizations, those nonprofit boards on which women are equitably represented appear to be community based, with relatively small budgets and influence. Except on local health and human service boards, there are few cases of boards with parity for women and men trustees.

National, regional, and local women's organizations are led by women with authority and responsibility. They are run by and for women, at least in part because women have been blocked from such leadership roles in other major institutions. The organizations have served as "parallel power structures" for women (McCarthy, 1990; Scott, 1991). Of course, like men's organizations, women's groups (such as the American Association of University Women at the national level or local programs working against domestic violence or rape) tend to be gender segregated.

Women of color serving as trustees are almost invisible in the statistics. The scholarly work on black women and voluntary organizations is scarce and general but more developed than that for other women of color (Carson, 1987; Gallegos and O'Neill, 1991). Scott (1990) substantiates the historical importance of African-American women who joined together to create community and national associations that promoted civil and workers' rights, among other causes, in the nineteenth and early twentieth centuries. And Carson writes, "Notwithstanding the historic involvement of black women's organizations in charitable giving and voluntarism, little is known about the contemporary philanthropic activities of individual black women" (1987, p. 4).

Gender equity—like class, color, and ethnic diversity on boards—is far from having been achieved or even widely endorsed. The popular and promotional literature presents a picture of an integrated nonprofit field. Limited evidence suggests that voluntary organizations may be segregated by gender, class, and culture at the board, staff, and client levels. Few studies acknowledge, document, or investigate issues of homogeneity in regard to cultural differences and diversity (Erkut, 1990).

Women's board membership is both powerful and marginalized. Women's involvement in voluntary organizations may be widely recognized, but the kinds of nonprofits at which women usually hold leadership roles are assigned low status. In her otherwise thorough review and assessment of the literature on nonprofit boards, Middleton (1987, pp. 141–153) reinforces this perspective by referring to women only once: "Less vital nonprofits include social service agencies whose boards more often consist of women and of men with few corporate ties" (p. 140). Along with the scholars she surveyed, Middleton does not acknowledge the lack of gender analysis, nor does she question why women serve on less prestigious boards. Women were and are clearly barred from holding certain high-status board appointments.

Widmer, a leading scholar of nonprofit boards (1989, 1991) noted, "In the case of one board I observed, as this low-status board dealing with a 'women's issue' became more powerful—i.e., the budget grew, more professionals were hired, more technology was involved—the board became increasingly male" (C. Widmer, personal communication to author, 1992). More research needs to be conducted to understand whether what Widmer observed is part of a trend. Do women control boards that are less prestigious or, conversely, do women lose control of boards as the boards become more powerful?

Women are least likely to serve on power boards (Karpilow and Brootkowski, 1989, p. 23). Major corporate directorships are generally considered to be at the top of the board hierarchy. The women trustees hold few of these coveted seats. Forty percent of the Fortune 1,000 companies have no women directors (*Annual Board of Directors Study*, 1991). Thirty-one percent of the biggest foundations have no women trustees (Women and Foundations, 1991, cover flap). In local government, women are least well represented on planning commissions, which are "viewed as 'political plums,' . . . [and] are often seen as launching pads for political office" (Karpilow and Brootkowski, 1989, p. 22).

Policy-making boards of the most prestigious organizations with large budgets have always been dominated by upper-class white men. The homogeneous composition of traditional governing boards (Fenn, 1971; Hall, 1990, 1992; Middleton, 1987, p. 146) established and maintains a model for pervasive class, ethnic or racial, and sex discrimination throughout society. This chapter further explores what is known about women and boards, particularly in the nonprofit arena, and proposes the outline of a theoretical framework for bringing both the invisible and the recognized endeavors of women trustees into fuller view.

Gender as a Statistical Indicator

With the exception of the studies cited here, where well-organized trade associations have begun gathering and tracking basic board member statistics on gender and color, little in aggregate form is known about the trustees of the vast majority of more than 1 million nonprofit organizations in the country (Hodgkinson, Weitzman, Toppe, and Noga, 1992). Even when information is collected, it is rarely broken down by gender and color. Published data are almost never available on the percentage of trustees who are women of color, identifying ethnic or racial breakdowns such as African American, Asian, Latina, or Native American, much less in greater detail. Even more rarely are these ethnic or racial breakdowns compared for various categories of nonprofit organizations. In addition, the research that covers extended time periods is limited, so it is difficult to ascertain trends.

Some longitudinal statistics are available for higher education and foundations. Symphonies and United Way chapters are beginning to keep figures. For most arts organizations, churches, civic groups, hospitals, and social service agencies, data on board composition are not readily accessible. Where information on trustee makeup appears in the form of annual reports or tax returns, board members' names may not be publicly available, without going to each organization. More specific board information might be found in a state-by-state search. For example, detailed reports on boards may be filed with state charity boards. Yet no comprehensive data monitor board diversity.

Referring to college and university boards, Capek (1984) was among the first to note the scarcity of research on gender: "Content analysis of several major national trustee publications reveals, at best, benign neglect" (p. 48). In

1985, 20 percent of some three thousand college and university board members, both public and nonprofit, were women. Public higher education had a greater percentage of female trustees than did private colleges and universities (Association of Governing Boards of Universities and Colleges, 1986, p. 9). In a later publication, Capek compared 1977 and 1985 data from the Association of Governing Boards (AGB) that indicated that representation by women had increased 5 percent (Capek, 1988, p. 343).

The data on women of color on higher education boards also show low participation. According to the results of the 1985 AGB survey, 6 percent of college and university board members were African American and fewer than 1 percent were Hispanic. "The estimated number of other racial/ethnic groups' (Asian, Native American) members is three percent of the total" (AGB, 1986, p. 9). The inference from these statistics is that an extremely low percentage of women of color serve as trustees on college and university boards.

More research on trustees has been conducted in the foundation field than for any other nonprofit enterprise. There has been a slow but steady increase in the number of women on foundation boards over the years. In her groundbreaking study, Marting reports that in 1973, women constituted 18 percent of foundation trustees (Marting, 1976, p. 6). The most detailed longitudinal data on foundation board membership has been collected by the Council on Foundations (COF). By 1988, 29 percent (COF, 1988, p. 50) of foundation board members were women, a proportion that remained the same in 1990 (Boris, and others, 1990, p. 27).

This report found that only 2 percent of the responding foundations had African-American women on their boards. People in the category of "other" accounted for 2 percent of board membership (p. 27).

Women and Foundations/Corporate Philanthropy's (WAF/CP) 1989 survey of the top seventy-five corporate, community, and private foundations reported a lower representation of women, 20 percent, on governing boards than had the COF with a larger sample (WAF/CP, 1990, cover flap). In her chapter of the WAF/CP's 1990 study, Gittell (p. 6) observes, "The larger the foundation's endowment, the lower the percentage of women on its board. This fits with the theory that the more powerful the institution the less likely it will respond to pressure for diversity. Only five percent of the largest foundations' board members were women of color, and 69 percent of the major foundations had no trustees who were women of color." In 1991, WAF/CP updated its figures, using the top sixty-seven foundations. Women of color still held only 5 percent of the board seats. The percentage of foundations with no women of color on their boards dropped to 58 percent (WAF/CP, 1991, p. 17).

Limited national statistics on women and board membership are available for specialized nonprofit organizations. For example, in 1991, 41 percent of the members of 310 responding symphony orchestra boards were women. However, in what appears to be a trend in nonprofits, the smaller the budget of the symphony orchestra, the more women served on the board (American Symphony Orchestra League, 1991, p. 32).

In 1979, only 21.5 percent of the trustees of the largest 134 United Way chapters were women and 14.9 percent were minorities (Simpson, 1980, p. 80). In 1989, 26.2 percent of 425 local and state United Way trustees were women; for both sexes, 7.6 percent were black, 2 percent Hispanic, and 0.7 percent Asian American (United Way of America, 1989).

Few scholarly studies examine nonprofit organizations at the city level. Among the earliest, Babchuk, Marsey, and Gordon (1960) present data on 222 board members by gender for seventy-three civic organizations of a large northeastern city. The boards of the most important civic organizations had few women as members. The "most vital" agencies had the highest operating budgets. The nonprofit groups were run by men of high occupational status who also belonged to exclusive private clubs. The researchers found "that the higher the rank of the board, the higher the status of its members" (Babchuk, Marsey, and Gordon, 1960, pp. 402–403). Women trustees typically served on the boards of the lowest-ranked nonprofits. As indicated earlier, the whole issue of ranking in board membership is problematic.

Loeser and Falon's study (1978) of one hundred nonprofit organizations in the greater Boston area found that 23 percent of the board members were women. Nine of the boards they examined had no women members, while eight had more women than men trustees. Women were significantly less likely than men to be board officers. Loeser and Falon predicted that as women's status in the larger society improved, so would their representation on nonprofit boards of directors (1978). Unfortunately, there had been no comprehensive studies to prove or disprove their prediction.

Widmer surveyed ten boards of human service agencies in central New York State in 1983 and again in 1990. During that time period, 8 percent more women joined these local-level boards. The boards changed from 47 percent female in 1983 to 55 percent female in 1990 (Widmer, 1991). Of course, this was a period of severe cutbacks for human service agencies. Perhaps as budgets became smaller and human service organizations less powerful, more women become involved.

Abzug and colleagues (1992) examined the 1925, 1955, and 1985 boards of an art museum, a hospital, and United Way chapters in Boston and Cleveland. Gender was one variable they included: "As boards come to match the diversity of a service population with board member diversity, it is predicted that the traditional male stranglehold over such boards will be challenged. Evidence suggests that, indeed, female membership on boards of trustees has increased significantly across the time periods studied (Phi = .154)" (Abzug and others, 1992, p. 13). An additional finding was that women serve on art museum and hospital boards to a greater extent than people of color, whose memberships tend to be limited to federated charities (Abzug and others, 1992, p. 22). Boards of art museums probably are dominated by upper-class patrons, whatever their gender.

In two statistical studies of voluntary associations, McPherson and Smith-Lovin (1982, 1986) treat gender as a major analytic category. Their finding, that women participate in smaller organizations than men (1982, p. 898), was based on a representative probability sample of Nebraskans in 1977. Men belonged to large core economic groups, whereas women were concentrated in smaller community and domestic associations (1982, p. 890).

In another study of ten Nebraska communities, the authors show that almost one half of the groups in their sample of nonprofits had exclusively female members, while only one fifth of the groups had solely male members. Along with Loeser and Falon, they view this phenomenon as a mirror of larger society: "The voluntary sector tends to reflect the sex segregation in other domains of our society. It divides men and women into separate domains even more effectively than does the occupational structure. Furthermore, it acts to maintain the status differences that such segregation implies, by creating networks of weak ties that restrict men's and women's information and resources to the domains that are traditional for each. In this arena, as in so many others, separate is probably not equal" (McPherson and Smith-Lovin, 1986, p. 77).

If volunteer women are underrepresented in policy-making positions, tend to belong to smaller community-based organizations that are less integrated or less powerful, and tend to operate as leaders in sex-segregated contexts, a strong case can be made that there is institutionalized sex discrimination in the nonprofit system.

Comparing Statistics on Women Policy Makers

Based on the statistic that women comprised "only 1.8 percent of the directors of the top [Fortune] 1,300 [business] boards" in 1979, Schwartz publicly called for corporate America to open its boardroom doors to women (1980, p. 6). By 1991, Korn/Ferry International estimated that 7 percent of all directors of Fortune 1,000 companies were women. Limited evidence suggests that at the largest corporations, the more female board members there are, the better the hiring practices and personnel policies are for women (Catalyst, 1988; Konrad, 1990).

A sizable literature has been emerging on the topic of women and government appointments to boards, commissions, and cabinet-level offices (Carroll, 1987; Martin, 1989). It is not the intent of this chapter to review all the literature but rather to suggest some comparable directions for future research on gender and nonprofit board membership.

Information gathered about public boards suggests that adding women and people of color as trustees has significant benefits. There is "growing evidence that women bring new perspectives to public policy" (Kleeman, 1987, p. 199). Women have had different experiences, information networks, and management styles than men (p. 200). Kleeman writes, "The career backgrounds of women office-holders mirror those of American women in general, and differ significantly from those of male office-holders . . . [who have] careers in law, insurance or real estate[;] the women are much more likely to come from traditionally female professions—teaching, social work, clerical work and health care. These 'women's jobs' expose women to perspectives, problems and needs which most men seldom encounter" (p. 201). A study of women on public school boards indicates that nonprofit "organizations such as the PTA, the League of Women Voters, and the American Association of University Women have become important training grounds for female board members" (Marshall and Heller, 1984, p. 27).

One of the most detailed studies of gender and public boards was undertaken in 1988 by the California Board and Commission Project, made possible by 1974 legislation requiring the maintenance of public records on appointments. The research found a "significant underrepresentation of women on both statewide and local boards and commissions" (Karpilow and Brootkowski, 1989, p. i). It is worth noting that as more women are elected to public office, more women tend to be appointed in other capacities (p. 23). Karpilow and Brootkowski note, "At the state level, women held only 27.6% of all board and commission appointments. In . . . counties, women held 34.3% of all board sets. In . . . cities, women held 35.5% of advisory positions. Women did not reach parity, or 51%, on any board type at the state level. In counties, women only reached parity on one type of board: health and social services. In cities, women only reach parity on health and social service boards and library boards. At all levels of government, the representation of women decreased dramatically on boards advising in women's non-traditional areas of employment" (1989, p. i). Gender balance with men was closest for African-American women appointees, but Latinas were underrepresented in general. In comparison to men, women were likely to hold advisory rather than regulatory positions and less often re-

196

ceived salaries. In California, women tended to be appointed to boards and commissions that were associated with traditional activities for women (Karpilow and Brootkowski, 1989, p. 14).

If women bring unique perspectives to appointive office, the same is probably true for female corporate directors and nonprofit trustees. In fact, women often serve as nonprofit board members before they join a corporate or public board (Fisher, 1987, p. 38; Marshall and Heller, 1984, p. 27). When women join boards, they seem to have come from traditional women's occupations or roles and to be more attuned to issues affecting women and children. Whether women trustees are more concerned about gender equity and cultural diversity is an issue that merits further research.

Class Connections to Women's Board Membership

Because of wealthy women's higher class status and funding capabilities, they often are trustees of nonprofit organizations. Based on limited literature, this appears to be especially true in arts and cultural groups. In addition, women on the boards of family foundations are in their positions because of their kinship ties and class privilege.

One aspect of the complexity of the gender and class intersection is that with the exception of the feminist funding movement (Johnston, 1990; Margolis, 1983; Odendahl, 1990, pp. 187–208; Teltsch, 1980), upper-class women do not usually donate money or sit on the boards of nonprofit organizations that benefit women. The class interests of

affluent women are stronger than their gender consciousness (Beauvoir, 1952, p. 697; Odendahl, 1990; Steinem,
1986).

More than thirty years ago, Moore (1961) researched the
"women's boards" of big Chicago hospitals. She described
how upper-class women, who came from families that
founded the hospitals, readily moved into leadership positions at these elite institutions (1961). Although Moore
was studying women-only boards, her analysis was class
based: "There are hundreds of private health and welfare
agencies in Chicago, from health foundations to settlement
houses, to many of which auxiliary women's boards are
attached. In this complex of associations the upper-class
hospital board stands near the top of the hierarchy of prestige. . . . [They] originally granted substantial administrative authority to their women, authority which, though
in most cases it has declined, has far from disappeared in
the last seventy-five years" (p. 593). In contrast, according to Moore, the women's boards of middle-class hospitals were charged with raising money but had little authority over internal operations and little influence in the wider
community (p. 593). Upper-class boards were more selective in their recruitment strategies than middle-class institutions. By participating on the boards of voluntary associations, upper-class women were brought together and
sorted according to prestige. Those women with the most
memberships on highly regarded boards were considered
to have the most status.

In 1979, Ratcliff, Gallagher, and Ratcliff presented evidence that suggested that upper-class men dominated the

boards of civic organizations. Through citations of earlier research, their paper only alludes to women's lack of influence, although upper-class women participated extensively in the nonprofit arts, cultural, educational, and social service organizations they investigated (Ratcliff, Gallagher, and Ratcliff, 1979, p. 301). Their study is an example of how gender is left out of the analysis of power in the nonprofit arena or elsewhere and points to why so little is known about women and voluntary boards.

Ratcliff and colleagues gathered data on the directors of bank boards in St. Louis. The directors were apparently all men (the authors made no reference whatsoever to gender in their sample). The authors matched and counted the number of civic board memberships the men also held in United Way agencies, arts and education organizations, and business policy associations. Although their research was innovative and they asked pertinent questions, because their sample was limited to men, they could draw no conclusions about the roles or power of women. A shortcoming of their study was that they appear to have made the assumption that women do not count and hence there is no reason to count them.

In contrast, in a 1982 article, Jenner reports on a survey of the Association of Junior Leagues. She classified the all-women members of the Junior League as predominantly white and upper middle class. Of 292 respondents, 42 percent were trustees of nonprofit organizations (p. 32), with an average of three board memberships (p. 33). She investigated their motives for service and identified their voluntarism as comparable to a career (pp. 35–36).

Covelli (1989) studied women with multiple nonprofit directorships. Her sample was based on 1979 and 1981 board data in a large North American city. Covelli interviewed sixty-seven women who had served as trustees on several boards, some of which were high status. The research had two goals, to look at board composition in terms of class and culture and to analyze the motivations of the women who participate on nonprofit boards. Covelli found that "female volunteer directors are largely drawn from affluent professional and corporate families" (p. 24). In addition to class, the women tended to be well educated and "Anglo-English." There were only four women of color in the study.

Covelli (1989) found the boards, and the board recruiting methods, to be exclusive, narrow in focus, conserving, and not representative of the community. Covelli concludes that the main function of the boards was class and cultural legitimation: "This study argues that women who take on community leadership roles (volunteer directorships in particular) are motivated to do so because of class cultural incentives: noblesse oblige, duty to community and prestige. These combine with incentives for personal achievement in ways which, at once, serve to reproduce upper class prerogatives for community leadership roles and maintain the volunteer board status quo" (Covelli, 1989, p. 24).

Concurrently, feminist social scientists were focusing on upper-class women and their nonprofit activities. As a result of patterns of wealth distribution in the United States, the vast majority of rich women are white. Independently, Ostrander (1984), Daniels (1988), and Odendahl (1990) conducted in-depth research on affluent women volunteers. Ostrander (1984) details the link between wealth and board membership in a report of thirty-six interviews with privileged women in an unidentified city. According to Ostrander, "Upper-class women move quickly into leadership positions on the boards of their organizations. From these positions, they influence organizational operations and policy, and carry out what they perceive as their primary task—fundraising" (1984, p. 112). She argues that such volunteer work upholds, perpetuates, and contributes to the justification of class privilege (p. 138). Through their social networks, wealthy women "can exercise private control over community organizations. This private control aims to set [a] policy agenda that direct[s] the paid staff; it also seeks to keep broader based, non-upper-class . . . community input out of organizational decisions" (1984, p. 138).

Daniels presents a picture more empathetic to the perspectives of the seventy affluent women in a large northwestern city where she conducted research. In her 1988 book, Daniels shows that female philanthropists are not simply "lady bountifuls" as the stereotype would imply. The long hours they worked as volunteers, primarily at the board level, provided them with personal credibility and added meaningful purpose to their lives. "The work these women do, however, is complicated by their own resistance to any class analysis of it," Daniels added. "They prefer to view their service as being in the interest of the entire community rather than a special segment within it.

201

They ignore—or deny—any suggestion that their privileged position may be part of the problems they wish to solve" (p. xxi). Daniels, like Jenner (1982), argues persuasively that affluent women's serious nonprofit work deserves the distinction of a career.

Odendahl's 1990 book was among the first to examine power specifically in connection with wealthy people and their involvement with nonprofits. Odendahl and her project team interviewed 140 multimillionaires, fifty-six of whom were women. The wealthy women felt they had fewer options than their husbands or brothers "owing to a relatively rigid division of labor by gender in the upper class" (p. 5).

All three scholars agree that upper-class women have less status than their husbands, although wealthy women often work full time at their volunteer endeavors. Wealthy men are powerful in the business world as well as in the nonprofit arena. Only two of Daniels's informants served on the boards of business corporations. This finding hints at something that was not elaborated. There seems to be a widely held, but untested, assumption that in the American context, authentic power and status can only be gained through for-profit endeavors. Nonprofit activities are thought to be auxiliary, just as women are considered to be auxiliary to their husbands, brothers, and fathers.

The women Odendahl studied (1990) were prominent at both the local and the national level. They were trained to take on cultural responsibilities as young adults and continued to work in philanthropy throughout their lives. This included serving on the boards of arts and health organizations, raising money for the same groups, and organizing charitable benefits and galas.

Women and Charity Galas

Scholarly or critical literature on the relationship between wealthy women and the lavish fundraising events they direct is even more scarce than research on women who serve on nonprofit boards. According to Haley, "The crucible of the wealthy elite in their pursuit of the status quo is the charity ball" (1992, p. 24). Gender is a major focus of Haley's analysis, because "the organizing committees for charity balls are dominated by women" (p. 11).

At least fifty upper-class women involved at the board level with the most prestigious nonprofit organizations were frequently mentioned in the popular press (Auchincloss, 1980, Birmingham, 1980, p. 234; Cox, 1987; Hopkins, 1986; Wilson, 1985, 1988). The board members overlap as the leadership core of benefit committees (Birmingham, 1980, p. 235). "Most of the ladies are on the boards of more than one charity; many have traded jobs back and forth over the years" (Hopkins, 1986, p. 51). They are in such demand that they do several charity balls a season. These female board members may influence the policy making of nonprofit organizations, but their board-level participation is often limited to the benefits they are planning.

An unspoken criterion for chairing a large charity event is having far-ranging contacts within the social network of giving and the respect of people with wealth (Odendahl, 1990, pp. 39–42). Along with knowing the right people, the chair of a ball or gala must be a detail-oriented manager. The time-consuming responsibilities of benefit chairwomen include all the organizational planning, which may involve delegating to other committee members or subcommittees such tasks as conceptualizing the theme, marketing, arranging catering, decorating, and entertainment, as well as formulating highly political invitation lists and seating arrangements. Not only must the socially prominent attend but beautiful young women and men, as well as celebrities, help make the events a success. At both the national and community levels, prestigious, high culture, and health groups rely on the fundraisers (Birmingham, 1980; Hopkins, 1986; Wilson, 1985, 1988). It is unclear whether the organizations choose the women to chair the events or the women choose the organizations they wish to benefit from their skills.

The women who run charity galas determine which kinds of nonprofits, whether arts or social services, deserve the benefits. They exclude certain causes from funding and visibility (Odendahl, 1990). There are definite hierarchies of charitable prestige. According to socialite Robin Chandler Duke, who champions less popular nonprofit organizations, "Certain charities here [in New York] are very elitist: the library, the Met, and so forth. Then there is another level, which consists of the various boys' and girls' clubs, and things like that. And then there's the tough stuff: the social issues that aren't socially acceptable. I've had *many* people say, 'Awfully sorry, Robin, but it's such an *ugly* issue. I'd just rather not get into it'" (Cox, 1987, p. 396). There is probably a relationship between the preferred charities and the most elite balls. The galas take on a purpose of their own, and it is rare, except with high culture organizations, that any tangible connection exists between the social event and the cause (Hopkins, 1986, p. 52).

Daniels (1985) addresses the influential role women play in fundraising events. She used data on seventy metropolitan women who volunteered for charitable causes. Daniels's focus was on validating the activities of these women: "Women who are successful in charitable work take pride in their ability to create organizations and plan benefits that support symphony orchestras, welfare services, and other community causes. However, some of these women depreciate their work as mere 'party giving' even as they stress its contribution to their community" (1985, p. 353). She recognizes the serious work involved in creating an ambiance of hospitality and compares women's roles in the home and family to their volunteer efforts. Daniels argues persuasively that heading fundraising galas is uniquely female, an extension of women's traditional roles in the family, home, and society.

As Daniels implies, producing lavish fundraising events is one way affluent women compensate for their powerlessness or invisibility in society. For example, when referring to charity balls, Mrs. Horace E. Dodge of Palm Beach, Florida, said: "The women are the generals down here. . . . They run everything. The men just become black-tied silent bystanders" (Dunne, 1986, p. 120).

The women who run the special events may also set other agendas, because they are privy to knowledge. According to one commentator on the gala scene, "Because of up-to-the-elbows involvement, they are on 'the cutting edge.' . . . They know about medical advances before those advances become widely known. They spot tomorrow's opera stars long before those young talents grace a major stage. They know which buildings will be saved, where the next public garden will be planted . . . and probably know where the bodies are buried" (Wilson, 1988, p. 194). The upper-class benefit circuit is an arena in which women hold considerable power, but they are constrained by the very rituals they produce.

The connection between the charity parties and upper-class expectations about femininity is strong. The Western ideal for a woman's body may be a particularly upper-class social construction. Wealthy women have the money and the leisure time required for certain practices to achieve a thin young look through constant exercise, cosmetic surgery, spas, and weight-loss programs (on demystifying beauty and femininity, see Bartke, 1988; Bartke, 1990, pp. 63–82; Bordo, 1990; Brownmiller, 1984; Chapkis, 1986; Morgon, 1991; and Wolf, 1991). Hopkins interviewed several benefit chairwomen and fundraising experts: "'Beautiful young people change the whole tone of your party,' says Budd Calish [a fundraising expert]. 'It's not as though men my age are going to rape them. They're just a necessary part of your decor.' At a benefit for cancer [attended by Hopkins], as a bevy of bare white shoulders passed by, a satyrish old man said appreciatively, 'Half-naked girls, *that's* what I like to see'" (1986, p. 52). In addition, the balls promote consumerism and contribute to wider standards of culture with regard to beauty, glamor, and fantasy. The choice of gala themes, designer gowns, and hairstyles, for example, influences trends in the fashion industry. Mrs. Ezra Zilkha, chair of the Metropolitan Opera's special event for several years and a woman who involves herself only in benefits that clear at least $1 million for the charity, said, "What would the fashion industry do if women didn't have to buy wonderful dresses to wear to [the balls]? Charity stimulates our economy" (Hopkins, 1986, p. 53).

Upper-class social rituals such as charity balls rely on complex leadership hierarchies, women's hard work, entertainment, and glamorous feminine images. Gala circuit chairwomen do have power, but it is gendered. The women channel their power into parties rather than policy. The feminine focus may be a kind of diversion that keeps them subordinate to the men of their class.

Toward Theory

To review and summarize, more women than men work for free in nonprofit organizations. As volunteers, women are less likely than men to be policy-making board members. They are more likely to be doing routine and undervalued work essential to the organization. Limited data indicate that women tend to be trustees of community-based nonprofits that have relatively small budgets and consequently few staff members and little influence. For upper-class women who serve on prestigious boards, the division of labor is often by gender. Women plan the parties, while men make the policies. Yet women's important contributions, whether at the grass roots or more privileged levels, are often unrecognized.

Upper-class women who put on lavish charity balls are

an example of a combination of class privilege and feminized power. The gala events, both in their organization and because of the money they produce, provide opportunities for women trustees to wield power.

The nonprofit system may have developed as an extension of gender roles and activities centered in the patriarchal family. Nonprofit boards, primarily comprised of men, perform the father role of decision making. Men are in public positions of authority to which women *seem* to be subservient. Women take on the mother role by tending to the everyday aspects of caregiving, the special events such as party giving, other socializing, and a host of routine duties.

Activities within the home and nonprofit system have less recognized status than those in the business or public spheres. Many like to think of the nonprofit arena as one that is compatible for women, perhaps precisely because it often incorporates an extension of the nurturing work women have traditionally done in the home. As more women assume leadership positions in nonprofit organizations, they may carry their traditionally subservient family status with them.

The proposition here is that the nonprofit system is gendered female. A gendered system involves hierarchical power relationships wherein men dominate women. In the same manner, business activities have always dominated and influenced nonprofit matters. As more women move into leadership roles in nonprofit organizations, the nonprofit arena may become increasingly feminized.

Could it be that the activities, concerns, and power of

voluntary organizations have been largely invisible, or considered auxiliary, precisely because women are so important to and sometimes prominent within the world of nonprofits? In other words, volunteering may be "trivialized in the dominant culture in part because it is associated with women" (S. A. Ostrander, personal communication to author, 1992) and family work. As increasing numbers of women serve as trustees, do the boards become less prestigious? Are authentic status and power limited to business activities or men?

It is probable that the nonprofit system is in the process of transition. Women are gaining more authority on boards and with voluntary organizations and are redefining family roles, but traditional patterns persist. As more women become trustees, the nature of trusteeship cannot help but change. Whether such change is positive for women and people of color is open to question. For example, individual board status may decline as more women assume powerful roles. When more women are in policy making positions, it is unclear whether they will substantially alter the goals and activities of nonprofits. Systems are slow to change when the dominant groups do not want to relinquish power.

A complete understanding of whether women board members are marginalized or powerful would require more comprehensive research and theory. Such endeavors should consider the complicated interaction of gender, class, ethnicity or race, and other variables. A paradigmatic component would be to identify gender, class, and ethnicity or race consistently as worthy of consideration in all studies of nonprofit endeavors (Carson, 1993). A truly holistic approach would include more than simply the analysis of board membership by these variables. Scholars would need to examine trusteeship in its full cultural context within the nonprofit system and the larger society (Hall, 1990, 1992). Are voluntary organizations predominantly gender-, class-, and color-segregated? Are institutional sexism and racism prevalent in nonprofits? What is power, and how does it operate in the nonprofit arena or wider society?

Better demographic data are needed on the numbers, class status, color, and ethnicity of women and men serving as trustees and volunteering in other capacities, as is statistical information on the organizations with which women are and are not involved. More information is needed regarding financial characteristics, size of staff, and levels of responsibilities, as well as such factors as community-based work versus national influence. Geographical differences must also be taken into account. Are women more active in board leadership roles in certain cities or states? Too often, research findings, which are usually limited to a specific geographic area, are applied as general findings, leading to oversimplified and inaccurate accounts.

A fuller view also requires the gathering and comparing of data across and not only within the business, government, and nonprofit sectors and across industries within these sectors. For example, college and university boards need to be compared with cultural, health care, religious, or social service boards. The nonprofit arena, taken by itself, or any sector for that matter, would appear one dimensional, a slice of what is really a larger, more complex and dynamic system. Cross-sectoral studies would account not only for the different types of sectors but also for how they coexist.

In addition, it is vital to examine further and in more detail the boards of nonprofits in a cultural context (Hall, 1992). There have been many board studies, yet they have been primarily managerial in scope. Research agendas should include consideration of different types of board cultures, which may or may not be driven by gender, class, and racial or ethnic considerations. How do boards resolve conflict? What types of pecking orders exist within and across boards? How important is the fluidity of the board? Is it a conserving or an advocacy board? What is the relationship between the chief executive officer (CEO) and the board? Does it matter if the CEO is a woman or person of color? What about board selection and recruitment, grooming, and training? How important are education and professionalism, as compared with class and color, in obtaining a trustee seat? To what extent do boards, board relationships, and multiple board connections enforce compatibility or similarity of board members?

Power bases have been institutionalized and maintained by upper-class white men (Ostrander, 1987), excluding women, people of color, and poorer people. Throughout time, women have formed all-women boards, both for activist and conserving causes. The new organizations usually mirror traditional board structures, although alternatives are possible. Historian Kathleen McCarthy has noted that in the nineteenth century and today, women established parallel power structures in their nonprofit endeavors, because they were barred from participating in any other aspect of the public world (1990, 1991). Do nonprofits still offer parallel power structures for women, or does the concentration of women in this arena limit their opportunities elsewhere?

References

Abzug, R., DiMaggio, P. J., Gray, B. H., Kang, C. H., and Useem, M. "Changes in the Structure and Composition of Non-Profit Boards of Trustees: Cases from Boston and Cleveland, 1925–1985." Program on Non-Profit Organizations Working Paper No. 173. New Haven, Conn: Program on Non-Profit Organizations, Institution for Social and Policy Studies, Yale University, 1992.

American Symphony Orchestra League. *Policies & Procedures of Orchestra Governing Boards: A Survey and Study by the American Symphony Orchestra League.* Washington, D.C.: American Symphony Orchestra League, 1991.

Association of Governing Boards of Universities and Colleges. *Composition of Governing Boards, 1985: A Survey of College and University Boards.* Washington, D.C.: Association of Governing Boards of Universities and Colleges, 1986.

Auchincloss, L. "Brooke Astor: Because She Is New York's Own Lady Bountiful in the Midst of the Greed Decade." *New York,* April 25, 1988, p. 71.

Babchuk, N., Marsey, R., and Gordon, C. W. "Men and Women in Community Agencies: A Note on Power and Prestige." *American Sociological Review,* 1960, *44,* 399–404.

Baltzell, E. D. *Philadelphia Gentleman: The Making of a National Upper Class.* New York: Free Press, 1958.

Baltzell, E. D. *The Protestant Establishment: Aristocracy and Caste in America.* New York: Random House, 1964.

Baltzell, E. D. *Puritan Boston and Quaker Philadelphia: Two Protestant Ethics and the Spirit of Class Authority and Leadership.* New York: Free Press, 1979.

Bartke, S. L. "Foucault, Femininity, and the Modernization of Patriarchal Power." In I. Diamond and L. Quinby (eds.), *Feminism and Foucault: Reflections on Resistance.* Boston: Northeastern University Press, 1988.

Bartke, S. L. *Femininity and Domination: Studies in the Phenomenology of Oppression.* New York: Routledge & Kegan Paul, 1990.

Baughman, J. C. *Trustees, Trusteeship, and the Public Good: Issues of Accountability for Hospitals, Museums, Universities, and Libraries.* New York: Quorum, 1987.

Beauvoir, S. de. *The Second Sex.* New York: Vintage, 1952.

Birmingham, N. T. "Those Legendary Ladies Behind New York's Big-Time Benefits." *Town & Country,* September 1980, pp. 150, 234–237, 239, 241, 249–250, 252.

Bordo, S. "Reading the Slender Body." In M. Jacobus, E. F. Keller, and S. Shuttleworth (eds.), *Body/Politics: Women and the Discourses of Science.* New York: Routledge & Kegan Paul, 1990.

213

Boris, E. T., Brody, D. A., Guedj, K. R., Kamerer, J. B., and Ellis, M. R. *1990 Foundation Management Report.* Washington, D.C.: Council on Foundations, 1990.

Brownmiller, S. *Femininity.* New York: Fawcett Columbine, 1984.

Capek, M.E.S. "The Last Word." *AGB Reports,* November/ December 1984, pp. 46–48.

Capek, M.E.S. "Women as Trustees." In M. K. Chamberlain (ed.), *Women in Academe: Progress and Prospects.* New York: Russell Sage Foundation, 1988.

Carroll, S. J. "Women in State Cabinets: Status and Prospects." *The Journal of State Government,* 1987, *60*(5), 204–208.

Carson, E. D. "The Contemporary Charitable Giving and Voluntarism of Black Women." Paper prepared for the Center for the Study of Philanthropy, Conference on Women and Philanthropy: Past, Present, and Future, City University of New York, June 17–18, 1987.

Carson, E. D. "On Race, Gender, Culture, and Research on the Voluntary Sector." *Nonprofit Management and Leadership,* 1993, *3*(3), 327–335.

Catalyst. "Update: Women on Corporate Boards." *Perspective.* 60B, 250 Park Avenue South, New York, N.Y. 10002, May, 1988.

Chapkis, W. *Beauty Secrets: Women and the Politics of Appearance.* Boston: South End Press, 1986.

Council on Foundations. *1988 Foundation Management Report.* Washington, D.C.: Council on Foundations, 1988.

Covelli, L. "Dominant Class Culture and Legitimation: Female Volunteer Directors." In R. D. Herman and J. Van Til (eds.), *Nonprofit Boards of Directors.* New Brunswick, N.J.: Transaction, 1989.

Cox, C. "Who's Who in Charity?" *Vogue,* November 1987, pp. 396–399.

Daniels, A. K. "Good Times and Good Works: The Place of Sociability in the Work of Women Volunteers." *Social Problems,* 1985, *32*(4), 363–374.

Daniels, A. K. *Invisible Careers: Women Civic Leaders from the Volunteer World.* Chicago: University of Chicago Press, 1988.

Domhoff, G. W. *Who Rules America?* Englewood Cliffs, N.J.: Prentice-Hall, 1967.

Domhoff, G. W. *The Higher Circles: The Governing Class in America.* New York. Vintage, 1970.

Domhoff, G. W. (ed.). *Power Structure Research.* Newbury Park, Calif.: Sage, 1980.

Domhoff, G. W. *Who Rules America Now? A View for the '80s.* Englewood Cliffs, N.J.: Prentice-Hall, 1983.

Domhoff, G. W., and Dye, T. R. (eds.). *Power Elites and Organizations.* Newbury Park, Calif.: Sage, 1987.

Dunne, D. "The Women of Palm Beach." *Vanity Fair,* April 1986, pp. 68–71, 75, 120–121.

Erkut, S. *What Is Good for Women and Minorities Is Good for Business: What Corporations Can Do to Meet the Diversity Challenge.* Working Paper No. 218. Wellesley, Mass.: Wellesley College, 1990.

Fenn, D. H. "Executives and Community Volunteers." *Harvard Business Review,* 1971, *49*(2), 4–16, 156–157.

Fisher, A. B. "The Ruling Class: 395 Women Now Sit in the Boardrooms of America's Most Powerful Corporations. Who Are They—And How Did They Manage to Get There?" *Savvy,* September 1987, pp. 36–39, 97.

Gallegos, H. E., and O'Neill, M. *Hispanics and the Nonprofit Sector.* New York: Foundation Center, 1991.

Ghiloni, B. W. "New Women of Power: A Test of the Ruling Class Model of Domination." Doctoral dissertation, University of California, Santa Cruz, 1986.

Ghiloni, B. W. "The Velvet Ghetto: Women, Power, and the Corporation." In G. W. Domhoff and T. R. Dye (eds.), *Power Elites and Organizations.* Newbury Park, Calif.: Sage, 1987.

Gittell, M. "The Mysterious 7:3: The Token Representation of Women on Foundation Boards." In Women and Foundations/Corporate Philanthropy, *Far From Done: The Challenge of Diversifying Philanthropic Leadership.* New York: Women and Foundations/ Corporate Philanthropy, 1990.

Haley, M. "The Charity Ball as a Facet of Ritual Among the Philanthropic Elite." Unpublished paper, Arizona State University, May 1992.

Hall, P. D. "Understanding Nonprofits Trusteeship." *Philanthropy Monthly,* March 1990, pp. 10–15.

Hall, P. D. "Cultures of Trusteeship in the United States." In P. D. Hall (ed.), *Inventing the Nonprofit Sector and Other Essays on Philanthropy, Voluntarism, and Nonprofit Organizations.* Baltimore: Johns Hopkins University Press, 1992.

Hayghe, H. V. "Volunteers in the U.S.: Who Donates the Time?" *Monthly Labor Review,* 1991, *114*(2), 17–23.

Hodgkinson, V. A., Weitzman, M. S., and the Gallup Organization. *Giving and Volunteering in the United States: Findings from a National Survey.* Washington, D.C.: Independent Sector, 1992.

Hodgkinson, V. A., Weitzman, M. S., Toppe, C. M., and Noga, S. M. *Nonprofit Almanac: 1992–93: Dimensions of the Independent Sector.* San Francisco: Jossey-Bass, 1992.

Hopkins, E. "Our Ladies of Charity: Are Galas the Only Way?" *New York,* October 13, 1986, pp. 19, 48–53.

Jenner, J. R. "Participation, Leadership, and the Role of Volunteerism Among Selected Women Volunteers." *Journal of Voluntary Action Research,* 1982, *11*(4), 27–38.

Johnston, D. "Pulling Purse Strings." *Foundation News.* March/April 1990, pp. 32–36.

Karpilow, K. and Brootkowski, J. *California Women Get on Board!* Sacramento, Calif.: California Board and Commission Project, 1989.

Kleeman, K. E. "Women in State Government: Looking Back, Looking Ahead." *The Journal of State Government,* 1987, *60*(5), 199–203.

Konrad, W. "Welcome to the Woman-Friendly Company." *Business Week,* August 6, 1990, pp. 48–55.

Korn/Ferry International. *Annual Board of Directors Study of Fortune 1,000 Companies.* New York: Korn/Ferry International, 1991.

Loeser, H., and Falon, J. "Women Board Members and

Volunteer Agencies." *Volunteer Administration,* 1978, *10*(4), 7–11.

McCarthy, K. D. "Parallel Power Structures: Women and the Voluntary Sphere." In K. D. McCarthy (ed.), *Lady Bountiful Revisited: Women, Philanthropy, and Power.* New Brunswick, N.J.: Rutgers University Press, 1990.

McCarthy, K. D. *Women's Culture: American Philanthropy and Art, 1830–1930.* Chicago: University of Chicago Press, 1991.

McPherson, J. M., and Smith-Lovin, L. "Women and Weak Ties: Differences by Sex in the Size of Voluntary Organizations." *American Journal of Sociology,* 1982, *87*(4), 883–903.

McPherson, J. M., and Smith-Lovin, L. "Sex Segregation in Voluntary Associations." *American Sociological Review,* 1986, *51,* 61–79.

Margolis, R. J. "States of the Union Funding Feminists." *The New Leader,* May 30, 1983, pp. 10–11.

Marshall, S. A., and Heller, M. "Women on Public School Boards." *Education Digest,* 1984, *49*(6), 26–29.

Martin, J. M. "The Recruitment of Women to Cabinet and Subcabinet Posts." *The Western Political Quarterly,* 1989, *42*(1), 161–172.

Marting, L. "Women and Foundations: What We Now Know . . . What We Need To Do." Unpublished report, 1976.

Middleton, M. "Nonprofit Boards of Directors: Beyond the Governance Function." In W. W. Powell (ed.), *The Nonprofit Sector: A Research Handbook.* New Haven, Conn.: Yale University Press, 1987.

Mills, C. W. *The Power Elite*. New York: Oxford University Press, 1956.

Moore, J. W. "Patterns of Women's Participation in Voluntary Associations." *American Journal of Sociology,* 1961, *66*(6), 592–598.

Morgon, K. P. "Women and the Knife: Cosmetic Surgery and the Colonization of Women's Bodies." *Hypatia,* 1991, *6*(3), 25–53.

Odendahl, T. *Charity Begins at Home: Generosity and Self-interest Among the Philanthropic Elite*. New York: Basic Books, 1990.

Ostrander, S. A. *Women of the Upper Class*. Philadelphia: Temple University Press, 1984.

Ostrander, S. A. "Elite Domination in Private Social Agencies: How It Happens and How It Is Challenged." In G. W. Domhoff and T. R. Dye (eds.), *Power Elites and Organizations*. Newbury Park, Calif.: Sage, 1987.

Ratcliff, R. E., Gallagher, M. E., and Ratcliff, K. S. "The Civic Involvement of Bankers: An Analysis of Economic Power and Social Prominence in the Command of Civic Policy Positions." *Social Problems,* 1979, *26*(3), 298–313.

Schwartz, F. N. "From the Boardroom: More Accomplished Women Than Meet the Eye Are Ready for Effective Board Membership." *Harvard Business Review,* 1980, *58*, 6–8, 12, 14, 18.

Scott, A. F. "Most Invisible of All: Black Women's Voluntary Associations." *The Journal of Southern History,* 1990, *56*(1), 3–22.

Scott, A. F. *Natural Allies: Women's Associations in Ameri-*

can History. Urbana: University of Illinois Press, 1991.

Simpson, P. "Does United Way Cheat Women?" *Working Woman,* 1980, pp. 77–80, 82, 139.

Steinem, G. "The Trouble with Rich Women." *Ms.*, June 1986, pp. 41–43, 78–80.

Teltsch, K. "In Philanthropies, Women Move Up—Slowly." *New York Times,* August 8, 1980, A-18.

United Way of America. "Composition of United Way Board-Level Volunteers: 1987-1989." Alexandria, Va.: United Way of America, 1989.

Widmer, C. "Why Board Members Participate." In R. D. Herman and J. Van Til (eds.), *Nonprofit Boards of Directors.* New Brunswick, N.J.: Transaction, 1989.

Widmer, C. "Board Members' Perceptions of Their Roles and Responsibilities." *Association for Research on Nonprofit Organizations and Voluntary Action (ARNOVA) Conference Proceedings,* October 17-19, 1991, 145–160.

Wilson, J. "The First Ladies of Charity." *Town & Country,* June 1985, pp. 139–148.

Wilson, J. "Timeless, Tireless—and Terrific." *Town & Country,* September 1988, pp. 194–195, 270, 275–276.

Wolf, N. *The Beauty Myth: How Images of Beauty Are Used Against Women.* New York: William Morrow, 1991.

Women and Foundations/Corporate Philanthropy. *Far from Done: The Challenge of Diversifying Philanthropic Leadership.* New York: Women and Foundations/Corporate Philanthropy, 1990.

Women and Foundations/Corporate Philanthropy. *Making a Difference: The Impact of Women in Philanthropy.* New York: Women and Foundations/Corporate Philanthropy, 1991.

Zweigenhaft, R. "Minorities and Women of the Corporation: Will They Attain Seats of Power?" In G. W. Domhoff and T. R. Dye (eds.), *Power Elites and Organizations.* Newbury Park, Calif.: Sage, 1987.

7

Women
as Professional Fundraisers

Joseph R. Mixer

Significant changes are occurring in the roles of women as professional fundraisers. Women now outnumber men in professional fundraising associations and are enhancing their careers through additional fundraising networks. The glass ceiling separating women from top jobs is cracking. Salary inequities still exist but are narrowing.

The changes are occurring within a context of dramatic shifts in women's philanthropic activities. Women increased their giving in 1991, during a severe recession, to an estimated $28.3 billion—a 2.4 percent rise over 1989—while men decreased their giving 21.7 percent to $33.5 billion (Hodgkinson and Weitzman, 1992). Women are directing their gifts to their personal interests and concerns, moving beyond the influence of men. Women volunteers are asking women for sizable gifts. In short, a revolution is in the making, but it is not complete. Gender stereotypes remain major obstacles for women as professional fundraisers. Women fundraisers face inequities in opportunities, power, status, and compensation.

This chapter examines the changes taking place in the status of women as professional fundraisers and suggests policies and actions to improve conditions. Attention is drawn to psychological and social factors related to giving and getting money. For instance, beliefs about gender differences and roles strongly influence women's opportunities in the field. Perceptions of employers, boards of directors, career advisers, financial counselors, teachers, and parents shape the opportunities and conduct of women in philanthropy and fundraising. The socialization of women creates values and beliefs about funding roles that dominate performance and accomplishments.

Fundraising as a professional occupation for women became more commonplace in the early 1980s with a surge of female entrants. Only ten years later, women emerged as the majority of members in the largest associations of professional fundraisers. The field is closer to being pronounced "feminized," an occupation in which 60 percent of the workers are female (Conry, 1991).

This dramatic change comes after decades of male dominance, despite the singular accomplishments of prominent women leaders who raised substantial sums as heads of their agencies (McCarthy, 1990). When the YMCA needed more money in the early 1900s for buildings and capital, the organization launched the first whirlwind, intensive, communitywide campaign (Cutlip, 1965). Men became the professionals and solidified their role because of their connections with power structures capable of influencing public support and securing large sums. Women emerged gradually from clerical and support functions in the 1950s to supervise minor aspects of campaigns and to write grant proposals in the 1960s and 1970s. The wedge into professional status expanded rapidly in the 1980s with the explosion of nonprofit organizations, the decline in federal funding, and the demand for private support. Nonprofit organizations were hungry for people with some knowledge of fundraising to improve their revenues. Women provided a ready source, coming from a background of volunteer fundraising and participation in a multitude of workshops and training courses on funding.

Numerous issues arising from the phenomenon require discussion: the scope of feminization, salary inequities, the role of women of color, glass ceilings, occupational choice, barriers affecting choice, devaluation of status, stereotypical reactions, management capabilities, future opportunities, and measures to address inequities. The travails appear in every profession and occupation when women begin to outnumber men (Reskin, 1988).

Feminization of the Fundraising Profession

The extent of feminization becomes apparent when examining the several associations of fundraising professionals, frequently called *development* or *advancement officers.* Each succeeding survey of members discloses continuing and rapid demographic shifts.

The membership directory of the National Society of Fund Raising Executives (NSFRE) for 1991–1992 (National Society of Fund Raising Executives, 1991) shows that women comprise 52.2 percent of the total and that almost 30 percent of these women hold top-level positions in their respective nonprofit organizations—president, executive director, administrator, vice president for development, director of development, director of marketing and/or public relations, campaign director, and associate executive director. Another 1 percent hold the top or senior positions in consulting firms.

Unlike the situation in other professional associations, only 13 percent of women members of NSFRE occupy such lower-level positions as associate director of development, assistant executive director, director of annual giving, and director of special events. The relatively high cost of NSFRE membership, which is an individual responsibility, may deter membership by women with lower salaries. Additionally, women executives tend to join before other staff members (C. A. Looney, senior vice president, Saddleback Memorial Foundation, interviewed by author, 1992). An additional 7 percent of NSFRE membership are women who list no title, almost all of whom cite no employer. Presumably, these individuals are available for employment and value their continued contact with the profession. No data on their prior affiliations are available.

A 1992 survey of 12,600 NSFRE members found that women constitute a 57.6 percent majority (Mongon, 1992). The 5.4 percent differential from 1991 figures may be related more to different data bases than actual demographic change, because the 1991 figures came from a directory and the 1992 figures came from a mailing list sample. Some improvement in salaries occurred since the last survey, in 1988. The percentage of women earning less than $33,000 per year dropped from 49.5 in 1988 to 34.7 in 1992. The 1992 average for all women was $40,000, as compared to $52,000 for men. In the top bracket, over $75,000, women clearly suffered a disparity, with only 3.9 percent earning in that range, as compared to 20.2 percent of men. Additionally, fringe benefits received by women lag behind those of men, though somewhat less than in prior years. The most significant discrepancies occur in bonuses, tuition reimbursement, and travel expenses.

In the last few years, more women than men have achieved the status of Certified Fund Raising Executive (CFRE), a certification process developed by NSFRE and based on demonstrated competence, five years of service, and an extensive written examination. An advanced certification program, initiated in 1992 and even more rigorous than the CFRE process, drew eight women among eighteen candidates. Clearly, women are aggressively pursuing professional status and have the qualifications to succeed.

Other professional fundraising associations have similar programs in which women are correspondingly represented. The Council for Advancement and Support of Education (CASE), consisting principally of fundraising executives in colleges and universities, approached feminization in 1990 (McNamee, 1990). Women achieved a 54.7 percent majority of respondents in that year, whereas men had a 51.5 percent majority in 1986. However, women's salary averages and titles remained below those of men. In 1982, women's salaries averaged 20 percent less than men's; in 1986, 12 percent less; and in 1990, 14 percent less. The lower averages for women are attributable in part to youth and inexperience, but even when age, race, advancement experience, job tenure, and education were equal, women still learned $7,642 less than men. When the most powerful salary predictors (title, type of institution, and primary responsibility) were held constant, the gap narrowed to $5,136 less than the average man's salary.

Overall data on CASE members do indicate that women are younger and less experienced with shorter job tenure than men. This suggests that in succeeding years, women have a potential for gaining top-level positions as they mature in the field. However, women indicated that they were more likely than men to stay in their current job. Stationary status in fundraising jobs limits the variety of experience and deters upward mobility.

Similar feminization is evident in the hospital field, where the Association for Healthcare Philanthropy (AHP, formerly National Association for Hospital Development) reports that women outnumber men and that women's salaries are lower than men's for the same positions (as executives of foundations that are the fundraising agencies for hospitals and medical centers) and the same level of experience (Childress, 1992). The salaries of women with up to two years' experience in development and in serving as foundation executives fall 16.7 percent below those of men; the salaries of women with three to seven years of experience drop to 24.6 percent below those of men.

But women with eight or more years of experience are 11.8 percent behind men in salaries. The median salaries for women in these experience groups are $50,000, $53,000, and $67,500, respectively. Only 26 percent of respondents, both men and women, have been in development for eight years or longer. Hospital development is a young field: 71 percent of the programs are fourteen years old or younger. This suggests that women's prospects for closing the salary gap may improve with their number of years in the hospital development field.

A survey of a newer association of prospect research personnel, American Prospect Research Association (1992), discloses the same pattern of salary discrimination. This key occupation, which develops detailed data on prospects' interests, capacity to give, and personal links to their host organizations, was originally conceived as a clerical function relegated to women (E. Pfizenmaier-Henderson, consultant and second vice president, American Prospect Research Association, interviewed by author, 1992). Women comprise 81.4 percent of the 1,300 members of the association. The great majority (81.9 percent) of women members hold jobs that pay less than $35,000, while 46.1 percent of the men are paid more than $35,000. The formation of the association and its subsequent activities have brought significant recognition to the function of prospect research, moving it toward professional status.

Women of Color

Women of color form a small but growing group of professional fundraisers. While data on their presence remain elusive, membership surveys of the professional associations give some inkling of their numbers. The 1992 NSFRE roster includes 166 African-American, 34 Asian-American or Pacific Islander, 24 Hispanic, and 13 Native American women. Minority women comprise only 4 percent of all female members, an increase from the 1988 survey. The 1990 CASE survey lumps women and men together, reporting that all minorities constitute 4.5 percent of total membership, with an increase from 3.3 percent four years earlier. NSFRE sponsored a minority outreach workshop in 1991 that drew approximately two hundred minority fundraisers and would-be fundraisers; women at the workshop outnumbered men. The women came principally from small, grass-roots organizations.

Additional information on women of color comes from fundraisers in various ethnic groups who provide the following observations. According to Ruby Smith Love, a prominent consultant affiliated with Alford, Ver Schave & Associates (interviewed by author, 1993), African-American women fundraisers work in greater numbers in educational institutions and advocacy agencies such as black colleges, the United Negro College Fund, the Urban League, and the National Association for the Advancement of Colored People. Love said that African-American women fundraisers find it easier to relate to women of wealth than do their male counterparts. However, she said, both genders experience occasional difficulty in soliciting endowments and planned gifts because of donors' stereotypical views that African Americans have not had experience in managing large sums of money. At times, the stereotype makes it difficult to establish credibility early in relationships with donors.

Low salary levels and lack of flexible schedules deter women of color from entering the profession, according to Shirley Matthews, project manager of the United Negro College Fund (interview with author, 1993). The fund maintains an active program of internships for college students that brings them into professional work. All fund offices have women professionals. Working with these women on fundraising projects of the fund gives corporate leaders opportunities to see how capable the women are, and the leaders try to recruit them for their companies. Frequently, the attractiveness of corporate positions, salaries, and the recruitment efforts lure younger women from fundraising to business careers.

Notable philanthropic work is undertaken by national organizations of women of color (Hernández, 1991). The five prominent African-American sororities, with hundreds of local chapters and tens of thousands of members, raise millions of dollars for charitable works benefiting minority communities. The organizations rely principally on women volunteers, guided by only a few professional staff members. Direct mail, telemarketing, and personal solicitation, along with chapter fundraising events, are the principal methods used (W. Goff, executive director, Delta Research and Educational Foundation, and D. Parker, program executive, Alpha Kappa Alpha Sorority, Inc., interviews with author, 1993). Eighty to 90 percent of the money comes from members. Ten additional national organizations, among them The Links, the National Council of Negro Women, and the National Council of 100 Black Women, undertake advocacy projects, social and economic programs, legislative initiatives, and fundraising activities, primarily using their members (Hernández, 1991).

Latina fundraisers are significantly fewer in number and work principally in local social agencies and youth organizations. Lack of funding for development positions accounts for much of the void. More typically, Latinas doing fundraising are the chief executive officers, according to A. Martinez, executive director, Spanish Speaking Unity Council (interview with author, 1993). N. Lopez, director of development, National Council of La Raza, cites the difficulty in recruiting Latina women for fundraising jobs because of the perceived difficulty of the work, insufficient knowledge of philanthropy, and the lack of glamor compared to other occupations (interview with author, 1992). Gender and cultural biases among Spanish-speaking populations negatively affect women undertaking fundraising. "Old-boy networks" make it easier for men to work in the professions; women are viewed stereotypically as not appropriate for fund solicitation.

Asian-American women are also underrepresented in the profession. They too suffer from cultural biases that place them at a disadvantage in reaching sources of wealth, especially minority men (E. Marconi, fundraising consultant, Marconi West, interview with author, 1993). However, with the increasing numbers of women in corporations and foundations, the problem is easing. In fact, Marconi feels that minority women fundraisers are more comfortable in their roles than they were five years ago because of the presence of more women in the profession. Women find that male prospects become more amenable to solicitation for a donation when relationships have been established with their wives through volunteer service. In accompanying male volunteers on a fund solicitation, Asian-American professional women become resources and spokespersons for their agencies, answering difficult questions or providing detailed information that the male volunteers frequently do not know.

Professional Organizations for Women

Within the professional associations cited, women are restive about their lack of recognition, absence of efforts to correct inequities, and the limited number of women in leadership roles. They voiced their concerns during an ad hoc meeting of more than two dozen professional women during the 1992 International Conference of the National Society of Fund Raising Executives in San Francisco (Hall, March 1992).

The experience of inequity in the profession has inspired women fundraisers to form separate organizations to provide networking opportunities for jobs and information sharing, establish mentoring programs, gain recognition of women's competence in the field, report results of salary surveys, enhance career advancement, and equip members with negotiation strategies for salaries and benefits. One of the oldest associations, Women in Development of Greater Boston, celebrated its tenth anniversary in 1992 with more than 600 members representing nearly 250 institutions and organizations. The association's most recent salary survey (March 1992) shows its members competitive with national averages for women development professionals in the entry and mid-level positions. For senior-level women executives, the salaries are below the national average for all executives. Regularly scheduled meetings feature presentations on management skills and critical fundraising topics (Paresky, 1992). A similar organization, Women in Financial Development, serves about three hundred members in the New York metropolitan area with informational meetings, awards for outstanding performance, and job listings. The earliest association, Women in Development, is located in Chicago where its 160 members are grouped in four geographical areas for networking and discussing mutual interests.

The Glass Ceiling Factor

Membership rosters of the professional fundraising associations reflect a glass ceiling in the field. Men still occupy more than two thirds of top development and advancement positions at nonprofit institutions. The jobs are in the larger agencies, and the differential becomes more pronounced with increased size. Mongon (1992) notes that the longer tenure of men and their presumed effectiveness account for the difference.

The disparity exists also in the ranks of the big, well-established fundraising firms. The firms only recently began selecting women to direct capital campaigns and serve on major consulting assignments, according to G. Petty, senior executive, Ketchum, Inc. (interview with author, 1992). The inclusion of women came about because of pressure from client organizations, usually those that have prominent female constituencies, executives, or volunteer leaders. Several consulting firms cite moving as a greater problem for women than men with family obligations when it is necessary to move to different campaign sites for periods of six to eighteen months.

Some executive search firms still succumb to stereotypes and either do not include women candidates or send out a lone female on a panel of males to create the appearance of affirmative action for both the firms and the clients. The preferences of white-male-dominated boards of trustees contribute to the practice. Other firms make a conscientious effort to discuss agencies' needs, then provide candidates who meet those qualifications without regard to gender, according to C. Douglas of Cal Douglas & Associates (interview with author, 1993). However, even in these firms the relocation problem comes up frequently when the spouse is employed professionally. Nonprofit agencies have difficulty in placing professional spouses because of limited staff positions.

Inequality in top-level positions remains a challenge to women fundraisers. Dawn Marie Driscoll, a featured speaker at the February 1992 meeting of Women in Development of Greater Boston, urged her audience to build a presence in "the club," those circles of opinion leaders and power brokers that exist in every profession and community (Vincens, 1992). She recommended that women assist one another in identifying key leaders, cultivating them, and seeking leadership roles in their organizations. Working in "rain-making," or income-generating, specialties provides access to power, prestige, and advancement.

Cracks in the glass ceiling are appearing more frequently.

Women are rising through the ranks and by changing jobs to top fundraising positions at colleges, hospital foundations, and human service organizations. More women are becoming capital campaign directors. More women are gaining the mid-level experience and success necessary to move into top-level positions. The large reservoir of female talent has even caused some male development chiefs to complain about the future of the profession for men.

Occupational Choice

Personal and job characteristics shape occupational choice. Traditionally female professions are thought to attract those who want to work with people and help others (Eccles, 1987). Also, many traditionally female occupations allow part-time work and flexible hours. Women who want families often choose occupations in which future salaries are less likely to erode as the result of job interruptions (Olson, Frieze, and Detlefsen, 1990). Fundraising has job opportunities compatible with these interests.

By its nature, fundraising demands from all staff members a caring, helping, and nurturing relationship with prospects and volunteers. These qualities, coupled with appreciativeness and sensitivity—qualities often associated with women (Ruble, 1983)—facilitate the development of strong relationships with prospective givers. Men who do not exhibit or acquire the qualities soon find their production diminishing, and they are encouraged to find other employment. Fundraising is frequently depicted as a "people business" that requires the development of effective relationships with prospects and donors.

Entry into fundraising is attractive to women volunteers who have had experience in raising money. They capitalize on their knowledge of the field, relationships with wealthy individuals, and contacts with agency executives. The low salaries do not deter these women, because they come from unpaid assignments and even minimal pay adds to their financial circumstances and sense of self-worth. Many full-time positions develop for experienced volunteers who start as low-cost, part-time employees. Like bargain hunters, nonprofit employers welcome and exploit them.

The profession receives continuing attention as an opportunity for women. The July 1990 and 1991 issues of *Working Woman* magazine rank development officer (professional fundraising executive) as one of the twenty-five "hot" careers for women. The articles state that development officers can expect $14,000 to $21,000 for entry-level positions, $40,000 to $50,000 for five years' experience, and $60,000 to $125,000 for the most senior positions. This description and other reports of salary levels and career paths attract many female candidates.

The same magazine recently drew a more sobering picture of women in fundraising, citing potential for sexual harassment when asking for money, tougher qualification requirements, competition from men, and salaries lower than comparable business positions' (Tifft, 1992). The opportunities for satisfaction in fundraising also receive mention: working for a worthy cause, clear and measurable goals, quantifiable performance, and ready advancement based on results.

The NSFRE, CASE, and AHP surveys show that younger women and men are entering the profession. Growing awareness of professional opportunities in the field and the appeal of being of service come not only from published accounts about philanthropy and fundraising but also from the numerous college courses and research centers devoted to the study of philanthropy (Crowder and Hodgkinson, 1991).

Barriers Affecting Choice

The concerns and obligations that some women have for family and children appear to be incompatible with senior positions in fundraising. Furthermore, there is little evidence that husbands or male partners assume more responsibilities for home and child care when women work full time at any occupational level. Top development positions impose long hours, attendance at numerous evening and weekend events, and frequent out-of-town travel. Entry- and lower-level jobs permit more flexibility in hours and time devoted to the functions assigned, but the necessity of gaining competence and the field's reputation for commitment often conflict with a need for latitude. More freedom of operation occurs in newer and smaller agencies. Organizations with low budgets welcome part-time fundraisers who keep salary costs manageable while adding much-needed revenues.

The fundraising profession exhibits a high degree of turnover within its ranks, for both women and men (Walton, 1993). Membership rosters document the constant change of women in and between organizations, particularly in the newer and smaller agencies. Less movement occurs in well-established institutions such as colleges and universities. The profession's need for mobility presents serious constraints for women handling both careers and family obligations. Membership surveys show that the more successful fundraising executives make three to four job changes in their professional careers (Mongon, 1992). The best-paying jobs occur in limited numbers in any city or even metropolitan area, forcing women candidates to search even farther afield for openings. The more lucrative positions exist in the larger agencies which typically have widespread constituencies, and periodic travel from home offices becomes mandatory for fundraising executives.

The realities of the occupation often do not match expectations of female and male job seekers. Pressures for production of gifts, deadlines, poor management, lack of supervision and training, advancement barriers, personality conflicts, and excessive travel lead to resignations. Frequently, agencies seeking new professionals have organizational systems that are dysfunctional or chief executives who are unresponsive to the ingredients for successful fundraising (Walton, 1993).

For women wishing to remain in the profession, the turnover factor makes more acceptable the decision to exit for childbearing and then return. Yet few agencies have policies for maternity leaves and child rearing; thus, reentry usually means finding a new job. As a result, women are forced to work in a variety of organizational settings, which can become an asset to a fundraising career.

The socialization of women may create barriers to advancement in the fundraising profession (Fugate, Decker, and Brewer, 1988). One issue concerns risk socialization. Women from earlier generations were not trained to take risks or to see risk as an opportunity to demonstrate their capabilities. Every fundraising program contains risks of goal failures, expenses that exceed budgets, and volunteers who do not perform. Fundraisers need to accept the occupational risks, because success correlates highly with promotion. All fundraisers experience failures because of the many variables in the jobs and contexts. Exposure to pitfalls sharpens survival skills. For those women who are not raised to be comfortable with competition, the problem can be overcome by placing women in competitive situations, with mentors available for advice, and providing latitude for errors.

Support staff positions in development offices are not paths to top positions, because they involve little risk or competition. Gift-producing positions such as managing annual funds, originating special events, and especially creating major gift programs provide access to the higher levels. Directing small special purpose campaigns offers another effective route for gaining the exposure necessary. Women are recognizing these career opportunities and are exerting pressure for such assignments. The large number of job openings and the availability of women interested in and capable of filling them result in the feminization phenomenon.

Chusmir (1983) finds that women choosing nontraditional occupations have characteristics usually attributed to men. The "masculine" attributes are depicted by Ruble

(1983) as forcefulness, adventurousness, aggressiveness, self-confidence, independence, ambition, dominance, and inventiveness. Women with some of these qualities find ready acceptance in the fundraising field, providing that they also have the qualities mentioned earlier that men and women need in order to be effective with donors.

Established organizations reproduce themselves through the people in power (principally men) by mentoring, encouraging, and advancing those most like themselves (Grant, 1988). This factor presents a serious barrier to women and minorities in organizations dominated by white men. Yet senior male fundraisers are concerned about the paucity of male successors in competition with the predominance of competent women in mid-level ranks. Not surprising, Grant (1988) corroborates other studies, observing that the few women who achieve senior rank in organizations usually resemble the men in power. The fundraising profession is no exception.

Problems of Devaluation

Occupations in which women come to dominate end up being devalued in both prestige and compensation, according to many studies and common perceptions (Touhey, 1974; Reskin, 1988). Examples include librarians, dental hygienists, medical technicians, training and human resource personnel, and public relations specialists. An intriguing exception arose from an experiment with a hypothetical gender-neutral occupation evaluated by women and men (Johnson, 1986). Ratings of prestige and desirability of the constructed profession, both present and future,

241

did not differ significantly as a function of gender ratios. This suggests that gender bias in fundraising may become less pervasive.

In a comprehensive study of the reports on women achieving a majority status in fundraising, Conry (1991) compares the phenomenon with other female-dominated occupations. She cites the discouraging factors of occupational segregation, stereotyping of activities as "women's work," inequities of salaries and benefits, and devaluation of occupations. From this analysis, she questions the future status of the fundraising profession and the ability of women to gain parity with men in positions, functions, and salaries.

The prospect of devaluation is not yet certain for fundraising occupations. Certainly, evidence exists of discrimination toward women in salaries, benefits, and previously limited advancement to top jobs. Yet the high demand for development officers and the presence of affirmative action policies suggest countervailing forces. The *Chronicle of Philanthropy* (1992) listed 2,627 organizations that placed advertisements for development personnel during three years. Examination of the advertisements reveals a preponderance asserting equal opportunity policies. Nonprofit organizations become increasingly subject to government regulation in regard to affirmative action policies when they accept grants and contracts. This source of funds is now estimated to average approximately 38 percent of total revenues for charitable nonprofit organizations (Hilgert and Mahler, 1991).

People with money and power to compel action provide the fuel for successful fundraising efforts. Women development officers who direct, motivate, and influence these individuals acquire some of the luster associated with money and power. The transference of influence raises the status of women fundraisers within their agencies and within the broader community of civic leaders and donors. Income producers are highly valued by executives and board members of agencies existing on tight budgets, especially in times of competition and shrinking government resources. The increasing wealth of women and the amount of money they give provide an environmental context that enhances the success of women solicitors. Women are no less successful in obtaining gifts from their own gender than men, and in many instances they have the advantage of being viewed as kindred souls.

In light of these factors, the devaluation of status ascribed to other occupations because of feminization may be less threatening to fundraising. The professional development of fundraisers, coupled with the rigorous certification programs undertaken by all the major fundraising associations, will raise the status of individual practitioners and in the process deter devaluation.

Fundraising Stereotypes

The stereotypical view of fundraising is of an aggressive solicitor hounding a susceptible prospect by phone, mail, or in person. Such conduct is usually identified as masculine. Overlooked in this view are the fundamental and necessary processes of cultivating and involving prospects in the needs of the people to be served. Developing a relationship and commitment between prospects and clients in the donee agency brings about the willingness to give and satisfaction in doing so. The process relates to "feminine" characteristics of compassion, relatedness, and caring. Thus, women and men with these attributes have the ingredients for success.

Another stereotype claims that women cannot ask for large gifts. This fallacy began to unravel early in the 1980s with published testimonials about women's abilities to solicit major gifts. In the college environment, women have performed with distinction, according to Detmold (1981). He cites record sums raised by women presidents of small colleges. A lead story in the *Chronicle of Philanthropy* noted the impressive totals raised by Wellesley College with a staff of women fundraisers running its recently completed capital campaign (Hall, May 1992). In conducting hundreds of fundraising workshops, I have found women adept at mastering techniques of personal solicitation, the keys to major gifts.

Both women and men face negative stereotypes associated with raising money. Fundraising is often viewed in pejorative terms, such as begging, "tin cupping," and panhandling. Despite the need for revenue, board members and volunteer leaders dislike soliciting and avoid it when they can, according to B. Taylor, vice president, Association of Governing Boards (interview with author, 1992). Even chief executives of nonprofit organizations deprecate the function, putting up with it as a necessary evil.

The negative views capitalize on the lack of sufficient

knowledge of the field (Mixer, 1993). It is increasingly recognized that giving and getting donations are social exchange processes through which donors receive such valued satisfactions as self-esteem, achievement, status, and affiliation. When donors are perceived as benefiting from gift transactions, the negative views of presumed one-way transfers subside. Growing interest in research on fundraising indicates that the inadequacy of conceptual foundations will be remedied (National Society of Fund Raising Executives, 1992).

Powell (1988) documents the lack of evidence for the sex differences that are presumed to underlie stereotypes. Femininity and masculinity are attributes shared by both men and women in varying degrees of dominance, he reports. The expression of these qualities results from continuing socialization, prevailing cultural norms, and workplace environments. Powell notes that gender stereotyping diminishes as women and men work together, gaining an appreciation of the competencies of each other. Development offices, large and small, reflect the phenomenon.

Professional Fundraising: A Management Function

The basic functions of fundraising consist of identifying and projecting human and organizational needs (strategic planning and case development); identifying and cultivating people who have the capacity and interests to support those needs (prospect research and marketing); organizing human and physical resources to bring the first two elements together in social exchange relationships (governance, organizing, recruiting, training, and monitoring); and assessment of results and performance, followed by repetition of the process (evaluation and strategic planning) (Mixer, 1993). The elements of management envelop the central act of people asking for money. However, the definition says nothing about the culture, leadership style, and organizational behavior involved in nonprofit activities in which donors, volunteers, clients, and staff have a stake. The current and future status of women as professional fundraisers will depend on all these essential factors. Certainly, the growing number of female executives in development offices and in the larger worlds of business and government demonstrates their acceptance as managers.

Management style, coupled with organizational structure, is critical. Autocratic hierarchical attitudes and forms command less respect, reduce compliance, and diminish commitment. Newer styles that empower participants and link them in group efforts achieve greater results, especially in volunteer-centered organizations. Given the management nature of fundraising, the research and concepts about women as managers in general become relevant.

A debate rages over whether there are distinctive female characteristics that become more effective in the newer managerial environment. Loden (1985) provides psychological studies to support the position, citing the "female" qualities valuable to organizations: intuitiveness, sensitivity to the needs of others, greater capacity for working under stress, and the ability to juggle several things at once—all of which amply describe the demands that fundraising places on managers, both men and women. However, she cautions about the "dangerous game" of generalizing gender traits.

Freeman (1990) dismisses the idea of a uniquely feminine management style as another form of sexual stereotyping. Women and men are neither inherently aggressive nor inherently nurturing, she says, and personality traits can change as the situation demands. Successful women often take on traits considered masculine, becoming more ambitious and more task oriented. Preceding her in the late 1960s and early 1970s, feminist authors minimized the differences between men and women, leading to a notion of androgyny—male and female gender traits amalgamated in one personality.

More recently, some feminists have begun to emphasize a viewpoint that values the ways that women are purported to behave, feel, and think. Helgesen (1990) concludes from her research and case studies that feminine principles exist and reflect differences from men in thinking and acting in management roles. She asserts that "women are more caring and intuitive, better at seeing the human side, quicker to cut through competitive distinctions of hierarchy and ranking, [and] impatient with cumbersome protocols" (p. 1).

While the argument about differences and similarities of women and men in society and management roles continues, women demonstrate their effectiveness as professional fundraisers. They direct large and small campaigns, manage big and little development offices, and obtain major gifts. The challenge is to overcome prejudices and stereotypes that block opportunities to obtain positions and comparable economic rewards based on ability and success.

Conclusion

Actions to enhance women's role in professional fundraising can be adapted from a study by Catalyst, a nonprofit research organization that focuses on women's issues in the workplace (J. A. Lopez, 1992). The study recommends that women be more assertive in seeking jobs that give relevant experience for promotion, seek transfers to mainline positions (in fundraising: development director, director of major gifts, or campaign manager) that provide a variety of experience, ask for mentoring and career development programs, and promote discrimination awareness programs similar to those undertaken by leading businesses.

Establishment of career development programs in fundraising will give participants insights and knowledge of what they need to know and do to advance to higher jobs. Sponsors, men as well as women, in large nonprofit organizations can provide relationships that open doors to job opportunities in their institutions. Mentoring programs, particularly those established by female chief executives, can provide support, advice, and vision to women as they advance in their careers. Mentors must not be threatened by their protégés' potential for success as expertise is shared. Furthermore, mentoring cannot be institutionalized or it will lose its unique value. Rather, the examples set by top management will stimulate other managers to become mentors. In addition, organizations such as NSFRE actively promote mentoring across organizational, gender, and ethnic lines. Other associations have similar programs.

Giving and raising funds provide those opportunities that Johnson and Ferguson (1990) describe as personally fulfilling for women. Individual and social satisfactions accrue from getting and giving gifts that support desired ends. In their roles as fundraisers, women can use their talents to the fullest, gaining feelings of self-esteem, group endeavor, and beneficial purpose. Such satisfactions are often denied in other paid positions that women occupy. With women rapidly increasing their majority in the profession and gaining requisite experience and training, they are positioning themselves to enlarge the cracks in glass ceilings and reach more equitable rewards. The future looks promising, but hard work remains to overcome sex discrimination.

References

American Prospect Research Association. *Membership Survey.* Washington, D.C.: American Prospect Research Association, 1992.

Childress, R. *1992 Salary and Benefits Report, USA.* Falls Church, Va.: Association for Healthcare Foundation, 1992.

Chronicle of Philanthropy. Full-page listings of 2,627 organizations. *Chronicle of Philanthropy,* 1992, *IV*(17), 37–39.

Chusmir, L. H. "Characteristics and Predictive Dimensions of Women Who Make Nontraditional Vocational Choices." *Personnel and Guidance Journal,* 1983, *62,* 43–47.

Conry, J. C. "The Feminization of Fund Raising." In D. F. Burlingame and L. J. Hulse (eds.), *Taking Fund Raising Seriously: Advancing the Profession and Practice of Raising Money.* San Francisco: Jossey-Bass, 1991.

Crowder, N. L., and Hodgkinson, V. A. (eds.). *Compendium of Resources for Teaching About the Nonprofit Sector, Voluntarism and Philanthropy.* (2nd ed.) Washington, D.C.: Independent Sector, 1991.

Cutlip, S. M. *Fund Raising in the United States: Its Role in America's Philanthropy.* New Brunswick, N.J.: Rutgers University Press, 1965.

Detmold, J. H. "The Distinguished Record of Women in Fund Raising." In F. Pray (ed.), *Handbook for Educational Fund Raising.* San Francisco: Jossey-Bass, 1981.

Eccles, J. S. "Gender Roles and Women's Achievement-Related Decisions." *Psychology of Women Quarterly,* 1987, *11,* 135–172.

Freeman, S.J.M. *Managing Lives: Corporate Women and Social Change.* Boston: University of Massachusetts Press, 1990.

Fugate, D. L., Decker, P. J., and Brewer, J. J. "Women in Professional Selling: A Human Resource Management Perspective." *Journal of Personal Selling and Sales Management,* November 1988, pp. 33–41.

Grant, J. "Women as Managers: What They Can Offer to Organizations." *Organizational Dynamics,* 1988, *16*(3), 56–63.

Hall, H. "Fund Raisers' Group Accused of Slighting Women." *Chronicle of Philanthropy,* March 24, 1992, p. 22.

Hall, H. "Wellesley College Campaign Success." *Chronicle of Philanthropy,* May 19, 1992, p. 1.

Helgesen, S. *The Female Advantage: Women's Ways of Leadership.* New York: Doubleday, 1990.

Hernández, A. C. *National Women of Color Organizations: A Report to the Ford Foundation.* New York: Ford Foundation, 1991.

Hilgert, C., and Mahler, S. J. "Nonprofit Charitable Organizations, 1986 and 1987." *Statistics of Income Bulletin,* Internal Revenue Service, 1991, *11*(2), 63–76.

Hodgkinson, V. A., and Weitzman, M. S. *Giving and Volunteering in the United States: Findings from a National Survey.* Washington, D.C.: Independent Sector, 1992.

Johnson, K., and Ferguson, T. *Trusting Ourselves: The Sourcebook on Psychology of Women.* New York: Atlantic Monthly Press, 1990.

Johnson, R. D. "The Influence of Gender Composition on Evaluation of Professions." *Journal of Social Psychology,* 1986, *126,* 161–168.

Loden, M. *Feminine Leadership: Or, How to Succeed in Business Without Being One of the Boys.* New York: Times Books, 1985.

Lopez, J. A. "Study Says Women Face Glass Walls as Well as Ceilings." *Wall Street Journal,* March 3, 1992, p. B-1.

McCarthy, K. D. (ed.). *Lady Bountiful Revisited: Women, Philanthropy, and Power.* New Brunswick, N.J.: Rutgers University Press, 1990.

McNamee, M. "The Outlook for Women: Despite Their Increasing Number, Women Still Command Lesser Titles and Lower Pay." *CASE Currents,* 1990, *16*(8), 13–14.

Mixer, J. R. *Principles of Professional Fundraising: Useful Foundations for Successful Practice.* San Francisco: Jossey-Bass, 1993.

Mongon, G. J. *NSFRE Profile: 1992 Membership Survey.* Arlington, Va.: National Society of Fund Raising Executives, 1992.

National Society of Fund Raising Executives. *Who's Who in Fund-Raising: 1991–1992 Membership Directory.* Arlington, Va.: National Society of Fund Raising Executives, 1991.

National Society of Fund Raising Executives. *Research Agenda and Policy.* Arlington, Va.: National Society of Fund Raising Executives, 1992.

Olson, J. E., Frieze, I. H., and Detlefson, E. G. "Having It All? Combining Work and Family in a Male and Female Profession." *Sex Roles,* 1990, *23,* 515–533.

Paresky, S. "President's Report." *Women in Development News,* March 1992, p. 2.

Powell, G. N. *Women and Men in Management.* Newbury Park, Calif.: Sage, 1988.

Reskin, B. F. "Bringing the Men Back in: Sex Differentiation and the Devaluation of Women's Work." *Gender and Society,* 1988, *2,* 58–77.

Ruble, T. L. "Sex Stereotypes: Issues of Change in the 1970s." *Sex Roles,* 1983, *9,* 397–402.

Tifft, S. E. "Asking for a Fortune." *Working Woman,* November 1992, pp. 66–68, 94.

Touhey, J. C. "Effects of Additional Women Professionals on Ratings of Occupational Prestige and Desirability." *Journal of Personality and Social Psychology,* 1974, *29*(1), 85–90.

Vincens, M. "Shattering the Myth of the Glass Ceiling." *Women in Development News,* March 1992, p. 6.

Walton, C. "Accountability and Productivity in Fund Raising." *Fund Raising Management,* 1993, *23*(11), 38–40.

8

A Latina's Experience of the Nonprofit Sector

Antonia Hernández

All my life, I have followed nontraditional career paths. Almost daily, I challenge the barriers erected in front of me and defy the stereotypes with which people view me, a Latina living and working at the pinnacles of power in the United States. I deal with entrenched sexism as well as the cultural problem of being a Latina in what until recently has been a predominantly white Eurocentric society.

My desire to become a lawyer was premised on a simple belief—that the profession would provide me with the skills and the means to improve the quality of life for Latinos and society at large. But as a young woman, I naively believed that because I was going to devote my professional career to the public interest, I would not have to endure sexism and racism. I was wrong. The public-interest sector has been no different than the for-profit sector.

Throughout my nineteen years as a lawyer, I have had varied experiences. I have worked as staff attorney for the Los Angeles Center for Law and Justice, as directing attorney for the Legal Aid Foundation of Los Angeles, as staff counsel to the U.S. Senate Committee on the Judiciary, as a lobbyist in Washington, D.C., as a fundraiser, and, since 1985, as president and general counsel for the Mexican American Legal Defense and Educational Fund (MALDEF).

In these positions, I have interacted closely with a wide segment of society, including the corporate sector, government, and the philanthropic and religious communities.

To this day, I continue to wonder why it is that American society has yet to make significant progress in eliminating racism and sexism. The irony, in my mind, is all the more apparent in the nonprofit world, a segment of professional society that, because of its altruistic objectives, is seen as more enlightened and accepting of diversity.

As a Latina, I have often struggled to understand why I am treated differently by white males, who comprise the majority of the people I encounter in my professional role. Is it because of my ethnicity and my gender? Why should they make a difference?

Yet when I ask a white female, and they say they encounter similar attitudes, I find myself with the need to know which of the two evils—sexism or racism—is the more oppressive.

As a Latina, I am amused when non–Latinos lament the machismo in my community. Gender discrimination is a malady that, unfortunately, affects our entire society, and whether I am discriminated against by a Latino or Anglo male, the results are the same—doubt of my ability, betrayal, and anger.

What does all this have to do with the issue at hand? Everything. Our world, the nonprofit world, reflects the attitudes and behavior of society at large. If we, as a sector, are serious about addressing the problems, we must first disavow the myth that ours is a more perfect world. Then we must accept the notion that we, too, must deal with racism and sexism.

My experiences with racism and sexism have been, at times, amusing. Once I was refused entry to the lawyers' seating section in court because I was "too young and too pretty." What the white male bailiff meant, of course, was that I was Mexican. Some might conclude that the bailiff's comment was more sexist than racist, but as a woman of color, I cannot separate my gender from my ethnicity. I cannot report that the comment was less hurtful because it was directed at me as a woman rather than me as a Latina. The result was the same.

Another time, while I was working for the Senate Judiciary Committee, a colleague could not believe I was a lawyer. I had to show my bar card to convince him.

As counsel to the Senate Judiciary Committee, primarily responsible for immigration and refugee matters. I worked closely with the leadership of national nonprofit organizations concerned with these issues. Again, I was struck with how white and male the leadership was. I do not recall encountering individuals of color or women in positions of authority in the refugee and immigrant communities.

In regard to my contributions to the committee: Did it make a difference that a woman of color was involved in the decision-making process? A resounding yes. In looking at critical issues of immigration, my perspective on the plight of Mexican immigrants was in marked contrast to others', who were looking at the issue from an East Coast, turn-of-the-century immigration perspective. My contributions were based on working with thousands of immigrant families, both documented and undocumented. I knew firsthand what obstacles these individuals faced as they struggled to establish themselves in this country. I feel to this day that had it not been for my personal knowledge and experience, the strife of a sizable portion of the immigrant population of the United States would not have been addressed.

I customarily make light of being the "in" Latina. I am repeatedly invited to serve on boards and commissions or to speak and participate on panels as the only Latina or Latino. Inquiring diplomatically "Why me?" the usual response is that I am the best and there are so few qualified Latinas or Latinos. Quite a compliment.

Most foundations still do not have Latinas or Latinos on their boards of trustees. A study by Hispanics in Philanthropy, an organization devoted to increasing Latino participation in the funding community, found that less than 1 percent of foundation trustees are Latina or Latino. This mirrors the percentage of Latinas and Latinos who sit on boards of directors of major corporations, also holding steady at 1 percent.

Frustration with the lack of representation on nonprofit

boards led to the creation of the Leadership Development Program of MALDEF. Our goal is to train individuals in leadership and place them on boards and commissions in their communities. To date, more than sixteen hundred midcareer and grass-roots Latinos and Latinas have graduated from the program, with almost 50 percent attaining positions on such influential bodies as the United Ways of Los Angeles and Orange counties, the March of Dimes, and the American Red Cross.

Despite these advances, however, I am continually confronted with the reality that power and influence in the nonprofit world are still largely white and male.

When I first began my fundraising activities at MAL-DEF in 1984, I was astonished to learn that Latinos and Latinas received less than 5 percent of the grant money awarded; MALDEF received almost half of that. If the contributions of the Ford Foundation—the biggest grantor to the Latino community—were excluded, the amount of dollars going to the community would be minuscule.

As I traveled throughout the country seeking funds, I soon realized that my job was twofold—first, I had to educate the funding community about the Latino community and how we are not all immigrants or undocumented. In fact, the majority of the community is United States born; many go back fifteen generations. I also had to explain that we are not all farm workers or factory workers. Latinos are the most urban population in the country. Fewer than 15 percent work in agriculture.

Yes, we do need bilingual education and bilingual ballots for those in our community who have not yet learned

English, and no, we are not interested in forming a Quebec-like state of separatism. Our community was and is no different than other immigrant communities. We go through the same three-generation assimilation process that other immigrants go through. The difference is that the flow of immigrants is constant and since 1980 has increased and become more diversified.

As a Latina, I found myself not only having to explain who Latinos are but also to debunk the sexist and racist stereotypes that all Latinas stay at home raising children, hanging wash, and making tortillas. How was it that I became a lawyer? they would ask. Was that not unusual? Well, no more so than in the rest of society. When I entered law school in 1971, the percentage of women of any color studying to become attorneys was low. Sexism is a malady suffered by society at large.

I vividly recall my first experience with the nonprofit world, as a young Legal Aid lawyer. It happened in the mid-1970s, when I worked with a small, community-based organization seeking a grant from the United Way of Los Angeles. There were few Latino employees at the agency and next to none serving on the board of directors. Imagine, the largest nonprofit agency in Los Angeles County! With its low level of diversity, it might as well have been in North Dakota. The agency, administered primarily by Anglo males, had little understanding of my community or of me. Their interaction with us was bureaucratic, nonresponsive, and unsympathetic. Two years ago, as a member of the Los Angeles United Way board, I participated in a major strategic reassessment of the agency. Unfortunately, many of the same problems, including the lack of diversity in decision-making bodies, still existed.

In 1975, together with two other lawyers, I filed a class action suit against Los Angeles County Hospital, alleging the massive and coerced sterilization of Latinas. Most defendants were white men, including all five members of the county board of supervisors and the vast majority of doctors. More than one hundred interviews with poor Latinas who had been sterilized revealed a frightening picture. Throughout the many depositions of the physicians, together with their testimony during a three-week trial, it became clear that neither the representatives of county government nor the doctors at the county facility respected or cared for the patients. The doctors exhibited a total disregard for the physical and mental well-being of these women. As a young female lawyer representing the women, I was given the runaround and treated in a condescending manner. Was I treated with such disdain because I was a Latina, working for Legal Aid, and suing the predominantly male medical establishment? I do not know the answer, but fifteen years later, when I again sued Los Angeles County, alleging a history of discrimination in political representation, manifested by discrimination in the allocation of public services and resources, the board of supervisors still consisted of five white men. Their white male lawyers treated our legal team in a similar manner, with condescension and disdain.

What does the above have to do with the nonprofit sector? I take an expansive view of the nonprofit world. To me, working on behalf of the poor, whether it is in Legal

Aid, the United Way, or as a doctor in a county hospital, is work for the common good and in the public interest. There have been a few changes in the work force, but most things remain the same. Leadership positions and similar opportunities remain in the hands of white men. Opportunities for people of color, and specifically Latinas, in the nonprofit sector still remain low after all these years. For women like myself, the nonprofit sector remains a lonely place. When I look around, I can count on one hand the number of Latinas on large, well-established nonprofit boards or Latinas who are executive officers in these organizations.

How can the nonprofit sector change? The first priority must be to honestly talk about the barriers within the nonprofit world. Let's start by being honest. The aura of altruism surrounding the nonprofit sector is sometimes deceptive. Working in a nonprofit organization connotes working for the public good, for the betterment of the community, and fostering new ideals and principles to improve society. This is a squeaky clean description of the nonprofit sector that many are quick to believe. In reality, the nonprofit sector is not much different from the for-profit sector in the opportunities it provides for women, particularly in upper management. The openings are few and far between. Why? The male-dominated network is very much alive in nonprofit work, as in other areas of the workplace, providing its own selection criteria. The altruism associated with nonprofits often provides glossy covering that obscures the existence of this network.

In nonprofits, as in for-profits, white men predominate

in executive and upper-level management positions. The number of white females in midmanagement positions is increasing, but most women and people of color are in lower-level and volunteer positions. And, despite the battles white women have fought to reach middle management, their own brand of leadership exhibits the same stereotyping and condescension toward women of color that their male counterparts exhibit. Latinas face a double whammy, a structure dominated by white men and white women who admire their dark-skinned counterparts for the added burden of living in a macho Latino culture. There is no real difference or advantage for a minority woman in the nonprofit sector: the barriers remain the same as in the for-profit sector.

A closer look at the nonprofit sector shows that it does not adapt well to the needs of minority women. The upward struggle of minority women is dotted with obstacles and barriers by mainstream society and their own ethnic cultures. Freedom and empowerment are virtually nonexistent for most minority women in nonprofits. My own experience in working my way up the ladder to head one of the most successful civil rights advocacy organizations in the United States has its share of ups and downs and battling the status quo.

What, then, compels a Latina to enter the nonprofit sector? Why would minority women want to face the same barriers their counterparts face in the for-profit sector? Is it for an opportunity to get a foot in the door? For many individuals, it goes beyond just looking for a good steady job.

I have devoted more than half my life to working in

the nonprofit sector. I'm asked why I chose this path instead of another, perhaps one with greater financial rewards and certainly fewer demands on my time and my family. I felt I could make a change in society. The injustices, brutality, and discrimination against Latinos compelled me to take action. I remember thinking, "If I can get the skills to work within the legal system and work the system to change the rules and laws that govern society, I could do something to make my community a better place to live." That is what I sought to do and continue to do.

When I began working in nonprofits, few organizations offered women opportunities for work, much less management careers. When I entered the nonprofit sector, the number of women in the work force was growing. Between 1971 and 1981, the civilian work force grew by 31 percent. Women accounted for nearly 59 percent of the growth, and for the first time, more than half of working-age women were in the job market. In contrast, the number of working men actually dropped.

However, the numbers do not reflect what I mentioned earlier. The for-profit and nonprofit sectors still remain in the hands of men. According to recent findings by the U.S. Bureau of Labor Statistics, between 1981 and 1991 several alarming trends have appeared. The numbers of women in the work force have increased only 3 percent, from 43 percent to 46 percent of the total. And while the number of women managers has increased from 27 percent to 41 percent of the labor force, the number of senior executives who are women has risen by only 2 percent, from 1 percent in 1981 to 3 percent in 1991.

Changes in the workplace have added barriers to minority women in the nonprofit sector. Recession, mergers, corporate buyouts, and other economic factors have scaled down the for-profit sector. These factors have contributed to an increase in the number of nonprofit organizations operating in the workplace. But, as I pointed out earlier, increasing the number of nonprofit organizations does not mean more job opportunities or career possibilities for minority women. An increase in nonprofit organizations has provided additional work opportunities for mainstream women, but minority women, especially Latinas, have not been considered viable candidates to fill the newly opened positions.

In both sectors, Latinas remain in the lower hierarchy, more so than other minorities and Anglo or mainstream women workers. Some will state that the reason Latinas are not moving up the management ladder is because of our "traditional Latino values of family and culture." Well, the fact is, the economy has forced everyone to work. There are two-wage-earner Latino families, single-parent Latinas, and even latchkey Latino children. The Latino family comprised of a stay-at-home mother and a father who works in the fields or the factory disappeared years ago. Latinas have to work to support their families, just like everyone else today. The needs and aspirations of Latinas are no different from those of other women across the United States. We want to work and succeed and get ahead; our goals are the same.

With this in mind, we still must ask, Why do more women gravitate toward the nonprofit sector than to corporate America? Are we using it to establish ourselves in the workplace? Today, women comprise a large portion of the nonprofit sector. We are more than 60 percent of the 8 million nonprofit employees and 50 percent of the 90 million volunteer workers in the nonprofit sector. How can we explain women's concentrated presence in the non-profit sector?

One reason more women are found in nonprofit work is because it is the place we want to be. The majority of Latinas I have encountered in nonprofits are doing it because they want to. Whatever their private agendas, they wish to devote their careers to the nonprofit sector. It is a choice, not of economics but despite economics. The lawyers who work alongside me at MALDEF have forsaken the big bucks of private firms to be do-gooders like myself.

Women in nonprofits still must do what women in the for-profit sector have to do. But once women begin to achieve positions of authority, like me, things will change.

I view the world differently. I bring a wealth of ideas gained from experience, from the benefit of living in and knowing two cultures. This is why diversity is so impor-tant. We bring in something different. Is it better? I really can't say, but it is different. We must work to lead by the example of our ability to govern and nurture to everyone.

As we examine the role of women and the nonprofit world, I urge my colleagues to look within, not for the purpose of self-criticism but with the goal of improving and changing it for the better.

As workers in the fastest-growing sector of the econ-omy, we in the nonprofit world have a responsibility and a unique opportunity to lead by example, to serve as role models, to practice what we preach, to be inclusive, col-laborative, and agents of change.

9

Women and Volunteer Activity: One Practitioner's Adventures in Leadership

Barbara C. Roper

I have been a volunteer on many boards and for many causes. I was first aware of voluntarism during World War II as I watched my mother knit socks in the living room of our home in Pittsburgh. She was a volunteer for the Red Cross, and as part of her duties, she knit socks "for the boys in the service," as she used to say.

Mother was a dedicated volunteer all her life and instilled this habit in her children. As a child, I went with her to the blood bank at Red Cross headquarters in downtown Pittsburgh on Saturday mornings. After giving blood, donors were required to rest for at least half an hour, eat a sandwich, and drink a glass of orange juice. I was not old enough to give blood, but I sure could make a mean sandwich and pour orange juice from those big cans.

Voluntarism was also a school assignment. Upon reaching eighth grade, everyone was expected to do volunteer work. This could be as a candy striper at the hospital or as an assistant in church Sunday school classes, for story time at the library, or for special classes at the museum and zoo.

Through my high school years, I served as a volunteer at Presbyterian Hospital on Saturday mornings. Because candy stripers were part of the women's auxiliary of the hospital, we were allowed to attend those meetings, although we were not to hold office or vote. As part of that system, I saw how the auxiliary worked. I saw a totally volunteer organization take on a major responsibility in assisting the nursing staff and patients on nine floors of a big city hospital. In addition, the auxiliary ran a small business on the first floor. The gift shop and snack bar grossed close to $750,000 annually and was the major money maker of the auxiliary. The business required volunteers to select carefully the merchandise for sale, keep inventory records, and negotiate with food and flower vendors for the best prices and the freshest commodities.

I had a chance to work in all these areas over the years. I learned how volunteers were assigned, how their hours were recorded, and the consequences of a volunteer's failure to show up. I learned the rudiments of parliamentary procedure and how a skilled leader can keep a meeting on track when dealing with differences of opinion from strong personalities.

I also observed the power struggles over leadership roles, the pitfalls in the process of nominating leaders from various cliques in the organization, and the Peter Principle—

being promoted to the highest level of one's incompetence and remaining there. (It was not called the Peter Principle at the time, but it was nevertheless in operation.)

It has been many years since I left Pittsburgh. Since then, I have been a direct-service, a fundraising, and a policy-making volunteer for numerous groups, including the Orlando (Florida) Opera Board, the National Board of Laubach Literacy International, Eckerd College, and the national board of the Public Broadcasting System. I am also a founder of the Central Florida Commission on the Status of Women, dubbed "the SOW commission" by a number of men. The name, though defended as a joke, shows the attitude faced by black and white women on the commission and our need to organize and network, which we did.

The biggest and most important volunteer organization of which I have been a part is the YMCA. I am particularly pleased to have been the first woman to have reached the top of the organization as chair of its national board.

I was a member of a YMCA board in Florida in 1968 when the national organization first required annual certification by all YMCAs that they accept both men and women of all races at all levels of the organization.

Change came very late in the game, considering civil rights history and the leadership of many YMCA people in bringing both black and white women along in the organization. Sixty percent of the YMCAs were accepting women as members at the close of World War II in 1945.

One explanation is systemic—that YMCA action on the national level almost never dictates anything to the community YMCAs. It more often lags decades behind what local chapters are doing. For example, in 1957, women were formally accepted by the national YMCA when it removed the restrictive words "men and boys" from its constitution. At that time, more than 1 million women and girls were enrolled in Y groups and programs. Still, it was not until 1968 that the National Council demanded annual certification.

Another explanation is that the Y, since its origin in this country in 1851, got along by not engaging in debate on major questions of the day, such as slavery, child labor laws, women's suffrage, prohibition, unionization, and civil rights. Instead, independent Ys did what the community wanted. Some were on the cutting edge, and some would never be.

Perhaps the real explanation lies in what I experienced in Florida when the national edict came down. The men on the board realized that new facilities would have to be built for women. The price was more than they wanted to pay: an extra sauna, hiring another masseur, putting in another hot tub, and separate lockers and showers. "My wife will never come down here," a board member told me indignantly, "not until we hire a blind masseur."

Using more of my volunteer career as a case history, I would like to discuss how volunteering, under the right conditions, can help women and girls of all races and backgrounds acquire leadership skills (which I define as the ability to create change in a community) as well as help them grow personally (which I link mainly to creating self-esteem). Most of my examples come from the YMCA.

Because I address this issue as a practitioner, my ideas are based on personal experience. I suggest principles and practices that the voluntary sector can adopt to help make volunteering an effective course in leadership for women and girls. At the same time, I profile the type of organization that women should seek if they want their volunteer work to be fulfilling.

Background of the YMCA

The YMCA is the largest nonprofit community service organization in America. In 1991, it worked to meet the health and social service needs of 12.8 million men, women, and children in the fifty states. Its membership is third largest, behind the American Association of Retired Persons (32 million) and the American Automobile Association (28 million).

The Young Men's Christian Associations in this country today are not exclusively for the young—only half of their combined membership is seventeen or younger; not exclusively for men—47 percent are women; and not exclusively Christian—begun as a Protestant Christian evangelical organization, it today welcomes to its staff, membership, and boards those of all faiths or no faith. Its historic name, though no longer descriptive, has never changed and probably never will.

Today's Y is a community-based, volunteer-led association that promotes good health, strong families and children, and sound communities. It operates alone or in collaboration with other community agencies. It helps people develop values and behavior that are consistent with Christian principles. It is not itself a church or the representative of any particular creed. No one is turned away for inability to pay. Ys are intensely self-directed in control, outlook, financing, and services, aiming to match their programs to community needs.

Recently, the National Board of YMCAs adopted a vision statement for the associations. It sees the Y in the next few years as the national leader in preventive social services for children and families at risk, basing its approach on developmental programs and on cooperative community development. The Y already is the country's largest provider of health and fitness classes, aquatics, youth sports, and camping. A more surprising fact is its status as the largest provider of child care in the country.

Y programs also serve active older adults and people with disabilities. Literacy and job training programs help young people and families with low incomes. The programs vary from community to community. They are as diverse as infant mortality prevention, international exchange, environmental education, substance abuse prevention, and overnight camping for seniors.

The Y is also one of the country's largest voluntary organizations. In the average Y, a volunteer board sets policy. The executive manages the operation with full-time and part-time staff members and volunteer leaders.

According to the *1991 YMCA Statistical Summary* (p. 9), the 2,078 YMCAs in the United States reported a total of 62,271 policy-making volunteers—the people who serve as board members, trustees, and committee members. But of those sixty-two thousand, only 28 percent were women.

The Ys also reported having 325,713 program volunteers

272

during 1991. These are the people who lead YMCA groups and classes as coaches and instructors, as well as those who serve as literacy tutors, youth mentors, group leaders, recycling center volunteers, and so on. Most Y program volunteers provide direct service. Of those reported, only 38 percent were women. This is probably because 50 percent of Y program volunteers work in youth sports, which attracts more men than women as coaches.

The Charge for the YMCA and Other Nonprofits

For the YMCA and other organizations to remain relevant and vital, I believe they must open the doors more widely to female volunteers as well as minority women and men. For the YMCA, it is simply a matter of catching up to the membership and staff demographics. Currently, women and girls make up 46 percent of the membership and 53 percent of employed professional staff.

And it is not simply a matter of opening the doors more widely but of making sure that the volunteer experience is significant and meaningful. No fluff and no bluff. It must meet an important need in the community, so that its success helps the female volunteer become a better leader and more confident of her power to bring about positive change.

Such meaningful experience can occur only if the culture of the organization supports a number of important principles and practices. By culture, I mean the board, volunteers, and staff, but in some cases culture may include the clients, members, donors, and others with a stake in the organization.

273

Five principles and their related practices have become apparent to me through personal experience. First among them is that voluntarism must be recognized as essential to a democratic society. Second, volunteers must be regarded as essential to the existence of a nonprofit organization. Third, female and male volunteers representing at least the cultural diversity of the community must be sought out and valued as much as white male volunteers. Fourth, nonprofits must spend time and money to identify, recruit, and train volunteers. And fifth, voluntarism must be viewed as a leadership training program, not as a cheap source of labor.

By acting on the principles, nonprofits can offer women and men a genuine opportunity for leadership training and personal growth.

Principles and Practices

Volunteering must be widely recognized as essential to a democratic society. Staff members and volunteers alike need to understand the context in which voluntary organizations operate in society. The United States is one of the few countries in the world with a long history of voluntary activity on a scale remarkable for its size and influence.

Modern thinkers and writers about the organization of American society seem to have spent more time lately examining the voluntary sector. But it is not some new pearl. It has been there at least since Benjamin Franklin and some friends began a mutual improvement society in Philadelphia and founded the first subscription library in the city in 1729. Members pooled their money, bought books in England, and passed them around.

People get together to do things—things they have decided are important and necessary. That is what a YMCA board is and what it does.

In the 1830s, Alexis de Tocqueville wrote in *Democracy in America:*

Nothing, in my opinion, is more deserving of our attention than the intellectual and moral associations of America. The political and industrial associations of that country strike us forcibly; but the others elude our observation, or if we discover them, we understand them imperfectly because we have hardly ever seen anything of the kind. It must be acknowledged, however, that they are as necessary to the American people as [political and industrial associations] and perhaps more so. In democratic countries the science of association is the mother science; the progress of all the rest depends on the progress it has made [1945, p. 118].

All nonprofit volunteers and staff members should have the chance to learn about the importance of voluntarism. They need thorough training and orientation, supplemented by reprints of magazine and journal articles. The role of voluntarism can also be found in the mass media in books such as *Managing the Non-Profit Organization* by Peter Drucker, certainly one of the most influential management consultants in the United States. In the preface, Drucker comments:

It is working as unpaid staff for a nonprofit institution that gives people a sense of community, gives purpose, gives direction—whether it is work with the local Girl Scout troop, as a volunteer in the hospital, or as the leader of a Bible circle in the local church. Again and again when I talk to volunteers in nonprofits, I ask, "Why are you willing to give all this time when you are already working hard in your paid job?" and again and again I get the same answer: "Because here I know what I am doing. Here I contribute. Here I am a member of the community." . . . The nonprofits *are* the American community [1990, pp. xvii–xviii].

Indeed, Drucker claims that nonprofits have a singular ability to offer leadership training. He even goes as far as to say that people must learn leadership through volunteering, because they are not learning it on their jobs:

The exciting thing, the new thing, is that we are creating a society of citizens in the old sense of how people actively work, rather than passively vote and pay taxes. We are not doing it in business. There is a lot of talk of participative management; but there is not much reality to it, and in many ways, there never will be. The pressures are perhaps too great. . . . But we are doing exactly this in the non-profit service institution where increasingly there are only leaders. These are people who are paid and people who are not paid. In a church there are a very small number

276

of people who are ordained, but 1,000 people who work and do major tasks for the church who are not ordained, never will be, never get a penny. . . . We are creating tomorrow's society of citizens through the nonprofit service institution. And in that society, everybody is a leader, everybody is responsible, everybody acts. Everybody focuses himself or herself. Everybody raises the vision, the competence, and the performance of his or her organization [p. 49].

Those who are part of the voluntary sector must be able to understand the important role that it plays in developing leaders through citizen participation. Without this understanding, they cannot fully appreciate the importance of volunteers to their organizations and will lose them, losing their strength at the same time. And without a high regard for volunteers at all levels of the organization, there is little chance for any volunteer job to mean more than passing time or balancing the budget with unpaid labor.

Volunteers must be regarded as essential to the existence of a nonprofit organization. Nora Silver (1988, p. 83) of the Volunteerism Project in San Francisco has described how unresponsive bureaucracies can form in nonprofit organizations. The bureaucracies seem to deplete the strength of caring and community that are nonprofit organizations' reason for being. She calls the phenomenon *professionalization.* Indeed, YMCAs have witnessed it over time.

The Seattle YMCA's Rick Jackson, speaking to the National Association of Student YMCAs in 1991, said that in the 1960s and 1970s, the voluntary associational character of the Y was replaced at a number of Ys by a department store mentality. YMCAs became a place to buy child care and fitness rather than a community to belong to and support financially.

In the late 1960s, the staff title of "secretary" was changed to "director." Whereas *secretary* connotes a servant's relationship to the volunteer board, *director* connotes a more powerful executive role—the beginning, perhaps, of forgetting who holds the ultimate legal authority in governing a nonprofit: the volunteers.

The signs of damaging professionalization are the telephones that ring forever; negative staff attitudes; the haughty idea that volunteers are a nuisance or, at best, amateurs stomping about with muddy boots in a private and very professional world; the belief that policy making should be done by passive uninterested board members who rubber-stamp staff recommendations without discussion; and the attitude that training volunteers is not worth the time and effort. These are almost natural tendencies in the nonprofit world, where professionals are likely to take ownership.

On the other hand, volunteers can do actual damage to an organization when they do not take board responsibilities seriously, do not pay attention at meetings, or show the rubber-stamp mentality. The recent problems at United Way of America show how damaging inattention can be. The national board of directors of United Way included top leaders in American business, the professions, labor, and industry. They appeared to be caught by surprise by questionable actions of their top executive, a dynamic and persuasive individual who was using the corporate model in working with his board.

I understand their meetings never lasted more than an hour and a half. The executive had won their trust and as busy highly pressured individuals, they apparently did not notice anything was wrong. This elite group abdicated its responsibility and never followed through on the commitment a board member makes in accepting that position.

It remains to be seen whether lawsuits will be filed and whether the directors are covered by directors-and-officers (D&O) insurance. But it is clear that board members can be sued for actions or inactions that lead to a problem and that they are responsible as the financial watchdogs and owners.

In today's legal world, where people and institutions are sued at the drop of a hat, directors and officers of a nonprofit have what insurance people call "a meaningful exposure to personal liability." This means that, as a loss-prevention strategy, expanded and meaningful volunteer training is more than a good idea; like D&O insurance, it is a necessity.

A board also has a clear moral responsibility that can disappear when lawsuits are filed.

The Y's national office, the YMCA of the USA in Chicago, is developing expanded training programs for staff and volunteer leaders. The programs will stress the line between policy and management, the responsibilities of directors, and the essential role that volunteers play in fulfilling the mission.

YMCAs seldom try to calculate the worth in dollars of the huge number of volunteers who support them. But it can be done fairly simply. Independent Sector calculates that an hour of volunteer time is worth $10.82—the average nonagricultural wage in 1990, including fringe benefits (Hodgkinson, Weitzman, Toppe, and Noga, 1992, p. 47). For simplicity's sake, take a modest one hundred hours a year per volunteer (a little less than two hours a week), price the work at $10 an hour, multiply, then multiply roughly four hundred thousand YMCA volunteers by $1,000, and the worth of their time is $400 million annually.

The figure, of course, is of little practical use, except to underscore two principles of charitable nonprofits: their profound voluntary nature and the vital necessity of training the people who run them, both staff members and volunteers.

The training of program volunteers is better organized than is training for staff members because volunteers often must be certified under local and state laws as instructors in a specialty. Policy-making volunteers, on the other hand, tend to be recognized community leaders, those in the professions, social activists, and longtime YMCA members.

As Drucker (1990, pp. 171–172) points out, nonprofit board members are a far cry from traditionally docile corporate directors. In nonprofits, directors must serve on committees, act as donors and fundraisers, and spread the word. They are the owners—the guardians, interpreters, and advocates of the mission of the organization. A climate of trust and partnership must exist between the board and the chief executive officer. Both sides should know what is expected of them and be careful not to breach the line between creating policy and actually running the organization.

Drucker notes:

> The tendency of so many CEOs is to try to have a board that won't do any harm because it won't do anything. It is the wrong tendency. [Nonprofit CEOs] depend on the board. Therefore you can be more effective with a strong board, a committed board, an energetic board, than with a rubber stamp. The rubber stamp will, in the end, not stamp at all when you most need it. . . . Good boards don't descend from Heaven. It requires continuing work [by the CEO] to find the right people, and to train them. . . . You take a great deal of time to keep the board informed but also to have a two-way flow of information [1990, pp. 178–179].

Most training programs that I have seen for staff members of nonprofits focus on how to manage volunteers. Good training is about working with, not using, volunteers. Volunteers should be treated as coleaders. When such a philosophy is not ingrained in the culture, it is nearly impossible to create meaningful roles for volunteers, female or male.

Female volunteers must be valued as much as male volunteers. Women who volunteer may face a double burden. They may have to overcome negative staff attitudes about their importance and the resulting resistance to their involvement. And on the policy level with an all-male board, they often encounter gender discrimination from the other board members. As more women arrive in top managerial and policy positions, such discrimination should naturally decline. But the sting of it is difficult to forget.

My first position on a YMCA board was offered to me after it was offered to my husband. Y leaders knew our family because I had enrolled our children in camp. Although I had selected the camp and had the closest contact with the Y staff, my husband was offered a seat on the board.

I was furious. He declined, suggesting another candidate, me, and they took him up on the offer. (Throughout my volunteer career, I have had to work hard to become Barbara Roper, as opposed to Bert Roper's wife. Even today, I find that some male volunteers are comfortable with female volunteers only if they are wives of their friends or business colleagues.)

After that, progress was slow. I rose from a seat on one of six or seven branch boards of the Orlando Y system to a seat on the Central Florida Metro YMCA board, the corporate parent for the branches. After several years on the board, I was asked to be its secretary. I accepted the offer, expecting that I would eventually be offered another leadership position.

In the mid seventies, when the chair of the metro nominating committee called me for the third year in a row and asked me if I would again serve as secretary, I said, "Wally, is there ever going to be a chance for me to be anything other than secretary of the board?" There was a long pause, until he replied, "Barbara, I don't think the board is ready for that just yet."

To this day, I am not sure what changed their minds. It might have been the influence of the executive director, a man who was one of my mentors. The next year, I was offered the vice chair on the board and a year later the top volunteer job, making me the first woman to chair that board.

In another instance, as the board chair for the local Public Broadcasting System (PBS) station, I faced similar sexism. I call it the Story of the Invisible Board Chair. During my term of office, I was invited to attend a meeting in Phoenix in 1971, along with the chairs of other television stations around the U.S. I took the invitation to our executive committee, which was otherwise all male.

At that time, our station was only about four years old. We had barely enough money to operate, let alone spend on meetings across the country. As the invitation was passed around the table, I became the invisible chair. The others started discussing who should attend the meeting. It was suggested that Joe could go because he had a business in Phoenix, and he could charge the expense to his company. Then someone remembered that Max had a meeting there the next week, and he could go out several days early, attend the conference, and play golf before the PBS meeting started.

I was dumbstruck. The invitation was addressed to me, the chair, and the men were deciding who among them should go. Finally, the treasurer of the board slammed his fist on the table and said that I should go and that the station should pay for my trip or no one should go. I went, and as a result of attending, was appointed to a task force of the national board of the Public Broadcasting System.

Within a year, I was elected to the PBS national board, on which I served for eleven years.

The treasurer who came to my assistance was mentoring in the best sense, and I never forgot the lesson. I might add that today, it would be my fist slamming the table.

Nevertheless, there are fair-minded people who will judge things on their merits and will take the time to show you the ropes. The point here is to persevere and gain the support of a mentor, male or female. A mentor can help a woman achieve status as a volunteer. I credit my mentors with helping me acquire the self-esteem and skills necessary to become a leader in the nonprofit sector.

Mentors listened when I told them of my ambitions, and I feel it is incumbent on protégés to do that. They saw doors that were open and suggested I go through them, although they also let me learn from my own mistakes. Mentors can be assigned, but I believe mentoring that evolves from mutual respect is the most effective kind.

Women must take responsibility in identifying other women and minority candidates for leadership roles. Men must also assume that responsibility. A word said at the right time and place about another person's ability can be invaluable.

Training is also necessary. While no training program "can make a fair man out of a sexist pig," to quote a friend of mine, I believe that attitudes and beliefs can be changed through continuing education. A start in this direction is the training course Women and the Y, which highlights the historical accomplishments of female staff members and volunteers. Its goal is to show that women should be included at all levels of decision making in the organization—member, volunteer, and staff.

In 1991, the YMCA held the first national and international conferences devoted to full participation of women in the Y. We pushed for review of personnel policies, changes in hiring practices, equal pay for equal jobs, and insisted on training sessions so employees would recognize and combat sexual harassment. The national organization must show the way. Because we are an association of YMCAs, we are not in a position to legislate and must create positive examples.

I hope that such training will continue. I also advocate strongly the continuation of regular training sessions for staff and volunteers on sexual harassment. I have faced much of it. The incident that perhaps shook me the most occurred after a dinner at a national PBS board meeting. I returned to my hotel room to find an executive from a national foundation in my bed, stripped to his underwear. When I opened the door and saw him there, I stepped back outside and told him I would give him two minutes to walk to the lobby and out of the hotel. He did.

While I do not feel that this particular event compromised my power or influence in that organization, I know that sexual harassment is a despicable barrier for many. I am not aware of any legal resource that female volunteers have when faced with this sort of thing. Perhaps there is some. But the fact that I am not aware of it is significant.

When sexually harassed female volunteers do not feel they have the legal protection that exists—at least on paper—for female employees, something vital is missing.

That is why the Y and other organizations must provide training on what sexism and harassment are and what volunteers can do if they encounter them.

Mentors and training programs must fight the battle against sexism, not only toward women but also men. Men are often excluded from direct service volunteer jobs because those jobs are seen as women's work. Until sexism in all forms is eradicated in nonprofits, women will not have an equal opportunity to become respected leaders and change agents.

I might add that most of the sexual harrassment is perpetrated as if great sport by men who think of themselves as daring. Snuggling someone on an elevator or pinching someone is not daring. It is assault and battery.

Nonprofits must spend time and money to identify, recruit, and train volunteers. Good volunteer development is like any other good human resource development. First and foremost, it costs money. Nonprofits must be able to bear the costs of travel, training, supervision, and placement, in addition to administrative costs such as work space and supplies.

Budgets, for example, should include a line item for volunteer travel costs. Basic expenses should be covered. The money should be monitored by the staff and board. If a volunteer chooses to give the cost back in the form of a donation to the nonprofit, that is fine, but no volunteer should be disfranchised from leadership because of a lack of money. This is especially important if we want to include women and minorities, many of whom may not have as many financial resources as white men.

Budgeting for volunteer travel and training is an investment in the future of the organization. Staff people move on to other jobs and other communities. Volunteers offer continuity. There was a time when YMCA staff members stayed at the same Y for twenty years—or an entire career. Now they come and go every few years, leaving the volunteers behind as the more community-anchored group.

If a nonprofit is unwilling to invest in the training and nurturing of competent volunteers, it is probably a weak organization.

Ultimately, policy-making volunteer leaders have the fiduciary responsibility for a nonprofit. They must understand what is going on, how their decisions affect the nonprofit, and how to prevent problems.

Policy volunteers must also set the tone for the organization by inviting both women and minorities to participate fully. Such diversity of experience, culture, economics, and influence can only strengthen the board.

So once again, all volunteers need to be trained and should expect to be trained. In the Y, our work with members often involves activities such as swimming, team sports, camping, youth legislatures, and senior citizen recreation, crafts, and day care. We would not consider sending a staff member or volunteer into a group of young people to play a sport unless we knew that leader was properly trained in safety, the rules of the game, and the interpersonal skills that help people build self-esteem, self-confidence, and self-determination. Why would we consider sending a policy-making or fundraising volunteer into a leadership role without training?

I believe that the YMCA of the USA has some of the finest staff training of any nonprofit in the country. We are often called upon in local communities to train staff and volunteers of other nonprofits. Still, I would like to see policy-making and fundraising volunteers in the YMCA given additional training in skills that would make them better Y leaders and better community leaders.

Let me illustrate what I mean. Years ago, in one of my first Y experiences, I was asked to help raise money for the sustaining drive at my local Y branch. Sustaining money is Y lingo for yearly gifts for the operating budget. It comes from community fundraising and underwrites valuable programs that cannot support themselves. It is also used for what we call *scholarships*—subsidies to people in the community who are unable to pay program fees. Most often, the sustaining dollars go to disadvantaged communities in the area. A common slogan is "Help send a kid to camp."

When I was asked to work in the sustaining campaign, I had never raised money before. The thought was intimidating. How do you ask someone for money and give them nothing in return? How would I know how much to ask for? What if I were a failure?

Our Y had a training session for all board members of the branch. We were allowed to choose who we would call upon for the donation. We reported back as a group each week during the campaign—a forty-five-minute session early in the morning or after work. Progress reports were sent out each week with notes and letters of encouragement. Morale-boosting calls were made by both volunteers and staff to those who were falling behind. It was a group effort, it was fun, and it was a personal challenge.

To my surprise, at the end of the drive I was presented with a plaque for bringing in the most money from new donors. It still hangs in my kitchen. I was proud of my first effort and have since been involved in raising thousands of dollars for the Y, my church, and many other organizations. I have also gone on to train others in fundraising for both capital and sustaining projects and have handled major projects as the lead volunteer.

I should say in passing that a willingness to try to raise money leads to the ability to raise money. That, in turn, will solidify anyone's position—male or female, minority or majority, staff member or volunteer, newcomer or veteran—in the nonprofit world. You are taken seriously.

My attitude has always been this: I want to be trained to do my part. I expect good staff support. I enjoy learning a new skill that can be used in another part of my life, and I am willing to take the time to learn.

I also believe that other volunteers like to be trained in skills that they can use elsewhere. I have had wonderful training as a volunteer in practical subjects such as *Robert's Rules of Order,* techniques for evaluating and writing job descriptions, and interviewing applicants for employment. I also learned about difficult people, effective listening skills, long-range planning, and human resource management, including equal pay, upward mobility, and so on.

All the training has made me a better board member and enhanced my business and leadership skills. Good volunteer training can do the same for other women.

Currently, I am leading an effort to establish a training certification program for YMCA volunteers. It would allow them to select a series of skills they would like to learn, attend a prescribed set of workshops, and be certified as a trained volunteer for the Y. I envision the training as encompassing such areas as finance, human resources, and board development.

For example, a YMCA financial volunteer would learn how to establish a budget, read a financial statement, and understand an audit. Human resources training would provide an overview of current trends, salaries, and availability in the job market for social service providers; laws that affect nonprofit organizations, their volunteers, and their staff; and a review of the kind of personnel policies that YMCAs should establish to protect themselves and their staff members. With each certification, I would expect the volunteer participant to donate a certain number of hours every quarter or every year, sharing their skills with boards of smaller Ys.

City residents often forget that the needs of nonprofits are just as great in smaller communities and rural areas. More than two thirds of the YMCAs in the United States are located in communities with populations of fewer than fifty thousand. The volunteers that make up nonprofit boards in the smaller communities may not have the access to training that those in a bigger city have.

Through this system of training, a truly committed volunteer could bring unusual expertise not only to her YMCA but to other nonprofits in the community—for example, the hospital, the PTA, and the library.

Like staff members, volunteers need to be carefully placed, oriented, and supervised. Volunteers need to be treated as professionals and held accountable for their performance. Recruitment interviews, job descriptions, and regular performance reviews of volunteers should not be seen as insulting or mistrusting but as a testament to the seriousness of the volunteer's contribution.

Voluntarism is a leadership training program. A nonprofit exists to meet community needs, always foremost in designing a volunteer's job. However, leadership development must also be a goal of any volunteer activity. In fact, the most fulfilling volunteer jobs are usually those that meet the most compelling community needs.

It should be clear by now that I am not an advocate of a volunteer activity for the sake of busywork. However, under the right conditions, even a job stuffing and collating could offer personal growth if, for example, it offered someone the chance to form a meaningful friendship with another envelope stuffer.

But personal growth is not synonymous with leadership. I believe that volunteer policy-making and fundraising jobs offer the most opportunities for leadership as well as personal growth. I also believe that women should volunteer for policy positions in organizations in which men are active as volunteers rather than restricting themselves to organizations dominated by women. This was a determination I made years ago, and I believe I am a better leader because of it. It is not because women's organizations with which I have worked (Junior League, League of Women Voters, American Association of University Women, hospital auxiliary, church, and PTA) do not offer growth—but simply that, overall, the organizations dominated by men have traditionally been more powerful and influential.

Once on a policy-making board, women should look to the finance committee and executive search committee, as well as the executive committee, for the best opportunities for leadership development. Membership on the executive committee, of course, usually results from chairing certain committees. Women would do well to gain membership on a committee on which they can excel and then aim to become its chair.

Whether in policy making, fundraising, or a direct service job, the volunteer's assignment should promote the organization as well as personal growth, self-esteem, and leadership. Some may argue that this is appropriate for an organization such as the Y, which has a stated goal of developing leadership skills, but that it would detract from the mission of a nonprofit such as a hospital or a women's shelter. I maintain that leadership development of volunteers should be a major goal of all nonprofits. After all, our ability to fulfill our mission is only as good as the people who carry it out. A well-run business recognizes that in the long run, human resource development is essential to high profits. So, too, a nonprofit should realize that human resource development, including volunteer development, is essential to achieving its goals and carrying out its mission.

Conclusion

To develop volunteers effectively, a nonprofit must abide by the principles and practices I have outlined, recognizing that voluntarism is essential to the nonprofit, that female and minority volunteers are equal to white male volunteers, that nonprofits must spend time and money on volunteer development, and that voluntarism is a leadership program, not a source of free labor.

As these principles are applied, nonprofits must take care to include those who have traditionally been excluded from leadership: women and girls, of course, but also ethnic and racial minorities. Similarly, in seeking opportunities for leadership and growth, women and minorities should seek out those nonprofits that take the principles seriously.

At its best, the voluntary sector is a school for democracy. But it can only be its best if it includes people of all kinds at all levels of decision making.

Finally, take chances. Do not sit back and hope something good will happen to you. Instead, set your goals and go for them.

References

Drucker, P. F. *Managing the Non-Profit Organization.* New York: HarperCollins, 1990.

Hodgkinson, V. A., Weitzman, M. S., Toppe, C. M., and Noga, S. M. *Nonprofit Almanac 1992–93: Dimensions of the Independent Sector.* San Francisco: Jossey-Bass, 1992.

Silver, N. *At the Heart: The New Volunteer Challenge to Community Agencies.* San Francisco: San Francisco Foundation, 1989.

Tocqueville, A. de. *Democracy in America.* New York: Vintage Books, 1945 [1835].

YMCA of the USA, Department of Research and Planning. *1991 YMCA Statistical Summary.* Chicago: YMCA, 1992.

10

Women's Power, Nonprofits, and the Future

Teresa Odendahl

In the early United States, women's primary avenues to power were through their voluntary endeavors and philanthropy. In the nonprofit arena today, women continue to have power: in numbers, as employees and volunteers, and because of their connection to money, as major donors and fundraisers. With notable exceptions, however, women do not tend to serve on the governing boards or in the top staff positions of the most influential or prominent nonprofit organizations.

Those who have studied nonprofits tend to focus on women leaders and the wealthy to a greater extent than the numerically more important and diverse women clerical workers, volunteers who take on routine responsibilities, or those who receive the services of nonprofit agencies. My own research is open to this charge. Despite these caveats and concerns, in this essay I present some of my notions of what the future will look like for women in the nonprofit field. The analysis is not comprehensive but based on both personal experience and my research.

In the next century, most women's opportunities will be less restricted to the world of nonprofits than in the past. While many women will undoubtedly remain involved in nonprofit activities at all levels, presumably women's power base in business and government will continue to expand. Still, change is slow and uneven. It took more than seventy years of organized struggle for women to win the vote and an additional three-quarters of a century for more than two women to serve at the same time in the U.S. Senate.

I have proposed, along with Steinberg and Jacobs in this book, that the nonprofit sector is gendered female. If this is the case, the future of the nonprofit sector will be reflective of more general changes, or lack thereof, in the social construction of gender. Gender is a basic organizing principle in all societies. Labor is divided according to gender. Status is conferred according to gender, with women holding subordinate status to men. Gender, as well as other axes of oppression such as race and class, is at the heart of power relations and has a bearing on the nature of the past and the future.

Invented largely by women, the activities undertaken by nonprofits are often associated with culturally assigned feminine qualities. Historian Sara Evans has described how, "By pioneering in the creation of new public spaces— voluntary associations located *between* the public world of politics and work and the private intimacy of family—women made possible a new vision of active citizenship" (1989, p. 3). Kathleen McCarthy's earlier work and contribution to this book further develop the history of women's nonprofit involvement (McCarthy, 1982, 1990, 1991). Yet despite women's historical and current prominence in the nonprofit sector, the composition of governing boards, where power is said to reside, still mirrors and supports pervasive class, ethnic-racial, and gender discrimination throughout the nonprofit system and society.

Our understanding of women in the nonprofit sector is complicated by issues of class and color. Women vary considerably from person to person, whatever their class, ethnicity, or race. They have different jobs, opinions, and personalities. Generalizations lead to contradictions and exceptions. Women of color have always been involved in nonprofit, self-help, and religious endeavors, but their voluntary or paid work is rarely acknowledged in the literature. In contrast, wealthy white women, because of their higher class status and funding capabilities, are often trustees of the more prestigious nonprofit organizations. Even when white women serve on major boards, however, they typically plan the parties while men make the policies. And poorly paid women of color often do work in wealthy women's homes, allowing the more privileged white women to volunteer. Where upper-class women exude glamor and glitz on the charity scene, women of color become invisible. The sector may be gendered female but colored white and ranked upper class in terms of ideology and image.

Thus, the future is likely to be different for women of color than it will be for white or rich women as compared to poor women. These, of course, are just the stark contrasts. Middle-class women, whatever their color, serve in limited numbers on boards. Middle-class women are the majority of volunteers with less status. And middle-class women hold the vast majority of non-executive, paid jobs. They are lawyers and secretaries. One problem with accurately presenting the nuanced relationships of class, color, and gender to nonprofit issues, or making predictions, is that there is little research directly on women as nonprofit consumers, employees, or volunteers. Do women of color gain power through their nonprofit activities, or are they less well off in the sector because of low wages? Do wealthy women exploit poorer women and men through their voluntary endeavors? Have white women advanced professionally at the expense of people of color, including other women?

Nonprofit activities are often an extension of work done in the family. In fact, voluntary organizations are patterned on the patriarchal family. Men are the fathers who make policy. Boards of the most prestigious organizations with big budgets have always been dominated by upper-class white men who have held on to their power. Women do important work but only in certain contexts and often with little recognition. When women take on leadership positions as staff members or volunteers in nonprofit organizations, they carry their assumed family status with them. Whether they are or want to be mothers, women "seem" to be, and in fact they do the maintenance and nurturing work associated with woman = motherhood.

Thus, while acknowledging women's agency in forming a new arena for the exercise of power, nonprofit activities may actually have limited many women, keeping them busy in a single arena doing the same kinds of things women do in the family. Nonprofit ideology and work reinforces gender stereotypes about women's proper roles. In addition, there is substantial evidence that the sector has assisted in the exploitation of the poor, people of color, and women (Funiciello, 1993; Katz, 1986; Piven and Cloward, 1971). To a large extent, both the "femaleness" and the potentially oppressive nature of many nonprofit enterprises may be explained by the lack of capital and the heavy use of voluntary labor. Women constitute the vast majority of nonprofit employees, whether they work for pay or not. Less than 9 percent of the nonprofit workforce is compensated. The Western cultural value of money is such that, like work in the home, work done for free is viewed as less valuable.

Furthermore, when compared to other economic sectors, nonprofit endeavors are generally thought to be derived from or subsidiary to government or money-making activities. There is a widely held, but unexamined, assumption that in the American context, real power and status can only be gained from for-profit endeavors. Nonprofit activities are auxiliary to "real life." If women want to be players, they must gain power in government and the for-profit sector.

Nonetheless, the nonprofit arena is apt to be a locus of the struggles for power in the future. The wealthy may increase their exercise of power through their voluntary endeavors (see Odendahl, 1990), and the not-so-new class war (Piven and Cloward, 1971 and 1982) may be waged in and around the nonprofit sector. The ideas that lead to equity are more likely to emerge from nonprofit than for-profit or government activities. Thus, the nonprofit sector is full of contradictions. It serves as an arena for creating a new kind of future for the poor, people of color, and women, while it is at the same time a nexus for many activities of the power elite.

Power in Numbers

Women comprise more than half the total population. Feminists and women's advocacy groups have long recognized that if women were to act in solidarity, they would be able to take the power that has been denied them. Once again, women are a diverse group with varying interests and perspectives. Although women have numbers on their side, they have not been unified.

In this regard, there will be a continuing and growing role for women's advocacy groups, almost all of which operate as part of the nonprofit world. The advocacy groups which bring women and others together, however, do not necessarily envision the same futures. The anti-abortion and pro-choice movements are a vivid example of a conflict in the larger society about the appropriate roles and power of women that is being played out in the nonprofit arena. In order to receive money and recognition, both sides are organized as nonprofits. Both depend on grass-roots and more elite support to maintain their operations. More money is being harnessed than ever before for "women's concerns," including what I see as opposing women's interests. But the connection of numbers, power, and funding is not necessarily clear. I start with the numbers, although much of the importance of numbers is a matter of perception.

Continuing with the current reproductive rights battles as illustrative, national polls indicate that more than 80 percent of all Americans favor women's right to choose whether to have an abortion (American Public Opinion Index, 1992, p. 6, 8; Gallup Poll, 1993, pp. 115–6; Harris Poll, 1992, p. 3). The anti-abortion movement has a relatively small but incredibly well-organized constituency that draws most followers from the religious right (also part of the nonprofit sector). One of the leading critics of the religious right, Suzanne Pharr, has written about the contradictions within church-based nonprofit activities:

While both the Christian Right and the Civil Rights movements of the 60's were church-based, they were completely opposite in point of view. The Civil Rights Movement put forth the message that true democracy calls for justice, liberation, and participation, and that call was heard by oppressed groups throughout the country, creating a basis for other movements, and giving hope to disenfranchised people for the future. The white Christian Right Movement put forth the message that inclusion and participation by diverse groups will destroy the order of the 40's and 50's when segregation was legally enforced, male authority was unchallenged by women as a class, and lesbians and gay men were invisible. It called for a return to the past.

301

During the 70's and 80's, the Christian Right had considerable success in their attack against the gains of the Civil Rights Movement. In particular, they gained strength through initiating a campaign against homosexuality led by Anita Bryant, the defeat of the ERA lead by the Eagle Forum, and the attack against abortion rights led by Operation Rescue [1992, p. 2].

The anti-abortion movement has made itself seem huge and effectively uses the media to assist in perpetuating that perception. Men hold more leadership roles in the movement than women and may participate in larger numbers. Media, public relations, and organizing strategy are more important than numbers for this movement (Petchesky, 1990, pp. 241–262).

Moving away from women's nonprofit causes, how do numbers apply to nonprofit workers? More than 5 million women are paid employees within the nonprofit sector, and another 50 million women volunteer each year. In this century, a shift has occurred—from genteel women volunteers actually running the agencies they formed to increasing numbers of women in paid professional and managerial roles. At the same time, the numbers of women in poorly paid clerical and care-giving jobs in the sector are rising. In hard economic times, the lower-status positions are frequently the first cut, and volunteers are sought to do the work. Thus, another tension exists in the nonprofit arena about the value of women's work and potentially between volunteers and paid employees.

Despite the massive numbers of volunteers, practical wisdom holds that as more women enter the paid labor force, they have less time to volunteer. An additional 10 million women entered the paid labor force in the last decade. By the turn of the century, just as many women as men will be employed for pay. Many agencies report a declining volunteer population, although this may be offset by increasing numbers of older and retired people working in voluntary capacities. In addition, many young people start their careers as interns and volunteers.

I predict that outside of board-level jobs, most of the meaningful or more responsible positions of authority within nonprofits eventually will be paid. As they are today, voluntary positions will largely be supportive. The better wages, status, and position parity for women managers and professionals in the nonprofit field, and access to more prestigious jobs, will continue to make such employment attractive, but—as Preston has pointed out in this book—more so for professional white women than professional women of color.

The trend is toward increasing feminization, professionalization, and racialism. This is evidence of the contradictions inherent in women's paid position in the nonprofit field. The apparent opportunities available to women are better for white than black women. According to Preston, "By 1991, in both the nonprofit and government sectors . . . 10 percent more black women than white women held the less prestigious clerical and sales jobs" (see Chapter Two). (We do not have enough information on other women of color.) I believe that when such an indication of inequity is present, it is incorrect to present the sector as good for working women.

At the same time, bigger nonprofit workplaces such as

303

hospitals and universities are and will be fertile grounds for unionization. Clerical and technical workers, nurses, and other medical personnel are among the occupations for which union membership can increase wages, benefits, and respect. Using clerical work as an example, 80 percent of all full-time workers and 86 percent of all part-time workers in this category are women. The earnings of secretarial and clerical workers, as with all other "women's" jobs, are central to family income. But wages are low: "[T]he median weekly earnings for full-time, non-supervisory secretaries and clericals in female-intensive occupations are $300 . . . Among the most successful strategies for increasing the earnings of secretarial and clerical workers is union membership or coverage by a union contract" (Institute for Women's Policy Research Fact Sheet, n.d.). A recent study indicates that union membership benefits all groups but provides the highest returns for black and Hispanic women and men (National Displaced Homemakers Network and Institute for Women's Policy Research, n.d.).

The Power of Money

Many women have more access to money than ever before. They are earning it, raising it, and giving it away. This would seem to indicate that women's power through money is increasing in the nonprofit arena. Yet women often do not have the same kind of control over their funds as men. Usually, even women's class status is attached to that of the men in their lives. For example, a low-paid woman clerical worker may well have middle-class status if she is married to a professional man. And a woman who does not earn any income may be considered upper class because of inheritance or marriage. Only poor single women are assigned lower-class status in their own right, a dubious distinction (Amott and Matthaei, 1991, pp. 24–25).

Women are increasingly supporting our families, and low-wage employment has risen, especially for mothers. "Women of color are four times more likely, white women three times more likely, and men of color 1.6 times more likely than white men to be low wage workers, when controlling for factors such as human capital, industrial structure, and demographics" (National Displaced Homemakers Network and Institute for Women's Policy Research, 1989, p. 19). Once again, the power of money depends on how much discretionary income women have and how they are able to use it.

Women's foundations and federations represent a new kind of philanthropy in which women of all classes are participating by donating money and time, as well as making decisions about grants and allocations. Nearly sixty funds, in different stages of development, belong to the National Network of Women's Funds. From 1985 to 1992, they collected cash contributions in excess of $80 million. Their primary goal is to target grants for women and girls in order "to change the conditions that keep women and girls from achieving their full potential" (National Network of Women's Funds, n.d., p. 5). Women's funds are attempting to redress the fact that in the last two decades, only 2 to 4 percent of institutional philanthropic money has gone specifically to programs for women and girls (Ford Foundation, 1979; Foundation Center, 1988). Many of these public women's funds are also committed to building bridges between women of all classes and races. Scholars need to learn more about the giving patterns of women. Mixer's chapter in this book indicates that fundraisers are beginning to recognize the benefits of targeting professional and wealthy women donors for gifts. With more women entering the labor force, more money will be raised through workplace contribution programs. Because of the availability of many different campaigns, I predict that women will be less likely to give to the United Way than their male corporate peers, and more likely to direct their gifts to alternative groups such as Women's Way and others represented by the National Alliance for Choice in Giving.

The remainder of this section focuses on wealthy women philanthropists, because they tend to exercise more power in the nonprofit arena than those in other classes. A woman who married a millionaire was candid: "Giving money is very powerful." But upper-class women are both privileged and subordinate. They have less authority and status than the men of their class. One woman of wealth told me, "Men who marry money suddenly wind up with power over that money, whereas women do not." And a wealthy woman fundraiser and giver said, "Most of the wives are not free to make the final decision. It always involves two calls. I call and they say, 'I'll ask my husband what I can give this year.' . . . I have not had one woman say to me, 'Yes, I will give you X number of dollars for my gift this year' . . . There is not much independent giving."

Through their donations and involvement in voluntary organizations, however, charitable rich women exert enormous influence in society. As philanthropists, they acquire status within and outside their class. I have the impression that wealthy women may be more prone to give to basic human services than the men of their class, but rich women also remain the champions and promoters of arts and cultural organizations at the community level.

Women play a particular role in passing the culture of the elite from generation to generation through the socialization of their children, the support of their husbands, and their nonprofit activities. Wealthy women are taught to become involved in charitable activities, but they are expected to support conventional causes, and often to do their work behind the scenes (Daniels, 1988; Ostrander, 1984). They may also identify women with new money and bring them into the culture of philanthropy.

Sallie Bingham, the well-known Louisville newspaper heiress who has questioned the privilege of her own and other women's wealth, has written, "Most rich women are invisible; we are the faces that appear behind well-known men, floating up to the surface infrequently, palely; the big contributors, often anonymous, to approved charities, or the organizers of fundraising events. Rich women have been so well rewarded by an unjust system that we have lost our voices; we are captives, as women are captives, of a system that deprives us of our identities" (1986, p. 48). In general, female philanthropists are not empowered. The women's movement came to them fifteen or twenty years later than to other classes. Wealthy women risk losing more economic security and status than other women in contesting a system that privileges them.

307

Whether they are the daughters, granddaughters, or sisters of millionaires, whether they have married up or down, elite women's lives follow similar patterns, because they are structured by gender, class, and culture. Their status is derived from that of the men: husbands, fathers, or brothers who made or manage the fortunes. Their class standing is contingent on having surplus money that they did not earn, much of which is tied up in trusts. Their cultural prestige is based on giving interest income away to the right causes and working as volunteers with nonprofit organizations.

Shaping a Future with Power for Women

We need to rethink the nature of power, although that is not the intent of this essay. I envision a future in which power is shared, distributed with some form of equity. I believe women will gain this new kind of power only in unity with all other oppressed peoples. I hope for a world that honors diversity and inclusivity. Thus, I see much of the work ahead in coalition among peoples of color, people with disabilities, people with various sexual orientations, and women globally. Through collective action, these groups need to be more vocal and demand recognition as well as equal representation.

I can envision several futures. In the one I want, a nonprofit sector might not need to exist. Women and people of all colors would have a wide range of options and opportunities. Status differences based on income and wealth would be minimal. The government would have full responsibility for seeing that no one, and especially no children, go hungry, live without roofs over their heads or in inadequate housing, or lack good education and health care. My dream for the future may not be widely shared. And, the realist in me recognizes that this is not necessarily the direction in which we are moving as a society.

My short-term view is cynical. I predict a continuing backlash which threatens to make even more stark divisions based on class, color, and gender. But I think this will be followed by more organized struggle against the forces of individual greed and self-interest. I still hold on to my utopian vision of equity and social justice as possibilities, given the right conditions. Nothing will change suddenly. It will take the organizing efforts, hard work, and votes of millions of dedicated people who finally will not stand for things the way they are. My daughter may help make a new world, but I do not expect to see the wide-ranging changes I hope for in my lifetime.

In a very real sense, a world with shared power has no need for a "gendered" sector, or a special place for doing "women's work." As I indicated earlier, however, the long-term advocacy that might accomplish these goals is likely to come out of what is called the nonprofit sector today. In any event, I urge women to continue making more inroads in the public arena, including politics. We need to vote our consciences, as well as be appointed and elected to office. We need to run companies of all sizes. We need to set up new methods of providing goods and services.

We need to advocate for more women of all abilities, ages, backgrounds, classes, colors, and sexual orientations on the boards of directors of nonprofit organizations. If

309

we were able to change the basic character of governing boards, then perhaps we could overcome other forms of inequity. I also support finding more democratic methods of forming boards, rather than the current standard of exclusionary, self-constituting bodies.

Nowhere is the principle of comparable worth more meaningful than in nonprofit jobs. We must develop systems, job evaluation or otherwise, for valuing women's work more highly and raising wages and benefits so that every adult makes a fair family wage. We also need to value voluntarism. Perhaps in the future, we could all work half time for pay and half time as volunteers. We would have time to be with our families and do the things we care about.

References

American Public Opinion Index 1992, Vol. 1. Bethesda, Md.: Opinion Research Services Publishing, 1993.

Amott, T. L., and Matthaei, J. *Race, Gender, and Work: A Multicultural Economic History of Women in the United States.* Boston: South End Press, 1991.

Bingham, S. "The Truth About Growing Up Rich." *Ms.* June 1986, pp. 48–50, 82–83.

Daniels, A. K. *Invisible Careers: Women Civic Leaders from the Volunteer World.* Chicago: University of Chicago Press, 1988.

Evans, S. M. *Born for Liberty: A History of Women in America.* New York: Free Press, 1989.

Ford Foundation. *Financial Support of Women's Programs in the 1970s.* New York: Ford Foundation, 1979.

Foundation Center. *Grants for Women and Girls.* New York: Foundation Center, 1988.

Funiciello, T. *Tyranny of Kindness: Dismantling the Welfare System to End Poverty in America.* New York: Atlantic Monthly Press, 1993.

Gallup, G. *The Gallup Poll, Public Opinion 1992.* Delaware: Scholarly Resources Inc., 1993.

Harris Poll, Charlotte, N.C.: Institute for Social Research, University of North Carolina, June 19, 1992, Creators Syndicate Inc., Microfiche, #51.

Institute for Women's Policy Research. "Research-in-Brief, Raises and Recognition: Secretaries, Clerical Workers and the Union Wage Premium." Washington, D.C.: Institute for Women's Policy Research, n.d.

Katz, M. B. *In the Shadow of the Poorhouse: A Social History of Welfare in America.* New York: Basic Books, 1986.

McCarthy, K. D. *Noblesse Oblige: Charity and Cultural Philanthropy in Chicago, 1849–1929.* Chicago: University of Chicago Press, 1982.

McCarthy, K. D. (ed.). *Lady Bountiful Revisited: Women, Philanthropy, and Power.* New Brunswick, N.J.: Rutgers University Press, 1990.

McCarthy, K. D. *Women's Culture: American Philanthropy and Art, 1830–1930.* Chicago: University of Chicago Press, 1991.

National Displaced Homemakers Network and Institute for Women's Policy Research. *Low-Wage Jobs and Workers: Trends and Option for Change.* Washington, D.C.: National Displaced Homemakers Network, n.d.

National Network of Women's Funds. *Changing the Face of Philanthropy: 1985–1992 Report.* St. Paul, Minnesota: National Network of Women's Funds, n.d.

Odendahl, T. *Charity Begins at Home: Generosity and Self-Interest Among the Philanthropic Elite.* New York: Basic Books, 1990.

Ostrander, S. A. *Women of the Upper Class.* Philadelphia: Temple University Press, 1984.

Petchesky, R. P. *Abortion and Woman's Choice: The State, Sexuality, & Reproductive Freedom.* Boston: Northeastern University Press, 1990.

Pharr, S. "The Christian Right: A Threat to Democracy." *Transformation* 7(5), September/October, 1992, pp. 1–9.

Piven, F. F. and Cloward, R. A. *Regulating the Poor.* New York: Pantheon Books, 1971.

Piven, F. F., and Cloward, R. A. *The New Class War: Reagan's Attack on the Welfare State and Its Consequences.* New York: Pantheon, 1982.

CONFERENCE PARTICIPANTS

Conference on Women, Power, and Status
in the Nonprofit Sector
November 15–18, 1992

Melanie Beene
Melanie Beene and
  Associates
Sausalito, CA

Robert O. Bothwell
Executive Director
National Committee for
  Responsive Philanthropy
Washington, D.C.

Betsy Brill
Director
Sophia Fund of the Chicago
  Foundation for Women
Chicago, IL

Eleanor L. Brilliant
Associate Professor
School of Social Work
Rutgers University
New Brunswick, NJ

Lynn C. Burbridge
Deputy Director
Center for Research on
  Women
Wellesley College
Wellesley, MA

Becky Cain, President
League of Women Voters of
  the United States
Washington, D.C.

Mary Ellen S. Capek
Executive Director
National Council for
   Research on Women
New York, NY

Emmett D. Carson
Program Officer
Governance & Public Policy
   Program
The Ford Foundation
New York, NY

Susan Church
Executive Director
The Michigan Women's
   Foundation
Lansing, MI

Stephanie Clohesy
Associate Program Director
W. K. Kellogg Foundation
Battle Creek, MI

Mary Anna Colwell
Consultant
Corte Madera, CA

Arlene Kaplan Daniels
Professor of Sociology
Northwestern University
Evanston, IL

Jean E. Fairfax, Director
The Black Presence in
   Organized Philanthropy
   Project
Association of Black
   Foundation Executives
Phoenix, AZ

Tracy Gary
Executive Director
Resourceful Women
San Francisco, CA

Margaret Gates
Executive Director
Girls, Inc.
New York, NY

Antonia Hernández
President & General Counsel
Mexican American Legal
   Defense & Educational
   Fund
Los Angeles, CA

Anne L. Hoblitzelle
Consultant
San Francisco, CA

Helen Hunt
President
The Hunt Alternatives Fund
New York, NY

Patricia F. Lewis
President and CEO
National Society of Fund
   Raising Executives
Alexandria, VA

Juanita Tamayo Lott
President
Tamayo Lott Associates
Silver Springs, MD

Brooke W. Mahoney
Director
Volunteer Consulting Group
New York, NY

Barbara H. Marion
President
Marion Fundraising Counsel
San Francisco, CA

Kathleen D. McCarthy
Director
Center for the Study of
    Philanthropy
The Graduate School
City University of New York
New York, NY

Joseph R. Mixer
Consultant
Berkeley, CA

Carol Mollner
Executive Director
National Network of
    Women's Funds
St. Paul, MN

Helen Neuborne
Executive Director
N.O.W. Legal Defense and
    Education Fund
New York, NY

Teresa Odendahl
Executive Director
National Network of
    Grantmakers
San Diego, CA

Michael O'Neill
Professor and Director
Institute for Nonprofit
    Organization Management
College of Professional Studies
University of San Francisco
San Francisco, CA

Susan Packard Orr
President
Technology Resource
    Assistance Center
Menlo Park, CA

Susan Ostrander
Professor
Sociology Department
Tufts University
Medford, MA

Anne E. Preston
Associate Professor
W. Averell Harriman School
    for Management and
    Policy
State University of New York
Stony Brook, NY

Barbara C. Roper
Chair, National Board of
    YMCAs
President, Contour Groves
Winter Garden, FL

Judith Saidel
Executive Director
Center for Women and
    Government
State University of New York
Albany, NY

Bernice Sandler
Senior Associate
Center for Women Policy
    Studies
Washington, D.C.

Cecilia M. Sandoval
Senior Vice President of
    Planning and Community
    Service
United Way of Los Angeles
Los Angeles, CA

Kary Schulman
Director, Grants for the Arts
San Francisco Hotel Tax Fund
San Francisco, CA

Ronnie J. Steinberg
Professor
Department of Sociology
Temple University
Philadelphia, PA

M. Frances Van Loo
Associate Professor
Haas School of Business
    Administration
University of California
Berkeley, CA

Candace Widmer
Associate Professor of
    Human Services
Elmira College
Elmira, NY

Nancy Wiltsek
Charitable Contributions
    Consultant
RCM Capital Management
    Charitable Fund
San Francisco, CA

INDEX

A

Abel, E. K., 137, 148
Abramovitz, M., 146, 148
Abzug, R., 193, 212
Acker, J., 92, 93, 96, 99–100, 101, 113–114, 155, 178
Addams, J., 3, 81
African-American women: on boards, 186, 191; early roles of, 3–4, 32, 123–124, 166; fundraising by, 230–232; in labor market, 42, 47, 50, 52, 59, 69–70, 71; and occupational structure, 129–131, 137–138. *See also* Women of color
Alford, Ver Schave & Associates, and fundraising, 230
Alpha Kappa Alpha Sorority, and fundraising, 231
American Association of Retired Persons, size of, 271
American Association of University Women: boards of, 186, 196, 291; founding of, 168

American Automobile Association, size of, 271
American Female Moral Reform Society, history of, 19–20
American Prospect Research Association, and fundraising, 229, 249
American Public Opinion Index, 301, 310
American Red Cross: and diversity, 259; founding of, 3; volunteers for, 267
American Symphony Orchestra League, 191, 212
Amott, T. L., 305, 310
Anheier, H., 91, 101, 115
Appalachian women, quilts by, 28
Armstrong, P., 86, 114
Asian-American women: fundraising by, 232–233; and government employment, 124. *See also* Women of color
Asian Americans and Pacific Islanders in Philanthropy, 158, 178

Assimilationism, history of, 23–24
Association for Healthcare Philanthropy (AHP), and fundraising, 228, 238
Association of Governing Boards of Universities and Colleges: and fundraising, 244; and women members, 190, 212
Association of Junior Leagues, boards of, 199
Auchincloss, L., 203, 212

B

Babchuk, N., 192, 212
Baker, P., 26, 35
Baltzell, E. D., 185, 213
Barnett, R. C., 136, 137, 152
Barthel, D., 94, 114
Bartke, S. L., 206, 213
Barton, C., 3, 11
Baruch, G. K., 136, 137, 152
Baughman, J. C., 185, 213
Baumol, W. J., 140, 148–149
Bearse, P. J., 125, 154
Beauvoir, S. de, 198, 213
Beecher, C., 3
Benefits, and occupational structure, 135–136, 138–139, 147. *See also* Pay equity
Berg, B., 17, 19, 35
Bergmann, B. R., 95, 114, 133, 149
Bingham, S., 307, 310
Birmingham, N. T., 203, 204, 213
Black women. *See* African-American women; Women of color
Blegen, M. A., 134, 149
Block, F., 83, 84, 114
Boards of nonprofits: analysis of women on, 183–221; and class status, 184, 197–207; of colleges and universities, 189–190; current status of, 183–188; data needed on, 210–211; diversity on, 159, 258–259; of foundations, 190–191, 258; and gender as statistical indicator, 188–194; and history of nonprofits, 32–33; and power,

187–188, 191, 202, 207, 209; responsibilities of, 278–281; theory building for, 207–212; women policy makers on, 194–197; of women's organizations, 185–186, 196, 211–212
Bonavoglia, A., 175, 178
Bonilla-Santiago, S., 123, 149
Bordo, S., 206, 213
Boris, E. T., 190–191, 214
Boston area: board members in, 192, 193; fundraisers in, 233–234, 235
Bound, J., 40, 60, 76
Bowen, W. G., 140, 148–149
Brabson, H. V., 134, 137, 149
Brewer, J. J., 240, 250
Brody, D. A., 214
Brootkowski, J., 183, 188, 196–197, 217
Brownmiller, S., 206, 214
Bryant, A., 302
Burbridge, L. C., 14, 121, 135, 149, 165, 178

C

Cal Douglas & Associates, and fundraising, 235
California Board and Commission Project, 196–197
Calish, B., 206
Caminiti, S., 6, 15
Canada, nurses in, 86, 103–112
Capek, M.E.S., 189–190, 214
Carnegie, A., 23
Carroll, S. J., 195, 214
Carson, E. D., 124, 149, 166, 177, 178–179, 186, 210, 214
Catalyst, 195, 214, 248
Census of Service Industries, 73
Central Florida Commission on the Status of Women, 269
Central Florida Metro YMCA, board of, 282–283
Certified Fund Raising Executive, 227
Chapkis, W., 206, 214
Charity galas, and women, 203–207
Cherniss, C., 134, 136, 137, 149

Chess, W. A., 134, 136, 137, 151
Chicago: fundraisers in, 234; hospital boards in, 198; minority communities in, 177
Childress, R., 228, 249
Choy, S., 86, 114
Christian Right Movement, 301–302
Chusmir, L. H., 240, 249
City University of New York, Center for the Study of Philanthropy at, 25
Civil Rights Act of 1964, 39–40, 48, 70
Civil Rights Movement, 301–302
Clarke, L., 91, 114
Class status: and board membership, 184, 197–207; future for, 297–298, 304–305; in history of nonprofits, 21–22, 33; role of, 9
Cleveland, board members in, 193
Clinton administration, 146
Cloward, R. A., 299, 300, 312
Collaboration, history of, 18–25
Collectivism, history of, 17
Colleges and universities: boards of, 189–190; fundraising for, 227–228, 230–231, 244
Colored Female Religious and Moral Society, early role of, 3–4
Commission on Private Philanthropy and Public Needs, 155, 170, 179
Comparable worth: in future, 310; and job evaluations, 104–105
Compensating differentials: in nonprofits, 84–90; and occupational structure, 138
Conflict, history of, 18–25
Connell, R. W., 100, 114
Conry, J. C., 224, 242, 250
Cortés, M., 158, 179
Cott, N. F., 17, 19, 35
Council for Advancement and Support of Education (CASE), and fundraising, 227–228, 230, 238
Council on Foundations (COF), 190, 191, 214

Covelli, L., 184, 200, 215
Cox, C., 203, 204, 215
Crowder, N. L., 238, 250
Cutlip, S. M., 224, 250

D

Daniels, A. K., 9, 15–16, 81, 94, 101, 115, 171, 179, 183, 201–202, 205, 215, 307, 310
Davis, A. Y., 123, 149
Decker, P. J., 240, 250
Decorative art societies, history of, 27–28
Delta Research and Educational Foundation, and fundraising, 231
Demographics: aspects of changing, 155–182; background on, 155–157; conclusion on, 177–178; and data utility, 169–174; and expanding roles of women, 164–167; and feminization of fundraising, 225–228; implications of, 157–160; and nature of nonprofit work, 160–163; and women's organizations, 167–169, 175–176; of work force, 264–265
Derrickson, M. C., 122, 150
Detlefson, E. G., 236, 252
Detmold, J. H., 244, 250
Devaluation: in fundraising, 241–243; of women's work, 299, 302
DiMaggio, P. J., 91, 101, 115, 212
Diner, H. R., 33, 35
Discrimination, and occupational structure, 133–134, 137–138. See also Racism; Sexism
Dix, D., 3, 11
Dodge, Mrs. H. E., 205
Domhoff, G. W., 185, 215
Dou, T., 83, 115
Douglas, C., 235
Driscoll, D. M., 235
Drucker, P. F., 275–277, 280–281, 293
Duke, R. C., 204
Dunne, D., 205, 215
Dye, T. R., 185, 215

E

Eagle Forum, 302
Eccles, J. S., 236, 250
Eckerd College, board of, 269
Eddy, M. B., 3
Education, and labor market, 40, 50–52, 58
Educational services, occupational structure in, 126–127, 129–130, 131–132, 142, 144
Ellis, M. R., 214
Emily's List, 11
Employment. See Labor market
Empowerment, redefined, 175
England, P., 83, 115
Equal Pay Act of 1963, 40
Equal Rights Amendment, 302
Erkut, S., 187, 215
Estes, C., 91, 114
Ethnicity. See Race and ethnicity
Evans, S. M., 20, 35, 296–297, 310

F

Falon, J., 192, 194, 217–218
Farkas, G., 83, 115
Fastenau, P. S., 134, 150
Federal Reserve System, as nonprofit, 7
Feldberg, R., 90, 115, 135, 137, 143, 150
Feldman, P., 136, 137, 150
Fenn, D. H., 188, 215
Ferguson, T., 249, 251
Ferris, J. M., 141, 150
Fimian, M. J., 134, 150
Fisher, A. B., 197, 216
Flexner, E., 18, 36
Ford Foundation: grants from, 259, 305, 310; as nonprofit, 6
Foundation Center, 305, 311
Foundations: boards of, 190–191, 258; women's, 305–306
Franklin, B., 274
Freeman, S.J.M., 247, 250
Friedkin, R., 91, 102, 117
Frieze, I. H., 236, 252
Fugate, D. L., 240, 250
Fundraising: aspects of, 223–253; background on, 223–225; barriers to choice in, 238–241; charity galas for, 203–207; conclusion on, 248–249; devaluation of, 241–243; feminization of, 224, 225–229; functions of, 245–246; glass ceiling in, 234–236; as management function, 245–248; and occupational choice, 236–238; as social exchange, 245; stereotypes of, 243–245; training for, 288–289; women of color in, 229–233; and women's organizations, 231–232, 233–234
Funiciello, T., 299, 311

G

Gallagher, M. E., 198–199, 219
Gallegos, H. E., 124, 150, 186, 216
Gallup Poll, 185, 217, 301, 311
Gardner, I. S., 3, 24
Gaventa, J., 101, 115
Gender: concept of, 92–93, 112–113; division of labor by, 96–99, 202, 296; ignoring, 80–82; as statistical indicator, 188–194; and wage determination, 102–103
General Motors, as for-profit, 7
Gerson, J., 89, 115
Ghiloni, B. W., 183, 216
Giddings, P., 124, 150
Ginzberg, E., 124, 150
Ginzberg, L. D., 26–27, 36
Gittell, M., 172, 179, 191, 216
Goff, W., 231
Goldin, C., 39, 40, 43, 47, 76
Gordon, C. W., 192, 212
Government: employees of, 37–72; spending trends by, 139–146
Graddy, E., 141, 150
Grant, J., 241, 250
Gray, B. H., 212
Gray, D., 98, 115
Greene, S., 74, 77
Gronau, R., 133, 150–151

Growe, S., 98, 115
Guedj, K. R., 214

H

Hackett, E. J., 41, 60, 76
Haley, M., 203, 216
Hall, C., 151
Hall, H., 233, 244, 250–251
Hall, P. D., 81, 115–116, 188, 210, 211, 216
Hansmann, H., 141, 151, 163, 179
Harris, L., 301, 311
Hartmann, H., 96, 108, 120
Hayghe, H. V., 183, 217
Health services, occupational structure in, 126–128, 129–130, 131–132, 135, 139–141, 142–143, 145
Heinkel, J., 74, 77
Helgesen, S., 247, 251
Heller, M., 196, 197, 218
Henke, R., 86, 114
Hernàndez, A. C., 10, 231–232, 251, 255
Hewitt, N. A., 17, 20, 21–22, 33, 36
Hiestand, D. L., 124, 150
Hilgert, C., 242, 251
Hine, D. C., 32, 36, 124, 151
Hispanics in Philanthropy, 258. *See also* Latinas
History of nonprofits: aspects of, 17–38, 122–125, 161–162; background on, 17–18; collaboration and conflict in, 18–25; of collectivism, 17; conclusions on, 34–35; political and economic power in, 25–31; and practitioners, 31–34
Hodgkinson, V. A., 1, 16, 40, 76, 94, 102, 116, 125, 126, 140, 151, 157, 159, 162, 163, 170–171, 179–180, 183, 185, 189, 217, 223, 238, 250, 251, 280, 293
Hopkins, E., 203, 204, 205, 206, 207, 217
Hospitals: fundraising for, 228–229; and pay equity, 103–112
Howes, C., 134, 135, 154

I

IBM, as for-profit, 7
Independent Sector, and volunteers, 280
Independent sector: concept of, 155–156, 170–171; employees of, 156–157, 159. *See also* Nonprofit sector
Indian women. *See* Native American women
Institute for Women's Policy Research, 304, 305, 311–312
Internal Revenue Service, and tax exemption, 2, 6, 169
Irish-Catholic women, early role of, 4

J

Jackson, R., 277–278
Jacobs, J. A., 14, 79, 86, 88, 107, 116, 122, 296
Jang, D., 166, 180
Jayaratne, S., 134, 136, 137, 149, 151
Jenner, J. R., 183, 199, 202, 217
Jewish women, early role of, 4
Job evaluation system, and pay equity, 104–110
Johnson, G., 40, 60, 76
Johnson, K., 249, 251
Johnson, R. D., 241, 251
Johnston, D., 197, 217
Jones, C. A., 134, 137, 149
Jones, P. A., 136, 137, 151
Jones-McClintic, S., 141, 152
Junior League, boards of, 199, 291

K

Kamerer, J. B., 214
Kane, N. M., 136, 137, 150
Kang, C. H., 212
Kanter, R. M., 83, 97, 100, 102, 116
Karasek, R. A., 125, 154
Karl, B. D., 30, 36
Karnow, S., 124, 151
Karpilow, K., 183, 188, 196–197, 217

Katz, M. B., 123, 151, 299, 311
Katz, S. N., 30, 36
Ketchum, Inc., and fundraising, 234
Kettner, P. M., 141, 152
Kilbourne, B., 83, 115
Kimmich, M. H., 137, 151
Kleeman, K. E., 183, 195, 217
Konrad, W., 195, 217
Korn/Ferry International, 195, 217
Kraditor, A., 21, 36
Kramer, R. M., 141, 154

L

Labor donation, and pay equity, 88–89, 111
Labor market: analysis of, 39–77; background on, 39–42; black women in, 42, 47, 50, 52, 59, 69–70, 71; changing patterns in, 52–59; conclusion on, 70–72; data on, 42–44; demographics of, 264–265; managerial positions in, 47, 53, 55, 57, 58–59, 65, 67–68, 71; occupational distributions in, 44–59; participation in, 39–40, 125, 303; part-time workers in, 50–51, 62, 72; professional positions in, 45–48, 53–58, 66, 67; religious workers in, 66, 71; scientists and engineers in, 64, 68; and wage and salary comparisons, 42, 59–70, 75–76; young, inexperienced women in, 48–49, 55, 58, 66–68
Latinas: experiences of, 255–266; fundraising by, 232; history of commitment by, 123–124; and occupational structure, 129–131. See also Women of color
Laubach Literacy International, National Board of, 269
Leadership: principles and practices for, 274–292; voluntarism as training for, 270, 291–292
League of Women Voters, boards of, 196, 291
Lee, D., 166, 180

Legal Aid Foundation of Los Angeles, Latina lawyer with, 256, 260–261
Legal issues, for boards, 279
Legal services, occupational structure in, 126–128, 131–132
Levy, F., 139, 152
Links, The, and fundraising, 231
Loden, M., 246–247, 251
Loeser, H., 192, 194, 217–218
Looney, C. A., 226
Lopez, J. A., 248, 251
Lopez, N., 232
Los Angeles, minority communities in, 177, 256–266
Los Angeles Center for Law and Justice, 256
Los Angeles County Hospital, and Latinas, 261
Lott, J. T., 7, 155, 180
Love, R. S., 230
Lukes, S., 101, 116
Lummis, A., 95, 116
Lyon, M., 3

M

McCarthy, K. D., 10–11, 17, 26, 27, 36–37, 94, 116, 161, 162, 165, 171, 180, 186, 211–212, 218, 224, 251, 297, 311
McMurtry, S. L., 141, 152
McNamee, M., 227, 252
McPherson, J. M., 101, 119, 193–194, 218
Mahler, S. J., 242, 251
Majone, G., 125, 152
Majors, B., 87, 116
Managers: of charity galas, 204–205; and demographic shifts, 173; in female-intensive fields, 128–129; in fundraising, 245–248; in labor market, 47, 53, 55, 57, 58–59, 65, 67–68, 71; and pay equity, 95–96, 97, 107–108, 110, 112; styles of women, 12, 246–247
Maraldo, P. J., 137, 152
March of Dimes, and diversity, 259
Marconi, E., 232

Marconi West, and fundraising, 232
Margolis, R. J., 197, 218
Marsey, R., 192, 212
Marshall, N. L., 136, 137, 152
Marshall, S. A., 196, 197, 218
Martin, J. M., 183, 195, 218
Martinez, A., 232
Marting, L., 190, 218
Marxist analysis, of history, 18, 20
Massachusetts Institute of Technology, as nonprofit, 6
Matthaei, J., 305, 310
Matthews, S., 231
Medicaid, 140
Medicare, 140, 143
Medrich, E., 86, 114
Melosh, B., 97, 117
Mentors: in fundraising, 240, 241, 248–249; for volunteers, 283, 284, 286
Messing, S., 176, 180
Metaphors, and gendered nonprofits, 99–101
Metropolitan Opera, and charity galas, 204, 207
Mexican American Legal Defense and Educational Fund (MALDEF): Latina leader of, 256, 266; Leadership Development Program of, 259
Mexican American Women's National Association, founding of, 168
Middleton, M., 187, 188, 218
Mills, C. W., 185, 219
Mirvis, P. H., 41, 60, 76
Mixer, J. R., 13, 172, 176, 180, 223, 245, 246, 252, 306
Mollner, C., 176
Mongon, G. J., 226, 234, 239, 252
Moore, J. W., 198, 219
Moral reforms, history of, 19–20
Morantz-Sanchez, R. M., 22, 37
Morello-Frosch, R., 166, 180
Morgon, K. P., 206, 219
Mott, L., 11
Mueller, C. W., 134, 149
Muncy, R., 29–30, 37
Murningham, M., 156, 172, 175, 176, 180

N

National Alliance for Choice in Giving, and giving patterns, 306
National Association for Hospital Development, 228
National Association for the Advancement of Colored People, and fundraising, 230
National Association of Colored Women, founding of, 168
National Association of Student YMCAs, and volunteers, 277–278
National Coalition Against Domestic Violence, founding of, 168
National Congress of Mothers, and political power, 30
National Council of Jewish Women, founding of, 168
National Council of La Raza, and fundraising, 232
National Council of Negro Women, and fundraising, 231
National Council of 100 Black Women, and fundraising, 231
National Displaced Homemakers Network, 304, 305, 311–312
National Federation of Business and Professional Women's Clubs, founding of, 168
National Federation of Women's Clubs, and political power, 30
National Football League, as nonprofit, 6–7
National Institute for Women of Color, founding of, 168
National Network of Women's Funds: founding of, 168; goals of, 305, 312; power of beneficiaries in, 176
National Organization for Women, founding of, 168
National Society of Fund Raising Executives (NSFRE), and women fundraisers, 226–227, 230, 233, 238, 245, 248–249, 252
National Women's Political Caucus, founding of, 168

Native American women: and
government employment, 124;
lace by, 28. *See also* Women
of color
Nebraska, board members in, 194
Nelson, M. K., 137, 148
Netting, E. F., 141, 152
Networks: for displaced
homemakers, 304, 305, 311;
for fundraisers, 223, 233–234;
history of national, 27–28; of
women's funds, 168, 176, 305
Neuffer, E., 152
Neustadt, R. M., 152
Neverdon-Morton, C., 124,
152–153
New York City: charity galas in,
204; fundraisers in, 234; history of nonprofits in, 22;
minority communities in, 177
New York State, board members
in, 193
New York Stock Exchange, as
nonprofit, 7
Nightingale, F., 98
Nineteenth Amendment, and history of nonprofits, 30, 33
Noga, S. M., 1, 16, 125, 126, 140,
151, 157, 159, 162, 170–171,
180, 183, 189, 217, 280, 293
Nonprofit sector: attractions of,
41, 88–89, 125; background
on, 1–4; as category, 5–7;
charge for, 273–274; church-
based, 301–302; concept of,
2–3, 91–92; conclusion on, 15,
308–310; diversity in, 6–7,
158–160, 262–263; family pattern of, 298–299; future for,
295–312; and gender-neutral
explanations, 82–90; as gendered, 14–15, 90–102, 208–
209, 296; growth in, 40–41,
53; history of, 17–38, 122–125,
161–162; industries in, 43–44,
72–75, 91; in labor market,
39–77; Latina's experience in,
255–266; leadership for, 274–
292; market orientation of,
163; nature of work in, 160–
163; organizational structure
of, 121–154; paradox of
women and power in, 1–16,
95–96; and pay equity, 79–
120; size of, 3, 156; and social
context, 7–9, 10–11; themes in
study of, 4–15; volunteers in,
267–293; and wage determination, 102–103; women on
boards of, 183–221
North York Hospital, and pay equity, 103, 108
Noyelle, T. J., 125, 154
Nurses, and pay equity issues,
97–99, 103–112, 135

O

Occupational distribution: and
fundraising, 236–238; and pay
equity, 96–99; sectoral, 44–59
Occupational structure: analysis
of, 121–154; background on,
121–122; conclusion on, 146–
148; as female-intensive, 128–
132; implications of, 133–135;
and pay equity, 135–136, 147;
reasons for, 125–133; trends
and prospects for, 139–146;
and working conditions,
136–139
O'Connell, B., 156, 180
Odendahl, T., 9, 14, 16, 94, 117,
165, 171, 172, 181, 183, 184,
185, 197, 198, 201, 202, 203,
204, 219, 295, 299, 312
Olson, J. E., 236, 252
O'Neill, J., 133, 153
O'Neill, M., 1, 80, 117, 124, 141,
150, 153, 155, 161, 181, 186,
216
Ontario, Canada, nurses in, 86,
103–112
Ontario Hospital Association
(OHA), 104, 105, 108–111
Ontario Nurses Association
(ONA), 103–112
Ontario Pay Equity Tribunal,
108–109
Operation Rescue, 302
Orlando Opera Board, and volun-
teers, 269

Ostrander, S. A., 9, 16, 94, 117, 184, 201, 209, 211, 219, 307, 312

P

Palm Beach, charity balls in, 205
Parent-Teacher Association (PTA), boards of, 196, 290, 291
Paresky, S., 234, 252
Parker, D., 231
Pay equity: aspects of, 79–120; background on, 79–80; case study of, 103–112; comparisons for, 5, 42, 59–70, 75–76; conclusion on, 112–114; and demographic shifts, 159, 173; in fundraising, 227–229; in future, 303–304; and gender-neutral explanations, 82–90; and gendered nature of nonprofits, 90–102; and ignoring gender, 80–82; and male elite, 94–96, 113; and managers, 95–96, 97, 107–108, 110, 112; and occupational structure, 135–136, 147
Pendleton, G., 166, 180
Petchesky, R. P., 302, 312
Peter Principle, 268–269
Petty, G., 234
Pfizenmaier-Henderson, E., 229
Pharr, S., 301–302, 312
Philadelphia, volunteers in, 27, 274
Philanthropist, redefining, 175–176
Phillips, A., 90, 117
Phillips, D., 134, 135, 154
Pittsburgh, volunteers in, 267–268
Piven, F. F., 299, 300, 312
Pleck, J. H., 136, 137, 152
Polocheck, S. W., 133, 153
Powell, G. N., 245, 252
Powell, W. W., 80, 91, 102, 117
Power: access to, 2; background on, 1–4; and boards, 187–188, 191, 202, 207, 209; conclusion on, 15, 308–310; and demographic shifts, 155–182; distri-

bution of, 10–11, 111; future for, 295–312; kinds of, 25; meaning and uses of, 11–13; of money, 304–308; in numbers, 300–304; overview of, 295–300; paradox of, 1–16, 95–96; parallel structures of, 33, 186, 211–212; political and economic, 25–31; redefining, 174–177; sectoral analysis of, 5–7; shared, 308–310; themes in study of, 4–15
Presbyterian Hospital, volunteers for, 268
Prestige, and trivialization, 13–14
Preston, A. E., 5, 10, 12, 39, 41, 44, 60, 77, 82–83, 84, 85, 87, 88, 102–103, 117, 122, 124, 125, 138, 153, 172, 173, 181, 303
Priebe, J. A., 74, 77
Privatization, and nature of nonprofits, 162–163
Productivity, and nonprofits, 83–84, 141–142, 143, 147
Professionalization, development of, 277–278
Professionals: in labor market, 45–48, 53–58, 66, 67; and political and economic power, 28–30
Public Broadcasting System, boards of, 269, 283–284, 285

Q

Quality of Employment Survey, 85

R

Race and ethnicity: attention to, 32; and demographic shifts, 157–158, 177; importance of, 9–10. *See also* Women of color
Racism, in nonprofits, 255–266
Rand, as nonprofit, 6
Ratcliff, K. S., 198–199, 219
Ratcliff, R. E., 198–199, 219
Reich, R. B., 143, 153

Remick, H., 97, 99, 118
Reskin, B. F., 89, 97, 118, 225, 241, 252
Reubens, B. G., 124, 150
Reverby, S., 98, 118
Risk, and fundraising, 240
Rochester, New York, history of nonprofits in, 21–22
Rockefeller, J. D., 23
Role conflict, and occupational structure, 137
Roos, P., 97, 118
Roper, B. C., 14, 267, 282
Rose, M. S., 172, 175, 181
Rosenberg, R., 22, 37
Rossiter, M. W., 22, 37
Ruble, T. L., 236, 240–241, 252
Rudney, G., 73, 77, 80, 91–92, 102, 118

S

Saddleback Memorial Foundation, and fundraising, 226
Sage, M.O.S., 3, 81
Saidel, J., 185
St. Louis, bank boards in, 199
Salamon, L. M., 41, 77, 139, 140, 141, 153–154
Salaries. See Pay equity
Salem, D., 124, 154
Salem, Massachusetts, African-American women in, 4
San Francisco, volunteers in, 277
Sanger, M., 11
Sanitary Commission, history of, 27
Sapienza, A. M., 136, 137, 150
Schneiders, S., 95, 118
Schorr, L. B., 137, 154
Schreiber, R., 168, 182
Schultz, V., 88, 89, 118
Schwab, D., 106, 118
Schwartz, F. N., 195, 219
Scott, A. F., 17, 19, 20, 37, 186, 219–220
Seattle, volunteers in, 277–278
Separatism, history of, 20, 23, 33
Seton, E., 3
7-Eleven, as for-profit, 7

Sexism: in nonprofits, 255–266; and volunteers, 281–286
Sexual harassment, of volunteers, 285–286
Shaffer, R., 95, 118
Sheppard-Towner Infancy and Maternity Protection Act of 1921, 31
Shils, E., 108, 118–119
Silver, N., 277, 293
Simpson, P., 192, 220
Skocpol, T., 30–31, 37
Smith-Lovin, L., 101, 119, 193–194, 218
Smith-Rosenberg, C., 19–20, 37–38
Social context: and gendered ideologies, 101–102; for non-profits, 7–9, 10–11; for voluntarism, 274–277
Social reforms, history of, 19, 30–31
Social services, occupational structure in, 126–127, 129–130, 131–132, 135, 141–142, 145, 146
Socialization, and fundraisers, 224, 239–240
Spalter-Roth, R., 168, 182
Spanish Speaking Unity Council, and fundraising, 232
Stanback, T. M., 125, 154
Standard Industrial Classification, 73
Stanford Research Institute, as nonprofit, 6
Stansell, C., 22, 38
Stanton, E. C., 3
Steinberg, R. J., 14, 79, 84, 86, 88, 90, 97, 100, 101, 103, 104, 106, 107, 116, 119, 122, 296
Steinem, G., 198, 220
Sterling, D., 124, 154
Stevenson, Kellogg, Ernst and Whinney (SKEW), 105, 107, 108, 109
Suffrage movement, history of, 21, 30, 33
Summers, D., 83, 102, 116

Sunnybrook Hospital, and pay equity, 103
Survey of Job Characteristics, 85

T

Tax Reform Act of 1986, 162–163
Taylor, B., 90, 117, 244
Teachers Insurance and Annuity Association/College Retirement Equities Fund, as nonprofit, 6
Teltsch, K., 197, 220
Terrell, P., 141, 154
Third sector, concept of, 156. See also Nonprofit sector
Thomas, J. A., 134, 150
Tifft, S. E., 237, 253
Tocqueville, A. de, 6, 275, 293
Tomaskovic-Devey, D., 87, 119
Toppe, C. M., 1, 16, 125, 126, 140, 151, 157, 159, 162, 170–171, 180, 183, 189, 217, 280, 293
Touhey, J. C., 241, 253
Treiman, D., 96, 106, 108, 119–120
Turnover: in fundraising, 238–239; in nonprofits, 86–87, 134

U

Unions: in future, 304; and pay equity, 87, 103–112
United Kingdom: common law in, 26; nursing reform in, 98
United Negro College Fund, and fundraising, 230, 231
U.S. Bureau of Labor Statistics: and demographics, 171; and occupational structure, 142, 145n, 154; and pay equity, 73, 81; and work force, 264
U.S. Bureau of the Census, 44, 75, 124, 127n, 130n, 132n, 154, 157, 182; Current Population Surveys (CPS) of, 42–43, 60, 73, 74, 82, 171
U.S. Children's Bureau, in history of nonprofits, 30, 31

U.S. Department of Labor, 145n, 154, 173, 182
U.S. Senate Committee on the Judiciary, Latina counsel to, 256, 257–258
United Way of America: and boards, 189, 192, 193, 199, 220, 278–279; Latina's experience with, 259, 260–261; and women's giving, 306
Urban League, and fundraising, 230
Useem, M., 212

V

Vincens, M., 235, 253
Voluntarism Project, and bureaucracies, 277
Volunteers: activities of, 267–293; background on, 267–271; certification for, 289–290; conclusion on, 292–293; development of, 286–291; dollar worth of, 280; as essential, 277–281; and gendered ideologies, 101; and leadership training, 270, 291–292; and sexism, 281–286; social context for, 274–277; supervision of, 290–291; training for, 280–281, 284–285, 286, 287–288

W

Wages. See Pay equity
Wallace, R., 94–95, 120
Walter, W. L., 84, 119
Walton, C., 238, 239, 253
Weisbrod, B., 60, 77
Weitzman, M. S., 1, 16, 40, 73, 76, 77, 94, 102, 116, 125, 126, 140, 151, 157, 159, 162, 170–171, 180, 183, 185, 189, 217, 223, 251, 280, 293
Wellesley College, fundraising by, 244
Welter, B., 17, 19, 38
West, C., 92, 120
White, E. G., 3

White-collar workers, in labor market, 44–70
Whitebook, M., 134, 135, 154
Whitney, G. V., 3, 24
Widmer, C., 187, 193, 220
Willard, E., 3
Williams, C., 120
Wilson, J., 203, 204, 205–206, 220
Wolf, N., 206, 220
Wolfe, A., 125, 154
Women: background on, 1–4; on boards, 183–221; and charity galas, 203–207; collaboration and conflict for, 18–25; conclusion on, 15, 308–310; and demographic shifts, 155–182; devaluation of, 241–243, 299, 302; as donors, 24–25, 33–34, 164–165, 176–177, 223, 243, 306–308; as fundraisers, 223–253; future for, 295–312; history of, 17–38, 122–125, 161–162; and job satisfaction, 134–135; in labor market, 39–77; management styles of, 12, 246–247; meaning and uses of power to, 11–13; number of, in nonprofits, 1, 5, 12, 94; opportunities for, 296–297; and organizational structure, 121–154; paradox of, 1–16, 95–96; participation in work force by, 39–40, 125, 303; and pay equity, 79–120; as policy makers, 194–197; positions of, 6, 13; property rights of, 26; roles of, 2, 3–4, 15, 123, 164–167; and shared power, 308–310; and social context, 7–9, 10–11; themes in study of, 4–15; and visible work, 79–120; as volunteers, 267–293; wealthy, 203–207, 306–308
Women, Power, and Status in the Nonprofit Sector conference, 9–10, 11
Women and Foundations/Corporate Philanthropy, 158, 159, 182, 188, 191, 220–221

Women in Development, and fundraising, 234
Women in Development of Greater Boston, and fundraising, 233–234, 235
Women in Financial Development, and fundraising, 234
Women of color: on boards, 186, 190, 192; and discrimination, 137–138; in fundraising, 229–233; future for, 297–298; history of commitment by, 123–124; racism and sexism for, 255–266. See also African-American women; Asian-American women; Latinas; Native American women; Race and ethnicity
Women's Christian Temperance Union: and collaboration, 18; and political power, 30
Women's College Hospital, and pay equity, 103
Women's Exchanges, and economic power, 28
Women's International League for Peace and Freedom, founding of, 168
Women's Legal Defense Fund, founding of, 168
Women's organizations: boards of, 185–186, 196, 211–212; and demographics, 167–169, 175–176; and fundraising, 231–232, 233–234; and leadership training, 291
Women's Way, and giving patterns, 306
Work force. See Labor market
Work load, and occupational structure, 136–137, 143
Wuthnow, R., 101, 120

Y

YMCA of the USA, 293; background of, 270–273; and certification, 289–290; charge for, 272, 273–274; first fundraising

by, 224; local boards of, 282–283; national board of, 269–270, 272, 279; professionalization of, 277–278; and staff mobility, 287; and training, 279, 288; and Women and the Y, 284–285
Yoshihara, N., 124, 151

Youmans, S., 14, 165, 172, 181, 183
Young, D. R., 125, 135, 138, 154

Z

Zilkha, Mrs. E., 207
Zimmerman, D. H., 92, 120
Zweigenhaft, R., 184, 221